REFASHIONING BEN JONSON

Also by Julie Sanders

BEN JONSON'S THEATRICAL REPUBLICS

Refashioning Ben Jonson

Gender, Politics and the Jonsonian Canon

Edited by

Julie Sanders

with

Kate Chedgzoy

and

Susan Wiseman

Published by PALGRAVE MACMILLAN
Houndmills, Basingstoke, Hampshire RG21 6XS and
175 Fifth Avenue, New York, N. Y. 10010
Companies and representatives throughout the world

PALGRAVE MACMILLAN is the global academic imprint of the Palgrave
Macmillan division of St. Martin's Press, LLC and of Palgrave Macmillan Ltd.
Macmillan® is a registered trademark in the United States, United Kingdom
and other countries. Palgrave is a registered trademark in the European
Union and other countries.

Outside North America
ISBN 0–333–67072–8

In North America
ISBN 0–312–21167–8

This book is printed on paper suitable for recycling and
made from fully managed and sustained forest sources.

A catalogue record for this book is available from the British Library.

Library of Congress Catalog Card Number: 97–40505

Transferred to digital printing 2002

Printed and bound in Great Britain by
Antony Rowe Ltd, Chippenham and Eastbourne

Contents

Acknowledgements

The initial idea for this book was allowed a 'test-run' at a major conference at the University of Warwick in January 1995. The editors would like to thank those organizations and departments which made that event the success and pleasure that it was – the Centre for the Study of the Renaissance and the European Humanities Research Centre at the University of Warwick, with special thanks to Peter Mack, J.R. Mulryne, Margaret Shewring, and Charmaine Witherall (without whom it certainly would not have been possible). Julie Sanders would also like to express deep gratitude to John Higham and Jane Clinton who took over the running of the event on the weekend concerned, allowing her to avoid complete collapse!

A number of the speakers on that occasion have essays in this book, but there are others whose contributions we must acknowledge. To all those who came, spoke, chaired, and made tea, many thanks, but special thanks to Martin Butler and Richard Dutton for their support, then as now. Inevitably, since that event, many others have also contributed to this project in ways both practical and supportive: the editors would therefore like to thank their colleagues in the Departments of English at both Keele University and the University of Warwick, and their editor at Macmillan, Charmian Hearne, who has been there from the start and whose presence at the original conference, as well as her ongoing professionalism and care, was, and is, much appreciated.

Janet Clare's chapter is a revised version of one which appears in *Contexts of Renaissance Comedy* which she co-edited with Roy Eriksen (Oslo, 1996). It is reproduced here with the kind permission of the University of Tromsø Press. Thanks are also due to Macmillan Press for permission to reprint the chapter by Richard Dutton.

Finally, Julie Sanders would like to say an especial thank you to Kate Chedgzoy and Sue Wiseman for all their help, advice, phone calls, love, and support. She claims sole ownership of any remaining errors.

Notes on the Contributors

Tom Cain is Head of the Department of English at the University of Newcastle, and editor of the recent Revels edition of *Poetaster* (Manchester, 1995). He has written and edited books on Tolstoy, Hilliard, Jacobean and Caroline poetry, and English culture in the seventeenth century. He is currently editing the manuscript poetry of Mildmay Fane and writing a book on the War of the Theatres.

Kate Chedgzoy is a Lecturer in the Department of English and Comparative Literary Studies at the University of Warwick. As well as being a co-editor of *Refashioning Ben Jonson*, she is the author of *Shakespeare's Queer Children* (Manchester, 1995) and co-editor with Melanie Hansen and Suzanne Trill of *Voicing Women* (Keele University Press, 1996).

Janet Clare is a Lecturer in English at University College, Dublin. As well as having published numerous articles on Renaissance and Commonwealth drama, she is the author of *'Art Made Tongue-Tied by Authority': Elizabethan and Jacobean Dramatic Censorship* (Manchester, 1990) and co-editor with Roy Eriksen of *Contexts of Renaissance Comedy* (Oslo, 1996) in which an earlier version of her essay appears here.

Richard Dutton is Professor of English at Lancaster University where he has taught since 1974. Recent publications include *Mastering the Revels: The Regulations and Censorship of English Renaissance Drama* (Macmillan, 1991), an edition of *Jacobean Civic Pageants* (Keele University Press, 1995), and *Ben Jonson: Authority: Criticism* (Macmillan, 1996) from which his essay here derives. He is also the general editor of the Macmillan *Literary Lives* series.

Robert C. Evans is a Professor in the Department of English and Philosophy at Auburn University at Montgomery. He is the author, amongst other things, of *Ben Jonson and the Poetics of Patronage* (Bucknell University Press, 1989), *Jonson and the Contexts of His Time* (Bucknell, 1994), and *Habits of Mind: Evidence and Effects of Ben Jonson's Reading* (Bucknell, 1995) and is currently editing the *Ben Jonson Encyclopedia*.

Kate McLuskie is Professor of English at the University of Southampton. She has written on Renaissance Dramatists and a study of Dekker and Heywood as professional dramatists. She is currently working on the commercialization of theatre in early modern England and is editing *Macbeth* for Arden III.

Clare McManus is currently a postgraduate student in the Centre for the Study of the Renaissance at the University of Warwick. Her doctoral research centres on the dynamics of elite female performance and cultural production in the early modern European court.

Helen Ostovich is an Associate Professor of English at McMaster University. She has published many articles on Renaissance drama, the most recent including 'Ben Jonson and the Dynamics of Misogyny: A Cultural Collaboration', *Elizabethan Theatre*, 15; and 'Mistress and Maid: Women's Friendship in *The New Inn*', *Ben Jonson Journal* 4 (1997). She has just finished preparing *Jonson: Four Comedies – Volpone, Epicoene, The Alchemist, and Bartholomew Fair* for Longman Annotated Texts and is currently working on the Revels Plays edition of *Every Man Out of His Humour* (Manchester University Press) which she hopes will be in circulation by 2000 – the four-hundredth anniversary of its original publication.

Julie Sanders is a Lecturer in English at Keele University. She has published various articles on late Jonson and Jacobean and Caroline Drama. As well as being a co-editor of *Refashioning Ben Jonson*, she has a monograph forthcoming from Macmillan entitled *Ben Jonson's Theatrical Republics*. She is currently working on a book on gender and community in Caroline Drama.

Susan Wiseman is a Lecturer in the Department of English and Comparative Literary Studies at the University of Warwick. She is a co-editor of *Refashioning Ben Jonson*.

1

Introduction: Refashioning Ben Jonson

Kate Chedgzoy, Julie Sanders, and Susan Wiseman

The concept of 'refashioning' is a loaded one in the context of the study of early modern literature. The title of this collection deliberately acknowledges the influence of that founding moment of New Historicist studies of the period, Stephen Greenblatt's *Renaissance Self-Fashioning*,[1] and yet it is necessary to observe that Greenblatt's text studiously avoided the self-avowedly paradoxical figure of Benjamin Jonson in its considerations of other literary, social and political shapings and fashioners of the Renaissance.

This collection responds to the significant absence of Ben Jonson in Greenblatt's seminal study but does not claim that New Historicism has passed him or his works by. Part of the refashioning project here is also to respond to, and in some sense move on from, the attention accorded to encodings of power in his work, in particular in his masques, but also by extension in his 'public' drama, as outlined and detailed by scholars such as Stephen Orgel and Martin Butler.[2] There is a need, expressed in a number of the essays included here, to view Jonson through a prism other than that of the court (and invariably the *Jacobean* court at that) and to widen our understanding of the spheres in which he operated. An awareness of the significance of popular culture to his compositions can enable alternative understandings of his local and national politics.[3] Such 're-readings' are already emerging in articles such as Leah Marcus's own 're-writing' of her earlier thesis on *Bartholomew Fair*[4] and in the attention now being (belatedly) paid to the significance of female patronage and writing in Jonson's career and self-formations.[5] In simple terms, then, this collection of essays seeks to subject Jonson's literary career to an historicized and self-consciously post-New Historicism reading.

1

The readjustment of the critical lens and the reinvigoration of debate on and around the figure of 'Ben Jonson' can and must be achieved in a multitude of ways – through a widening of the 'canon' of Jonson's work as it has been established, through a new focus on issues of gender and sexuality within that canon, thus allowing Jonson's work to become subject to diverse feminist and lesbian and gay critical practices, through a complicating of our political understandings of Jonson, and through the revival in the public domain of performances of plays until now neglected.[6] If the essays included here, including this introduction which suggests ways of 'refashioning' notions of the Jonsonian canon, authorship, and its engagement with questions of gender and sexuality, can contribute to that repositioning then our objective will have been realized.

I: RECONFIGURING THE CANON

Why is there a need at this time to reconfigure the Jonsonian canon? Such reconfigurations have occurred before and, indeed, the canon is in a constant process of reconfiguration and refashioning. We will hear at various points in this volume of Jonson's own interventions into the shaping and consolidation of his canon of work – in the printing of *Sejanus*, a collaborative text, as his sole work (see Evans and Dutton); in the suppression of the details of masquing occasions in the case of the printed texts of the masques for the weddings of Frances Howard (see Ostovich);[7] in the structuring and printing of his 1616 *Works* (see Sanders),[8] in his rewriting of *Every Man in His Humour* for that volume;[9] in his conscious omissions and suppressions in the same. We will also encounter historical reshapings and reconfigurations in the form of new or revised interpretations of certain plays, or even the favouring of certain plays for performance and revival (see Wiseman), or in the loss of the immediate (often political, frequently commercial) context of their initial composition and performance (see Cain, Dutton, and McLuskie).[10]

Yet there is also a need to consider the Jonsonian canon that has been constructed by our own age and academic context – one which clearly favours the dramas, and within that performance-based genre the 'middle comedies' of *Volpone*, *The Alchemist* and *Bartholomew Fair*, and which is only now beginning to include

Epicoene under that category. Easily available editions for undergraduate use are evidence of that intellectual trend, as are the plays that are regularly performed in the mainstream theatre.[11] This volume's concern is not simply to 'refashion' Ben Jonson for the current critical age; after all, other periods have consistently remade him in their image from the English Republic, the Interregnum, and the Restoration onwards (see Wiseman). Rather, it is the aim of this collection to be self-reflexive, self-conscious about the process of 'refashioning', subjecting that critical practice to rational critique.

Few essays in this collection focus on 'mainstream' plays, although the volume does, it should be confessed, reinforce the dramatic focus: other works will, we hope, take up the gauntlet and re-establish Jonson's poetry and prose as central to the canon as our own era defines it.[12] Richard Dutton's essay here concentrates on the 'Epistle to *Volpone*' partly in order to detach it from the direct concerns of the play and apply it to the micropolitical context of the moment in which Jonson authored that preface. Kate McLuskie employs *Bartholomew Fair* to explore the economic base of Jonson's theatre-writing. Elsewhere, however, the concern is to retrieve less-discussed texts for study: the masques for Queen Anne are subjected to a potentially recuperative feminist reading (see McManus), as is Jonson's 'last' Jacobean play, *The Devil is an Ass* (see Ostovich). Janet Clare reconsiders readings of *Cynthia's Revels* by locating the play in a tense relationship with the 'Cult of Elizabeth I'. Tom Cain relates *Poetaster* to the fall of Essex. The Roman tragedies are reclaimed as important registers of political concerns in the seventeenth century (see Evans and Wiseman) and the oft-neglected late plays are represented by Julie Sanders's re-reading of the signification of print for Jonson in his Caroline period, as represented in the stage operations of *The Staple of News*. The choice of texts for discussion is then an integral part of the refashioning process we are undertaking here.

The question of editions is a vital and significant one where Jonson is concerned. C.H. Herford and Percy and Evelyn Simpson's monumental collected works remains the standard edition, but this is scarcely a student-friendly edition, with its many volumes, its elaborate and separately collated notes, its old spelling, and its now occasionally anachronistic decisions (not least the placing of *A Tale of a Tub*, now recognized as a late play of considerable import, as one of Jonson's earliest – and by implication immature – productions).[13]

The middle comedies have seen numerous reprintings but the fate of the other plays has been considerably more erratic. The variety of editions employed by the contributors here is further proof, if it were needed, of the problematic and diffuse availability of Jonson in textual form. The two-volume *Selected Plays of Ben Jonson* edited by Martin Butler and Johanna Proctor went some way to redressing the balance, providing easily accessible editions of *Sejanus, The New Inn,* and *A Tale of a Tub* amongst others,[14] and the single scholarly Revels editions have recently provided us with versions of *The New Inn, The Staple of News, The Devil is an Ass,* and *Poetaster,* with *The Magnetic Lady,* and *Every Man Out of His Humour* promised for the future.[15] These as a group however constitute costly and disparate purchases that exclude for the most part the student population, meaning that university courses of necessity resort to the available and affordable option of the one-volume middle comedies when devising course syllabuses. As well as the new scholarly edition of the Complete Works being planned by Oxford University Press to replace Herford and Simpson, an undergraduate Complete Jonson would seem to be a desirable option for those hoping to expand the canon of Jonson texts that are studied and taught prior to postgraduate research.[16]

The need to refashion the canon is a genuine one, however, and inspired not solely by economics, but also by the concerns of our critical moment which find a focus in previously underrated texts such as the masques and the late plays with their interest in communities and in questions of performance, specifically female performance. By widening the canon we also expand our understanding of the carefully fashioned Jonsonian career as one that passed through many phases, spanning the Elizabethan, Jacobean, and Caroline eras, and stretching as far as the years of the Ship Money debate and the controversies over Charles I's Personal Rule in the decade prior to the civil wars. By reinstating texts that explore questions of women's social and marital constriction, or their performative silencing, so we start to revise the traditional understanding of Jonson as an aggressively masculine writer and to debate the misogyny that has previously been ascribed to his work. A new Jonson emerges who is alert to the socio-political contingencies of his age(s), who is empathetic towards the female condition (not least due to the significance of the network of female patrons and authors he moved within), and whose politics are far from being overtly absolutist or even monarchist. In the process, the deconstruction of the 'absolutist' understanding of Jonson redefines our understanding of his negotiations with his audiences. This Jonson no longer seems to be the anti-theatrical tyrant that dominated critical accounts for so long, but one involved in the complex process of the multiple production of meaning that is intrinsic to the theatrical experience.[17] This is a pluralist Jonson we are acknowledging; and alongside this revelation, a number of 'Jonsons' emerge who influenced subsequent writers and ages and we begin to understand how each age, as with Shakespeare, has refashioned Jonson according to its own concerns and interests. In the late 1990s when the consolidation of women's rights is underway in Western culture, so literary criticism is beginning to abandon the monotone cry that women of the Renaissance were oppressed by patriarchal society in favour of a wholly more shaded and nuanced version of events that recognizes diversity between decades, and even years, in terms of their social signification for women, and also between social groups; our awareness, until now limited, of the complexity of female representation in the Jonsonian canon needs to be readjusted accordingly. Masque studies have been central in inaugurating that readjustment of focus, and once again the increasing availability of printed editions is assisting the expansion of the community of study in that field.[18] In a decade when the fate of the monarchy and the future of political republicanism is also a concern so Jonson's complex negotiations with the politics of his own age provide a site for self-exploration and questioning. His later plays concern themselves with issues such as the freedom of the press, the role of print in the formation of popular culture, localism and local politics, sexism, and even environmentalism in the underlying theme of fen drainage in *The Devil is an Ass*.[19] We refashion Ben Jonson then according to the needs and concerns of our own micropolitical moment and this volume is anxious to recognize the contingencies of our own project. We do not offer a final or complete Jonson: like the broken compass that served for his emblem, Jonson's circle remains engagingly broken and incomplete, open to the revisions, reconfigurations, and refashionings of ages to come.

II: REFASHIONING AUTHORSHIP: JO(H)NSON, PRINT, AND PLAYHOUSES

One way in which Jonson is perpetually refashioned is in terms of our understanding of him as an author. What is, what was, an 'author'? As indicated by several of the essays in this volume (Dutton, McLuskie, Sanders), Jonson holds an important place in the debate as both symptom and agent, exemplifying and acting upon the ways in which authorship, cultural production, economic, and social relations, and taste meet to produce the early modern idea of the 'author' – one on which many later understandings and myths of creativity were founded. The question of 'authorship' is a place where Jonson criticism and wider concerns about the nature of 'authors' intersect; the self-fashioning and fashioning of Jonson as an author has been reinterpreted through the growth of critical texts on authorship.[20]

As a self-creator, Jonson might be linked to figures analysing the early modern potential for self-shaping, like Mosca and Iago (two figures compared in Greenblatt's brief reference to Jonson in *Renaissance Self-Fashioning*). But the ferocious conflicts played out in Jonson's quest for primacy are different from those fictional creations. Jonson's self-shaping as an author indicated a desire to produce an ideal image of the author fixed, unmoved, unperturbed, but it was also marked by the knowledge of the commercial relations of the public theatre; these two aspects of Jonson's analysis of authorship are in tension.

In terms of the claim to elite aesthetic primacy, Jonson's very name – manufactured by him from the quotidian 'Johnson' – is a provocation to think about him as a hybrid mixing creator and product. 'Jonson' excises paternity, staking a claim to be self-shaping, even unique, once rid of that unnecessary 'h'. Indeed, because Jonson's mother remarried after Benjamin's birth, the name of Jonson's biological father has not survived. The removal of the 'h' took away associations with a loathed stepfather. The change was solidified in the 1616 folio when plays previously published in quarto by 'Johnson' reappeared, edited, under 'Jonson'. That the folio was able to transfix and render permanent 'Johnson''s transformation into 'Jonson' indicates the central role of print and the importance of print in influencing and shaping the way his 'work' – and the name which authorized it – was understood.

Jonson's production of his *Works* in 1616 asserts the authorial name's hybrid status as part individual, part brand-named product, for sale in the literary marketplace.[21] The myth of authorship built into the idea of the *Works* worked; for, though Samuel Daniel amongst English poets had previously published his *Works* (1601), Jonson (hostile to Daniel) managed to shape the act as his because he seemed to have been the first to understand such publication as imbued with the implications of authorship and imbricated with claims to taste, decorum, literary and market value.[22] As Joseph Loewenstein points out, Jonson had been using print to stake a rivalrous claim to primacy in the earliest years of James's reign, when he published the texts of his masques – *Entertainments* – supervising and organizing the printing process to produce a printed text which aimed to present his masques as 'transhistorical ... antioccasional ... antitheatrical'.[23] While it seems logical that Jonson's work for the court should play an important role in his claim to authorship, it is clear that the context of this claim to lofty decorum was a frantic scrabble to triumph over his rivals, first Daniel, and later his collaborator, Inigo Jones, and to maintain patronage at court. The masques selected for inclusion in the 1616 Folio were, as David Riggs notes, chosen for their potential to maintain his position in favour.[24] Thus, the attempt to arrest the circulation of value and preserve his texts as a standing monument to the timeless quality of cultural value was tied to the very focus which ensured that no such certain fixity could be achieved.

Under scrutiny, Jonson's claim to literary authorship – not to texts or plays but *Works* (which transcend cultural moments rather than being bound by them) – seems like a conjuring trick (or like the very choreography and aesthetic harmony of Jonson's own ephemeral and illusionistic court masques) which, to appear effortless and magical, must be viewed from one angle only: regarded from any other viewpoint, the labour, conflicts, and paradoxes of the claim become visible. Jonson 'made' himself an author and, in doing so, though he did not invent the category of authorship, gave the role a reinforced claim to transcend the market and a commercial viability. The new category, which denied the moment and the market, was paradoxically founded upon the interaction of market and literary value: in enhancing the 'name of the author' as adding value to the named product Jonson's elite authorship sought to derive benefit from the very commercial relations which it in part disavowed.[25] Any space of authorial 'independence' claimed by Jonson was bound to such paradoxes.

What did it mean for Jonson to publish his *Works*? It is in part evidence of the success of Jonson's project to reshape English literary culture in line with his views on taste and decorum, realigning English aristocratic culture with admired classical antecedents – Martial, Horace, Sallust. The Folio did situate Jonson's name with the 'best' of the classical authors; but in what sense were such authors best? Best for what? Classical writers, both comic dramatists and writers on the state and politics – Menander, Aristophanes, Sallust, Tacitus – were far from stable values as they were used in a gentleman's education and thereafter by those gentlemen as a corpus of writing with which to interpret local and national politics in the present. Even, perhaps especially, in the separable aesthetic sphere Jonson invites us to imagine as the true domain of authorship, 'economic political interest ... and the related economic or political profit, constitutes one of the bases for evaluating the [aesthetic] producers and their products'.[26] Jonson, a bricklayer's child, was educated at Westminster school, where acquisition of classical learning meant that a particular text or author might function simultaneously politically and as an object fetishized in the emergent Jacobean aesthetic sphere of libraries and collections.[27] Cultural value and pragmatic applicability were bound up together in the readers' understanding of classical and European writers, and of Jonson too. So the realm of literary taste was bound to questions of civic duty and conflict, and even the classical texts with which Jonson's *Works* might compete were highly valued precisely *because* they were used in contemporary cultural and political polemic. Although Jonson's idea of authorship may have embraced the production of literary texts as a kind of pure surplus to culture, beautiful but not applicable to life, that was not how his texts were read by contemporaries or by successive generations. Indeed, that claim to transcend was, again paradoxically, a 'move' in a cultural game which was itself inevitably bound to the shifting networks of patronage, and through that to national politics.

Even as the folio *Works* represents the apotheosis of this new author it also registers an epistemological crisis in how writing is to be understood. The Folio is produced not by a clarification of what it meant to be an author – rather than writing parts of plays or poems for patrons – but from an increasingly confusing set of disjunctions and imperatives about the changing status of the writer. Thus, Jonson's career is a symptom both of the transformation of social, economic and cultural relations and of an attempt to arrest, stabilize and produce coherence out of an interaction between old and new where even what is old and what is new is unstable.

The traditional dichotomies of this confusion are: patron versus market (here it is hard to say which is old, and which is new); print versus manuscript; folio versus quarto; court versus 'public' theatre;

play versus masques; Whitehall versus suburbs. Add to these the
tensions in the economic relations which underpin them – town
versus country; mastered versus masterless; rooted versus travel-
ling; elite versus serving – and we can see a very confused economic and ideological situation developing during Jonson's lifetime.
Out of this confusion emerge not only the 1616 Folio but masques,
elegies, and *Bartholomew Fair*. Jonson is in a way author of each of
them but, clearly, a masque is not authored in the same way as a
play for the commercial theatre, and a play performed in a theatre
and at court is, of course, transformed once transferred into a
highly organized 'second edition' in folio form.

Thus, the very claim to coherence that the 1616 Folio seems to
signal is simultaneously an index of the many different systems of
authorship co-existing at the moment at which it was produced. It
would be a mistake to suggest that the Folio denies the different
kinds of writing that it represents, for it is clearly marked by its own
attempt to produce itself as without origin. What *has* been problematic has been the willingness of some Jonson critics to take Jonson's
claim to lofty decorum and authorship at face value and to deny the
tensions and inconsistencies that make Jonson's disavowed participation in the full range of practices of authorship so fascinating.
Such critical writing has led Jonathan Haynes to argue that the
emphasis on the 'moral and formal in Jonson' is 'worn out'.[28]

Critics who oppose the view that Jonson stands for decorum use
a rather different canon of Jonson texts – the comedies of his mid-
career (*Bartholomew Fair, Volpone, The Alchemist*). Such critics argue
that 'plays make sense only in relation to the historically actual
practice of theatre' – a stumbling block in Jonson's attempt to reify
the value of his comedies in timeless print.[29] Against a printed,
tidied, perhaps ossified Jonson, some critics assert that the populist
and carnivalesque energies of Jonson's plays produce audience
pleasure despite the generic gestures towards decorum.[30] As Tom
Hayes suggests, some such critics take up a Gramscian reading of
carnival in Jonson's plays, using these texts to 'locate resistance to
the dominant culture'.[31]

This version of Jonson, as an author whose texts are animated by
the very indecorous energies they disavow, can be tested by
reading one of the central texts in the production of the 'populist'
Jonson: *Bartholomew Fair*. *Bartholomew Fair* troubles the idea that
Jonson became 'decorous' at the time of the 1616 Folio because it is
roughly contemporaneous with it, though not included. From the

early volume of *Entertainments* to the folio *Works*, Jonson used his court entertainments and products to stake the claim of authorship, yet he was simultaneously working in the 'public' theatre, first as a player and then as a playwright. Writers were paid for scripts and dramatic companies had some protection from their relationship to aristocratic figures, but the whole enterprise – as Kate McLuskie points out in this volume – depended on the reaction of a paying audience. The 'attention of the audience is the *materia prima* of the theatre' and inattention, as in the case of Jonson's unpopular tragedies, meant poor receipts.[32]

This produces a very different set of relations between author and audience from those found in the assertion on the title-page of Jonson's folio *Works* that, in Horace's words, he was willing to write for the few. In the emergent capitalist institution of theatre, one in which Shakespeare was a shareholder and Jonson had been a mere actor, a very different concept of authorship existed.[33] At virtually the same time that he made such a significant contribution to the fashioning of the idea of the 'author', Jonson also worked for playhouses which, under the dual pressure of audience response and capitalist formation, tended to undermine, fragment, and reshape the very discrete literary units on which the 1616 Folio staked its claim to authorship.

The dynamics between the audience and the subject of the play were crucial to the new theatres and as early as the late 1590s the sense that it was possible to stage London to London audiences emerged, and Jonson's relationship to theatre fashion existed within a context in which Londoners felt that their concerns and relationships were being represented, albeit satirically, on the stage. If audiences were not exactly authors or patrons, they were nevertheless part of the complex relationships of control and identification in the production of Jonson's 'city texts', and their involvement is analysed in the 'Induction' to *Bartholomew Fair*. Arguably, the middle comedies use this intense audience–play relationship to negotiate a complex and sometimes metadramatic interplay of identificatory responses, satiric prompts, stereotype, and set piece. These plays offer a complex understanding not only of drama, but of its relationship to and representation of the driving forces – economic, sexual, and status-concerned – of extra-theatrical relations. In *Bartholomew Fair* Jonson seems to elaborate this awareness of a specific dynamic to offer another theory of authorship for the commercial stage – one linked explicitly to place and to social relations rather than the Folio's claim to timeless value.

In *Bartholomew Fair*'s prolonged 'induction', or framing of the play, first the Stagekeeper and then the Bookholder (Prompt) and Scrivener come on to draw up articles of agreement by which the play may be seen. Plays (and especially masques) which exist as illusions (or in the case of early modern comedy often as partially, intermittently illusionistic) by concealing the conditions and labour involved in their production are here reconfigured so that when the Stagekeeper opens proceedings he signifies simultaneously as 'play' (fictional representation of Stagekeeper) and as 'real' stage-keeper. He is not only metatheatrical, acting as theatre calling attention to itself, but constitutes a staging of the social and material circumstances in which theatre was produced. He addresses the audience:

> Gentlemen, have a little patience, they are e'en upon coming, instantly ... But for the whole play, will you ha' the truth on't? (I am looking lest the poet hear me, or his man, Master Brome, behind the arras) it is like to be a very conceited scurvy one, in plain English. When 't comes to the Fair once, you were e'en as good go to Virginia for anything there is of Smithfield ... he has not convers'd with Bartholomew-birds, as they say; he has ne'er a sword and buckler man in his Fair, nor a little Davy, to take toll o'the bawds there, as in my time, ...[34]

The Stagekeeper delays the play and *is* the play. He initially appears to be comparing the play to 'Smithfield' itself, to the actual fair, which Jonson's play is as like as to 'Virginia', but it turns out that that placed 'reality' which escapes Jonson's text is itself already in a way textualized and codified in the activities of 'sword and buckler' men and 'little Davy' which, as types, characterize the fair as already involved in modes of representation. The stagekeeper's inadequate understanding of the power of inversion to defamiliar-ize social relations is suggested by his nostalgia for representations of the Fair in which 'punks' were 'sous'd by my witty young masters o' the Inns o'Court' – a comic process which does not, as Jonson's play does, invert the structures of authority, or call attention to the sadistic excesses of the desire to punish both the body and social inferiors. Clearly, the Stagekeeper's commentary addresses the nature of the emergent canon of plays for the public theatre and the relationship between fashion, genre, and audience expectation – something taken up in greater detail by the Scrivener, who follows the Stagekeeper onto the stage.

The Scrivener draws up a contract between play and audience, a contract which makes explicit the link between the price of a seat and access to judgement:

> It is further agreed that every person here have his or their free-will of censure, to like or dislike at their own charge, the author having now departed with his right: it shall be lawful for any man to judge his six pen'orth, his twelve pen'orth ... provided always his place get not above his wit.
>
> (Induction, ll. 86–92)

Commercial relations of authorship in the public theatre are repre-sented back to the audience in a way that taunts them by making their assumed stupidity pleasurable to them. They may pay high prices to attend but 'place' in the hierarchy of seating arrangements guarantees nothing in relation to the hierarchy of wit – and makes that baiting pleasurable. Most significant in the 'comic contract' is the claim that 'the author having now departed with his right' the audience are free to judge and censure. This claim implies the lack of authorial control over the 'read' product in a way that forcibly reminds us of Barthes's understanding of the text as repeatedly reborn in the imagination of the reader, whose 'authorship' of the play was at the cost of the 'death of the author'.[35] Yet it is embed-ded in a sequence which mimics a contract between play and author, and one which attempts to delimit and encroach upon the freedom of audience members to 'read' the play ignorantly, to ask for different conventions, or to inappropriately over-read 'hidden' meanings. If the Induction acknowledges the place of the author in commercial culture it also simultaneously offers a critique of the audience's control and ability to censure simply by paying and – cunningly – makes that very critique pleasurable to the audience within the terms of commercial theatre.

Jonson's analysis of authorship within the theatrical cash nexus is as acute as his elaboration of elite authorship. Moreover, Jonson seems to be asserting himself as an innovator and addressing the very changeability of taste and fashion that the *Works* was striving to refuse, a changeability whereby innovation and improvement can be posed in terms of the 'conflict between two aesthetics' with 'orthodox art' (the kind that the Stagekeeper and some of the audience are characterized as preferring) 'continuously pushed into the past' by the attempt of an aesthetic faction to uphold a new legitimacy – as *Bartholomew Fair* partly presents itself in the Induction.[36]

As Haynes notes, the economic relations Jonson represented, as much as those he worked within, were unstable; the 'fairgrounds of Smithfield ... were being encroached upon by the expansion of the city; and in the year of the play the fairground was paved for the first time and improved in various other ways'.[37] As opposed to the emphasis on transcending time in the folio *Works*, Jonson is sharply aware of contingencies like the spatial situation of *Bartholomew Fair* and of the fact that, in representing Londoners to Londoners in his use of the Fair, he is participating in a circuit of pleasure permitted by and representing the economic and social relations existing within the theatre.

Thus, the play participates in and critiques the fantasy that this pressurized fair space is one in which usual economic relations are suspended. The play seems to be equivocal about the carnival and economic nature of the fair, especially whether it is a place where bargains are to be had by those who maintain quotidian, opportunistic, economic logic rather than succumbing to carnival inversion. Critics who want to read the fair as an utopian space driven by carnival energies do so by neglecting the hybrid nature of the fair and the spatial and economic relations of its survivors and those who make it productive. The emphasis is on contingency, space, and time. Yet the chaos and lack of decorum is as carefully plotted as a masque is choreographed and the fair is bound to the question of commercial authorship through the Induction.

Thus the 'counter-canon' of comic Jonson does not, as some critics seem to suggest, provide an ideal free space of commentary on social relations. However, these plays – *Bartholomew Fair*, *Volpone, The Alchemist* – do provide an insight absent from, or at least suppressed in, some of Jonson's other plays into social relations, into the economics and aesthetics of the playhouse, and into his own jockeying to make *his* product capture the market. The close terms on which audience and play coexisted in popular theatres makes a theory of sole authorship to an extent redundant. That Jonson's most successful comedies were produced in this complex field swept by fads, gimmicks, and relatively swift changes of taste – and within which he strove to position himself as an innovator – troubles the account of him as a self-generated author, beyond temporal and economic constraints.

How, if at all, are the tensions between the different kinds of authorship and Jonson's highly analytical commentaries to be reconciled? Some critics locate a decisive shift of emphasis from public theatre to elite servant towards the end of what can profitably be understood as a 'career' in writing and authorship. However, this image of Jonson relies on the *Works* as epitomizing Jonson's projects and setting the trajectory for the whole of Jonson's subsequent career. This interpretation is troubled by the late poetry and by his returns to the playhouses with *The Staple of News* in the first years of the reign of Charles I.

The paradoxes of Jonsonian authorship have structured the course of Jonson criticism to the extent that Terry Eagleton sees the split in critical understandings of Jonson as an author as divided into 'classical humanists and romantic populists', with neither group holding a tenable view of the 'dramatist himself, who is both protégé of the powerful and petty bourgeois entrepreneur, dissident intellectual and part of an expanding capitalist enterprise'.[38] One way in which this volume aims to return to the question of Jonson's authorship and 'career' is by indicating that while it is possible to interpret Jonson's career as acting out a division between the demands of decorum expressed in *Works* and of the playhouse, or as an author whose energies can be understood as carnivalesque before 1616 and after that moment suggesting a more decorous and courtly aspect, each of these positions constitute a simplification of the field in which Jonson was operating. As the essays in this volume make clear (especially Dutton, McLuskie, Sanders) it is necessary to attend to the continuing highly analytical and sophisticated and yet fierce and contradictory problematic of Jonson's relation to authorship throughout his career.

To return to the 1616 *Works* around which so much Jonson criticism circulates: the reception of this volume itself indicates the impossibility of its attempt to wrest a permanent literary value from a changing market. After the claim to permanence staked in the *Works* the author was still alive – and was to live on for many years.[39] As Jennifer Brady puts it, 'the *Works* supplanted Jonson as the authority that coerced' and stood in the way of the next generation of male authors, as Nicholas Oldisworth lamented:

... For shame, engrosse not Age,
But now, thy fifth Act's ended, leave the stage,
And lett us clappe.[40]

Notably, Oldisworth addresses the problem of Jonson's longevity in relation to his *Works* in terms of the 'public' theatres, reasserting the claims of occasion, impermanence, event. Although in the *Works* he had created a monument to himself as one kind of author, his career continued to be constituted (though perhaps to a lesser extent and in different ways) by the dynamic between the forces of decorum and dissolution, acknowledged in the late poems in *Underwoods* in which, as Jennifer Brady notes, the 'body of the poet is a mortifying spectacle'.[41]

III: RECONSIDERING JONSONIAN SEXUALITIES

The essays in this volume testify that the diverse and energetic refashionings of the Jonsonian canon have transformed the academic and theatrical meanings of Jonson for our time. But what is surprising about this process is that the engagement with lesbian and gay scholarship and queer theory which has recently proved so fruitful for the study and staging of many of Jonson's contemporaries has not so far made a substantial impact upon Jonson studies. Indeed, the question of sexuality has only occasionally been raised in relation to Jonson's texts; where it is addressed, it is most often within a feminist framework which critiques Jonson's representations of female sexuality, and his depiction of relations between men and women with reference to that key institution of heterosexuality, marriage. The valuable work done in this area by a number of feminist critics is extended in the current volume by the contributions of McManus, Ostovich, and Sanders, which both re-examine Jonson's works in the light of some of the most recent developments in feminist theory, and extend the range of Jonsonian texts to which feminist concerns have been addressed.[42]

Feminism, though, is principally concerned not with sexuality but with gender, and intimately related though these matters are, it is politically and analytically crucial to distinguish between them. Clearly, in the gendered world of early modern England – as in our own time and place – the discussion of sexuality has very different implications for men and women. Outside the context of feminist criticism, however, it remains the case that there has been surprisingly little discussion of homoerotic, masculine, or perverse sexualities in Jonson. Taking by way of example three of the most magisterial and influential studies of early modern sexualities to have been published in recent years, Bruce Smith's *Homosexual Desire in Shakespeare's England*, Jonathan Goldberg's *Sodometries*, and the collection edited by him, *Queering the Renaissance*, Jonson merits a mention, often merely in passing, on just 16 pages out of a total 896, lagging well behind his most obvious rivals, Marlowe and Shakespeare, with many dozens of references each.[43] These books are by no means untypical in their sidelining of Jonson. This situation is perhaps all the more surprising since Edmund Wilson's celebrated account of Jonson's anal eroticism in his essay 'Morose Ben Jonson', first published as long ago as 1938, might have seemed to open up the possibility of installing Jonson at the heart of the queer canon.[44] In fact, Wilson is at pains to stress that the Freudian notion of anal eroticism should not be taken as indicative of homosexuality. Invoking Wilson's essay, Jonson's biographer David Riggs summarizes the character traits typical of the anal-erotic personality as 'pedantry, a tendency to hoard up knowledge, obstinacy and irascibility';[45] pre-eminent here are obsessional forms of social behaviour, rather than a desire to participate in sodomitical pleasures. In strictly Freudian terms, this is reasonable enough; yet it is tempting to give the Freudian screw another turn, and ask why these critics are so keen to both invoke and repudiate Jonsonian anality.

Undoubtedly, Jonson's plays do demonstrate a certain fascination with the multifarious pleasures of anality. But it is not necessary to secure this interest in the playwright's own psyche in order to undertake a queer reading of his texts. One of the key tenets of queer theory has been the separation of identity claims from textual inscriptions of desire in all its forms, along with the problematization of assumptions about how modern understandings of sexual desire and identity map back onto the early modern past. The moment of lesbian and gay critical scholarship which began to investigate traces of homoeroticism in Renaissance drama was initially driven by a form of identity politics which sought to find literary precursors and to isolate poignant or affirmative moments of the textual representation of same-sex love, which seemed to hold out the possibility of achieving a certain recognition of one's desires and sense of self in some of the most prestigious texts of the literary canon. This project is reminiscent of the earlier stages of feminist criticism, in that it seeks to combine a recuperation of homosexuality with a critique of negative representations of it. In its most straightforward and unsophisticated form, this approach to sexuality in literature is summed up by Christopher Robinson:

> Lesbians and gay men need to become better acquainted with creative writing by and about homosexuals because literature is a mirror of society's perceptions. Studying it helps us to understand how and why homosexuals have represented themselves, or have been represented by heterosexuals ... There is a need for critical works written from a specifically gay perspective on *any* sort of literature, because traditional criticism is partisan, writing to a hidden agenda ....[46]

It is perhaps hardly surprising that among Renaissance dramatists it has been Marlowe and Shakespeare, rather than Jonson, whose plays have seemed most responsive to this kind of reading. There are no equivalents in Jonson to the wistful Antonios of *Twelfth Night* and *The Merchant of Venice*, no moments which collapse together the homosocial and the homoerotic with such a powerful charge as Aufidius's greeting to Coriolanus (*Coriolanus* IV.v. 102–36), nothing like the desire between Edward and Gaveston. In the Jonsonian canon, the plays which seem to lend themselves most easily to a reading in the light of the concerns of the lesbian and gay movement as outlined by Robinson are undoubtedly *Volpone* and *Epicoene*, both of which contain a number of remarkably matter-of-fact intimations of homoerotic behaviour, yet these are scarcely scenarios which offer confirmation of the priorities of a modern movement grounded in identity politics. We shall return below to the ways in which the homoeroticism of *Epicoene* and *Volpone* can be read. Here we want to propose that although Jonson has been relatively neglected – and perhaps with good reason – by lesbian and gay scholarship, nevertheless the rather different intellectual and political investments of the queer critical project may make this an appropriate moment to refashion our understanding of Jonsonian sexualities.

The literary-critical and historical work stimulated by queer theory is distinguished by two key areas of difference from the earlier (but by no means superseded) lesbian and gay scholarly project. One of these differences is encapsulated by the insight, borrowed here from Corinne Blackmer's work on opera, that on stage *'queer sexuality* is no longer a noun that belongs to the identity of the paradigmatic "gay man" or "lesbian", it rather describes a dynamic musical-theatrical mode of socially organizing and dramatically performing erotic pleasure and intimacy in which *power freely circulates and is freely exchanged'*.[47] The utopianism of Blackmer's faith in the free circulation of power is out of place in relation to Jonson, where the erotic is constructed and expressed precisely through power relationships. More generally, though, this disengagement of the sexual from the notion of dramatic character, to which it was firmly anchored in earlier phases of work on lesbian and gay issues in early modern literature, recasting it as the textually diffused circulation of libido, seems very apt to Jonson.

The second aspect of this difference can be understood in terms of the distinction between minoritizing and universalizing accounts of sexuality which Eve Kosofsky Sedgwick formulated in her influential *Epistemology of the Closet*.[48] The minoritizing understanding of sexuality – which is, Sedgwick suggests, the prevalent 'common-sense' perception of sexuality in the modern West – holds that there are distinct populations of persons whose sexual and social identities are primarily organized around their desires for the same or the other sex. It is this understanding of sexuality which underlies the search by lesbian and gay scholars for precursors in, for example, the literature of the Renaissance. The universalizing account, on the other hand, is founded in the Freudian diagnosis of 'the supposed protean mobility of sexual desire and ... the potential bisexuality of every human creature'.[49] This latter insight speaks less to the notion that everyone would find a stable home in the affirmation of a secure bisexual identity, and more to a sense that, as Sedgwick puts it, 'sexual desire is an unpredictably powerful solvent of stable identities'.[50] It is this universalizing construction, then, that accords with the emphasis which the queer critical/historical project places on tracing the workings of disruptive, perverse, or non-normative desires in texts and situations, regardless of the conscious identifications and affiliations of the personages concerned. In a moment, we will sketch some of the ways in which such an approach can facilitate a refashioning of the erotics of the Jonsonian canon. But first we wish to highlight another crucial aspect of the queer project, namely that in unchaining the textual articulation of queer desires from homosexual identities, it opens up the possibility of queering heterosexuality, and thereby disposing altogether of the distinction between normative and transgressive sexualities. We propose, then, that despite the comparative irrelevance of the concerns of the lesbian and gay movement to Jonson, since there is effectively no normative heterosexuality in his works, he is in a sense one of the queerest of Renaissance writers.

What does it mean to say that there is no depiction of normative heterosexuality in Jonson? Clearly, we are not suggesting that all liaisons between men and women in his plays are actually homoerotic relationships in disguise, or that his works offer an unproblematic celebration of polymorphous perversity. Nor do we mean to make the anachronistic claim that Jonson sought programmatically to challenge the status of marriage as a dominant institution of early modern society. What we do want to suggest, though, is that although the centrality of the institution of marriage is taken for granted (albeit in an often corrupt manifestation: witness the much-handled marriage licence of *Bartholomew Fair*), there is no endorsement of heterosexual love, no celebration of heterosexual romance. Rather, we would argue that Jonsonian libido characteristically finds textual expression in two forms, which are not necessarily incongruent with heterosexuality, but in which the question of the gender of the chosen object is not primary: namely, fetishism, and relations which are structured through differentials of power. To speak of the latter in terms of sadomasochism would be unnecessarily provocative; it would also disguise the extent to which these differentials are not merely a function of the erotic dynamics of the relationship, but are embedded in the social worlds of these plays.

Two of the plays which offer themselves most readily to queer readings are the already-mentioned *Epicoene* and *Volpone*. In his recent article on the homoerotics of mastery in Renaissance satire, Mario DiGangi elaborates a sophisticated reading of these plays which links queer sexualities with the eroticization of differentials in power and status.[51] He argues that the homoerotics of mastery has two aspects, both pertinent to a discussion of sexuality in Jonsonian drama: the homoerotic potential within the power structure of master–servant relations (and *Sejanus* is another play in the Jonsonian canon which invites the application of this model of reading), and the importance of homoerotic dynamics within satiric plots which typically involve the assertion of social and dramatic mastery. Like much recent work in this field, DiGangi's article reads the dramatic representation of desire in the context of new insights drawn from social history, in this case the changing conditions of personal service in early modern England. DiGangi perceives the meanings of same-sex desire as contingent upon their interrelations with social structures and values which are not necessarily primarily concerned with the sexual. This leads him to distinguish sharply between the meanings of the traces of male homoeroticism he finds in *Epicoene* and *Volpone*:

> In *Volpone*, an erotically disorderly master–servant relation is integral to the social disorder threatened by class mobility and the non-reproductive (or monstrously reproductive) household. The erotically orderly relation between master and servant in *Epicoene*, on the other hand, bolsters the social order by re-establishing an heir's proper inheritance and by allowing him to humiliate disorderly men and women.[52]

DiGangi's persuasive account can be further nuanced by taking age difference as a further significant aspect of the eroticization of social distinction; this is pertinent to readings not only of the Volpone–Mosca relationship but also to that between ageing Emperor Tiberius and his Machiavellian upstart advisor Sejanus in Jonson's under-explored tragedy. Stephen Orgel has, however, recently taken this even further, suggesting that the rivalrous yet sustaining male homosocial communities which recur in Jonson's plays *are* potential sites of homoeroticism.[53]

We have been speaking here of the homoerotics of mastery, but the volatile and socially charged erotics of heterosexual mastery are, of course, no less relevant to a discussion of Jonsonian sexualities. In this acknowledgement of the imbrication of sexual desire with social structures, the queer project rejoins the feminist examination of gender and sexuality mentioned earlier. Nevertheless, the near-exclusive focus on masculine homoeroticism in the present discussion is no accident. Outside the context of heterosexuality – and more particularly the manoeuvrings around marriage and cuckoldry which are the staple of certain forms of comic drama – Jonson's plays, prior to his Caroline drama at least, demonstrate almost no interest in female sexuality. The early comical satires are decidedly homosocial in their emphases and the middle comedies (and tragedies), as we have seen, circulate on and around the erotics of master–servant relationships rather than male–female ones. Only in the post-1616 Folio texts do questions of female sexuality emerge with any genuine force and once again the politics of canon-formation have had their role to play in the suppression of study or contemplation of these aspects. Paradoxically, Jonson's 'Epigram on the Court Pucell', one of the occasional poems which are also relatively marginal to his canon, has recently taken on a certain fetishized status in discussion of early modern female eroticism, and has thereby achieved an ironic importance as the embodiment of one key aspect of Jonsonian sexuality. It was suggested earlier that the libidinal force of Jonson's texts is often inscribed in fetishistic form: amongst the plays, *Volpone* and *Epicoene* are, again, prominent examples, while Michael McCanles has offered a detailed reading of a number of poems as well as *The New Inn* as inscriptions of a fetishistic sexuality which is marked by class as well as sexual difference.[54] In the 'Epigram on the Court Pucell', Jonson accuses the object of his censure, Cecilia Bulstrode, of perpetrating a lesbian rape in the act of her usurpation of the pen. Writing is construed here as a masculine prerogative, enacted in the form of a sexual relation with the muse: 'What though with Tribade lust she force a Muse,/And in an Epicoene fury can write news/Equal with that, which for the best news goes'.[55] What gives this poem its pertinence to the current discussion is its use of the single word 'tribade', which according to the historian of lesbianism Emma Donoghue was established in the English language by the late sixteenth century as a term evoking lesbian acts and identities.[56] Jonson's deployment of the notion of lesbianism as insult suggests that, at least in the context of the courtly coteries in which he and Bulstrode both participated, its meaning would be immediately intelligible. The 'Epigram on the Court Pucell' therefore seems to signal the existence of a world, scarcely attested in other early modern literary and historical sources, in which female homoeroticism is acknowledged as a meaningful possibility. In consequence, the poem has become fetishized in the context of modern discussions of sexuality, in that the mere use of the word 'tribade' by such a prestigious author as Jonson makes it a precious commodity; yet the attenuated nature of the invocation of lesbianism means that it is hard to do anything with the text beyond passing it from hand to hand as a cherished yet taciturn fragment of evidence. In its marking of the seductions and the difficulties of the project to refashion Jonsonian sexualities, the 'Epigram on the Court Pucell' seems like an appropriate place to conclude what is really a plea for new beginnings.

Notes

1. Stephen Greenblatt, *Renaissance Self-Fashioning: From More to Shakespeare* (London and Chicago: University of Chicago Press, 1980). Greenblatt has dealt with Jonson on other occasions, most notably in his articles, 'The False Ending in *Volpone*', *Journal of English and Germanic Philology*, 75 (1976), 90–104, and 'Loudon and Loudon', *Critical Inquiry*, 12 (1986), 326–46, making the dramatist's absence from the seminal text of New Historicism all the more surprising. The top-heavy emphasis of much subsequent New Historicism-inspired criticism on Shakespeare cannot be blamed on Greenblatt, but the absence of the playwright most frequently seen as Shakespeare's 'Other' always excepting his appearances in his constrained capacity as court masque-maker, is intriguing and deserves further comments. Julie Sanders is personally indebted to Stephen Greenblatt for illuminating discussion of these matters.
2. See, for example, Stephen Orgel, *The Jonsonian Masque* (New York: Colombia University Press, 1965; repr. 1981); Martin Butler, 'Late Jonson', in *The Politics of Tragicomedy: Shakespeare and After*, ed. by Gordon McMullan and Jonathan Hope (London: Routledge, 1992), pp. 166–88; 'Stuart Politics in *A Tale of A Tub*', *Modern Language Review*, 85 (1990), 12–28. Butler's work, it should be said, can itself be categorized as post-New Historicist and is itself in debate with Orgel's, but in respect of its endorsement of court-centred readings of Jonson we include it here alongside the former.
3. William E. Slights makes a related point in *Ben Jonson and the Arts of Secrecy* (London and Toronto: University of Toronto Press, 1994).
4. Leah Marcus, 'Of Mire and Authorship', in *The Theatrical City: Culture, Theatre, and Politics in London*, ed. by David L. Smith, Richard Strier and David Bevington (Cambridge: Cambridge University Press, 1995), pp. 170–81; the same volume also includes an essay reconsidering Puritan stereotypes in Jonsonian drama by Patrick Collinson: 'The Theatre Constructs Puritanism', pp. 137–69.
5. Previous articles had stressed the latent and sometimes blatant misogyny of Jonson's work: see, for example, Kathleen E. McLuskie, in *Renaissance Dramatists* (Hemel Hempstead: Harvester Wheatsheaf, 1989) and Karen Newman in *Fashioning Femininity and English Renaissance Drama* (Chicago: University of Chicago Press, 1991). A sea-change is occurring however and a major contributor to this has been Helen Ostovich – see her 'The Appropriation of Pleasure in *The Magnetic Lady*', *Studies in English Literature* 34 (1994), 425–42 and her essay here. See also Barbara Smith, *The Women of Ben Jonson's Poetry* (Aldershot: Scolar Press, 1995), although the scope of her project is limited; Katherine Eisaman Maus in *Inwardness and Theater in the English Renaissance* (Chicago: University of Chicago Press, 1995); and Julie Sanders, '"The Day's Sports Devised in the Inn": Jonson's *The New Inn* and Theatrical Politics', *Modern Language Review*, 91 (1996), 545–60; and her 'Women and Theatre in Late Jonson', forthcoming.

6. Recent revivals of *The Devil is an Ass* (Royal Shakespeare Company, 1995) and *The Magnetic Lady* (University of Reading, 1996) have begun that project with aplomb.
7. See also David Lindley, 'Embarrassing Ben: Masques for Frances Howard', *English Literary Renaissance* 16 (1980), 343–56.
8. See also Jennifer Brady and W.H. Herendeen (eds), *Ben Jonson's 1616 Folio* (Newark, NJ: University of Delaware Press, 1991).
9. See [A.] Richard Dutton, 'The Significance of Jonson's Revisions in *Every Man In His Humour*', *Modern Language Review*, 69 (1974), 241–9; the parallel edition ed. by J.W. Lever (London: Arnold, 1971); and Chapter 2 in Julie Sanders, *Ben Jonson's Theatrical Republics* (Basingstoke: Macmillan, 1998). The performed version of *Every Man in His Humour* is invariably the London-based 1616 version and that tendency is mirrored in printed versions of the play.
10. A related project underlies Robert C. Evans, *Jonson and the Contexts of His Time* (Lewisburg: Bucknell University Press, 1994).
11. Michael Jamieson's edition of *Three Comedies* (featuring *Volpone, The Alchemist, Bartholomew Fair*) (Harmondsworth: Penguin, 1966) is consistently reprinted. The G. Wilkes edition of *Five Plays* (Oxford: World's Classics, 1981) for the World's Classics series, which to its credit made *Every Man in His Humour* and *Sejanus* available to a wider audience in addition to the three central comedies, has recently been superseded in that series by Gordon Campbell's edition of *The Alchemist and Other Plays* (Oxford: World's Classics, 1995) which inserts *Epicoene* at the expense of those earlier plays, thus securing that play's status as a 'middle comedy' and its presence on undergraduate courses. James Knowles includes *Every Man in His Humour* (the folio edition?) in his edition of four citizen comedies for the series (forthcoming) but again this is spreading the availability of texts between editions which will prohibit student purchase. Helen Ostovich has recently prepared an edition of the middle comedies (including *Epicoene*) for Longmans, continuing the tradition of republishing only certain plays.

Cheap editions tied into the Royal Shakespeare Company and Royal National Theatre performances of *Volpone* and *The Devil is an Ass* and published by Nick Hern have recently entered the market, but these are provided with only limited notes and scholarly material. Theatre productions, *The Devil is an Ass* apart, remain somewhat unadventurous where Jonson is concerned. The RNT has produced *Bartholomew Fair* and *Volpone* (twice, most recently directed by Matthew Warchus in 1995) in recent decades; the RSC has more ambitiously produced *Volpone, Every Man in His Humour* (dir: John Caird), *The New Inn* (dir: John Caird), *Epicoene* (dir: Danny Boyle) – although it should be noted that this production was denied a transfer from Stratford-upon-Avon to London, a spectacular version of *The Alchemist* (dir: Sam Mendes), and *The Devil is an Ass* (dir: Matthew Warchus). Plans to produce *Sejanus* are regularly cited, but have never come to fruition. Other productions of *Volpone* in the past decade

include those at the Almeida in Islington and the Birmingham
Repertory Theatre, touring productions by the English Shakespeare
Company and Greyeye. A recent conference at Reading entitled 'Ben
Jonson and the Theatre' heard frequent requests for productions of
the late plays, in particular *The Staple of News* and *The Magnetic Lady*,
endorsed by theatre director Peter Barnes, but it remains to be seen
whether mainstream or even fringe theatre will respond to that call.
12. Richard Dutton's *Ben Jonson: Authority: Criticism* (Basingstoke:
Macmillan; New York: St. Martin's Press, 1996) does much to re-
establish the significance of Jonson's prose.
13. C.H. Herford, and Percy and Evelyn Simpson (eds), *Ben Jonson*, 11 vols
(Oxford: Clarendon Press, 1925–52). Henceforth H&S. For persuasive
arguments against the H&S early dating of *A Tale of a Tub*, see Anne
Barton, *Ben Jonson, Dramatist* (Cambridge: Cambridge University
Press, 1984), pp. 321–37; and Martin Butler, 'Stuart Politics in *A Tale of
a Tub*'.
14. *Selected Plays of Ben Jonson*, ed. by Martin Butler and Johanna Proctor,
2 vols (Cambridge: Cambridge University Press, 1989).
15. *The New Inn*, ed. by Michael Hattaway (Manchester: Manchester
University Press, 1984); *The Staple of News*, ed. by Anthony Parr
(Manchester: Manchester University Press, 1988); *The Devil is an Ass*,
ed. by Peter Happé (Manchester: Manchester University Press, 1994);
Poetaster, ed. by Tom Cain (Manchester: Manchester University Press,
1995). *Sejanus*, ed. by Philip J. Ayres (Manchester: Manchester
University Press, 1990), was also issued but is now regretfully out of
print.
16. The new multi-volume and electronic text edition for Oxford is being
undertaken by Martin Butler, Ian Donaldson, David Bevington and
David Ganz. A conference relating to the project was held at the
University of Leeds in 1995, a report from which is included in the
Ben Jonson Journal 2 (1995), 233–7, along with Ian Donaldson's
reflections on the project (223–31).
17. John Creaser, 'Enigmatic Ben Jonson', in *English Comedy*, ed. by
Michael Cordner, Peter Holland and John Kerrigan (Cambridge:
Cambridge University Press, 1994), pp. 100–18.
18. As well as the standard edition of the *Complete Masques*, ed. by
Stephen Orgel (New Haven: Yale University Press, 1964; repr. 1975), a
number of masques texts are now available in a World's Classics
edition of *Court Masques*, ed. by David Lindley (Oxford: World's
Classics, 1995). Articles that have carried out the retrievalist project
on Jonsonian masques include Marion Wynne-Davies, 'The Queen's
Masque: Renaissance Women and the Seventeenth-Century Court
Masque', in *Gloriana's Face: Women, Public and Private, in the English
Renaissance*, ed. by S.P. Cerasano and Marion Wynne-Davies (Hemel
Hempstead: Harvester Wheatsheaf, 1992), pp. 79–104; Barbara
Lewalski, *Writing Women in Jacobean England* (Cambridge, MA:
Harvard University Press, 1993); and Kim Hall, 'Sexual Politics and
Cultural Identity in *The Masque of Blackness*', in *The Performance of
Power: Theatrical Discourse and Politics*, ed. by Sue-Ellen Case and

Janelle Reinelt (Iowa City: University of Iowa Press, 1991), pp. 3–18, although it is a marked feature of these articles that they remain reluctant to credit Jonson with any liberal humanism, preferring instead to credit Queen Anne and the performers, or subsequent reception of the texts.

19. The work of Martin Butler has been invaluable in reclaiming these late plays for attention; see, in particular, 'Late Jonson'; 'Stuart Politics in *A Tale of a Tub*'; and 'Ecclesiastical Censorship of Early Stuart Drama: The Case of Jonson's *The Magnetic Lady*', *Modern Philology*, 89 (1991/2), 469–81. See also Julie Sanders '"The Day's Sports Devised in the Inn"', and 'Local Government and Personal Rule in Jonson's *A Tale of a Tub*', *English Literary Renaissance*, 27.3 (1997).

20. See Roland Barthes, 'The Death of the Author', in *Image–Music–Text*, trans. by Stephen Heath (London: Fontana, 1977); and Michel Foucault, 'What is an Author?', in *The Foucault Reader*, ed. by Paul Rabinow (Harmondsworth: Penguin, 1986). Although the present article sees Jonson as caught in a field of competing understandings of authorship, Sara Van den Berg, in 'Ben Jonson and the Ideology of Authorship', in Brady and Herendeen, *Ben Jonson's 1616 Folio* (Newark, NJ: University of Delaware Press, 1991), pp. 111–38, makes a persuasive case for seeing Jonson, especially the Jonson of the 1616 *Works* as fulfilling Foucault's categories of authorship: 'Foucault argues that the humanist interpretation of the literary texts as the acts of a unique person rests on four distinct definitions of the word *author*: first, a constant level of value in a body of texts; second, a field of conceptual or theoretical coherence in those texts; third, a stylistic unity in their language; and fourth, a historical or circumstantial identification of writing as the person's distinctive act. Jonson's *Works* (1616) establishes and investigates the new ideology.' (p. 111).

21. See Richard Burt, *Licensed by Authority: Ben Jonson and the Discourses of Censorship* (Ithaca and London: Cornell University Press, 1993).

22. *The Works of Samuel Daniel* (1601); See Joseph Loewenstein, 'Printing and "the Multitudinous Presse": The Contentious Texts of Jonson's Masques', in Brady and Herendeen, *Ben Jonson's 1616 Folio*, pp. 168–91 (esp. pp. 169–73).

23. Loewenstein, 'Printing', p. 182.

24. David Riggs, *Ben Jonson: A Life* (Cambridge, MA and London: Harvard University Press, 1989), pp. 188–221.

25. For an illuminating discussion of the relationship of Latin and English, and commerce and authorship, on the title-page of the folio, see Van den Berg, 'Ben Jonson and the Ideology of Authorship', pp. 114–17.

26. Pierre Bordieu, *The Field of Cultural Production*, ed. by Randal Johnson (Cambridge: Polity Press, 1993), p. 46.

27. See Riggs, *A Life*, pp. 11–17.

28. Jonathan Haynes, *The Social Relations of Jonson's Theater* (Cambridge: Cambridge University Press, 1992), p. 4.

29. Simon Shepherd and Peter Womack, *English Drama: A Cultural History* (Oxford: Blackwell, 1996), p. vii.

30. See, for example, Peter Womack, *Ben Jonson* (Oxford, Blackwell, 1986).
31. Tom Hayes, *The Birth of Popular Culture: Ben Jonson, Maid Marian, and Robin Hood* (Pittsburgh, PA: Duquesne University Press, 1992), p. 3.
32. See Haynes, *Social Relations*, p. 4.
33. Thanks to Erica Sheen for discussion of this.
34. Ben Jonson, *Bartholomew Fair*, ed. by E.A. Horsman (London: Methuen, 1960; repr. 1979). Induction, ll. 1–15. Subsequent references contained parenthetically within the text.
35. See Barthes, 'The Death of the Author'.
36. Bourdieu, *The Field of Cultural Production*, pp. 101–2.
37. Haynes, *Social Relations*, p. 121.
38. Terry Eagleton introducing Peter Womack's *Ben Jonson*, pp. vii–viii.
39. See Jennifer Brady, '"Noe Fault, But Life": Jonson's Folio as Monument and Barrier', in Brady and Herendeen, *Ben Jonson's 1616 Folio*, pp. 192–216.
40. Nicholas Oldisworth, 'A Letter to Ben Jonson, 1629', quoted in Brady, 'Noe Fault, But Life', p. 194. See also Richard C. Newton, 'Jonson and the (Re)Invention of the Book', in *Classic and Cavalier: Essays on Jonson and the Sons of Ben*, ed. by Claude J. Summers and Ted-Larry Pebworth (Pittsburgh, PA: University of Pittsburgh Press, 1982), pp. 31–55.
41. Brady, 'Noe Fault, But Life', p. 199.
42. See, for example, the discussion of Jonson in the aforementioned McLuskie, *Renaissance Dramatists*; Newman, *Fashioning Femininity and English Renaissance Drama*; and Maus, *Inwardness and Theater in the English Renaissance*. See also Kim Hall, *Things of Darkness: Economies of Race and Gender in Early Modern England* (Ithaca, NY: Cornell University Press, 1995).
43. Bruce Smith, *Homosexual Desire in Shakespeare's England: A Cultural Poetics* (Chicago: University of Chicago Press, 1991); Jonathan Goldberg, *Sodometries: Renaissance Texts, Modern Sexualities* (Stanford, CA: Stanford University Press, 1992) and as editor, *Queering the Renaissance* (Durham, NC: Duke University Press, 1994).
44. Edmund Wilson, 'Morose Ben Jonson' (1938), Repr. in *Ben Jonson: A Collection of Critical Essays*, ed. by Jonas Barish (Englewood Cliffs, NJ: Prentice-Hall, 1963), pp. 60–74.
45. Riggs, *A Life*, p. 31.
46. Christopher Robinson, *Scandal in the Ink: Male and Female Homosexuality in Twentieth-Century French Literature* (London: Cassell, 1995), p. vii.
47. Corinne E. Blackmer, 'The Ecstasies of Saint Theresa: The Saint as Queer Diva from Crashaw to *Four Saints in Three Acts*', in *En Travesti: Women, Gender, Subversion, Opera*, ed. by Corinne E. Blackmer and Patricia Juliana Smith (New York: Columbia University Press, 1995), pp. 306–47 (p. 331).
48. Eve Kosofsky Sedgwick, *Epistemology of the Closet* (Hemel Hempstead: Harvester Wheatsheaf, 1991).
49. Ibid., p. 84.
50. Ibid., p. 85.

51. Mario DiGangi, 'Asses and Wits: The Homoerotics of Mastery in Satirical Comedy', *English Literary Renaissance*, 25 (1995), 179–208.
52. Ibid., p. 192.
53. Stephen Orgel, *Impersonations: The Performance of Gender in Shakespeare's England* (Cambridge: Cambridge University Press, 1996).
54. Michael McCanles, *Jonsonian Discriminations: The Humanist Poet and the Praise of True Nobility* (Toronto: University of Toronto Press, 1992), pp. 123–5.
55. H&S VIII, ll. 222–3. Spellings modernized but higher case marking out of 'Tribade' is retained for emphasis.
56. Emma Donoghue, *Passions between Women: British Lesbian Culture, 1668–1801* (London: Scarlet Press, 1993), p. 4.

2

Jonson's 'Comical Satires' and the Art of Courtly Compliment

Janet Clare

Accompanying the 1607 quarto of *Volpone* is a wealth of paratextual material which includes Jonson's dedication and lengthy epistle to 'the most noble and most equal sisters, the two famous universities', together with commendatory poems from fellow writers, Donne, Beaumont, Chapman, and from influential friends and patrons, Dudley Digges and Esme Stuart. The recurrent note is Jonson's classicism. The verse panegyric of the musician Edmund Bolton, which was later to preface the *Works* of 1616, proclaims Jonson as the first to study Greek antiquities and the monuments of the Roman theatre. Donne praises Jonson as a singular follower of the ancients who is yet an innovator, while Beaumont credits him with introducing a classic comic style hitherto unknown to the English stage.

In 1607, when *Volpone* was published, Jonson's reputation as a writer of classical comedy was based on a comparatively small corpus of plays: *Every Man In His Humour*, the three 'comical satires' – *Every Man Out of His Humour*, *Cynthia's Revels*, and *Poetaster* – and *Volpone*. His credentials as a writer of classical humanist comedy were undoubtedly established through his own vigorous self-promotion of his style and idiom. Through Prologues, Choruses, and comments on aesthetics within the dramatic narrative, readers and auditors are reminded of the classic comic tradition, recovered by the humanists, which Jonson is perpetuating.

My purpose in this essay is not to rehearse familiar details of Jonson's debt to classical authorities. Instead I propose to examine Jonson's strategic use of classical antecedents, specifically satire, in a contemporary Elizabethan context. Jonson's appropriation of such materials, it will be argued, rather than representing early experiments in comic theatre, gave him the initial opportunity to engage with courtly politics and, in particular, the cult of Elizabeth. The relationship between Jonson's ideal of artistic freedom of expression, which he identified with the norm of Greek and Roman theatre and articulated within all of the comical satires, and the reception of his imitative poetics will then be explored in some detail.

In classifying *Every Man Out of His Humour* on its title-page as a 'comical satire', Jonson was positing a new departure in English comedy. The term 'comical satire' draws attention to the mixture of linguistic and stylistic registers demonstrable in the play, while the alignment with comedy of the sub-species of satire also evokes the verse satire as practised by John Marston and Joseph Hall. Jonson's determination to write satirical comedy was a daring, as well as innovative, manoeuvre. The three comical satires – *Every Man Out of His Humour, Cynthia's Revels* and *Poetaster* – date from the final years of Elizabeth I, 1599 to 1602, a period which was deeply hostile to satirical drama. Jonson had already been imprisoned in 1597 for his part in *The Isle of Dogs*, a lost play which evidently, from surviving references to it, had satirical overtones.[1] It is well known that the ecclesiastical press authorities had placed a formal ban on the publication of non-dramatic satire in 1599 and that representative works by John Marston and John Davies were burnt in the Stationers' Hall, whilst other satiric works were confiscated.[2] There were even signs of a literary counter-reaction. Nicholas Breton, in the epistle and text of *No Whippinge nor Trippinge: But a Kinde Friendly Snippinge* takes issue with the cut and thrust of satire which takes 'a wicked course in shadowes of correction' and the humorist who makes 'loath'd behaviours plaie their parts upon a stage.'[3]

Jonson's edginess regarding his experimental drama is conveyed in the production of the texts. By way of defensive strategy, the plays were published with weighty paratextual material and choric interpolations defending the satirist's art and exalting satire's supposedly revered classical antecedents. Yet such apologies for satire coexist with the uncompromising stance of the satiric persona bent on exposing the corruptions of the times, producing an ambivalence of tone and meaning. Moreover, there are indications of Jonson adopting a progressively less controlled attitude towards the audience, a bold gesture in the context of opposition to all the comical satires.

It is, of course, in *Every Man Out of His Humour* that Jonson expounds his well-known definition of 'character' as a man possessed by 'one peculiar quality' that draws 'all his affect, his spirits, and his powers, in their confluctions, all to run one way',[4] a construction of character derived from classical origins. The title-page of the 1600 quarto carries the announcement 'with the severall Character of every person', which alludes to the short description of each character preceding the text; but both the term itself and the expositions recall the *Characters* of Theophrastus, a work published in 1592 with a commentary by Isaac Casaubon. In general, Theophrastus's 'Characters', such as Flattery, Obsequiousness, Idle Chatter, and Pennypinching, lend themselves well to Jonson's conception of a dominant 'humour'. But the focus in *Every Man Out of His Humour* is much more socially precise. Sordido, the ruthless and racketeering farmer, is reminiscent of the *personae* of formal verse satire found in Marston and Hall. There are ardent followers of fashion and would-be courtiers in Puntarvolo, Fastidious Brisk, and Fungoso, and those who are seeking patronage, Fungoso and Sogliardo. With the emphasis on class identity, embracing the farmer, merchant, knight and student, Jonson, in his representation of character, is less concerned with moral abstractions than with types who are identifiable with a specific social milieu.

The loose structure of *Every Man Out of His Humour*, essentially a series of encounters, is given a more formal framework by the Chorus, or Grex as Jonson terms it, which comprises Asper, the author/presenter, and, more prominently, his two associates, Cordatus and Mitis. The role of this Chorus is expanded beyond its precedent in Old Comedy to facilitate a discussion about the purpose and models of the satire. Its primary function becomes that of commentator rather than, as in the Aristophanic form, that of promoting the disputations of antagonists. In the opening Chorus, Asper spells out his intention to be uncompromising in his satiric purpose. His language will never be ground into 'oily colours', 'to flatter vice and daub iniquity'. Instead, 'he will strip the ragged follies of the time,/ Naked , as at their birth' (ll. 13–18). In response to Cordatus's cautionary rejoinder, he remarks ironically that he fears 'no courtier's frown, should I applaud/ The easy flexure of his supple hams' (ll. 27–8). Using the familiar metaphor, he determines to turn the stage into a mirror in which the audience shall 'see the times deformity/ Anatomized in every nerve and sinew' (ll. 120–21). Such a course Mitis deems highly provocative and warns: 'take heed/ The days are dangerous, full of exception,/ And men are grown impatient of reproof' (ll. 123–5). This enables Asper to make the satirists's distinction that exception will only be taken by:

> a sort of fools, so sick in taste,
> That they condemn all physic of the mind,
> ...
> Good men, and virtuous spirits, that loathe their vices,
> Will cherish my free labours, ...
>
> (ll. 131–5).

Such idealist notions of the effects of satire are typically Jonsonian but also represent an explicit attempt to control the reception and interpretation of the play.

Asper's own role is confined to his bold statement of intent in the Chorus prefacing the first act. After this, he assumes the part of Macilente, and Mitis and Cordatus take control of the commentary. Throughout their discourse, the play's genre comes under close scrutiny. Cordatus tells Mitis that he will refrain from any judgement of the play other than that it is somewhat like '*Vetus Comoedia*': this is a form which pleases Cordatus, but one which, he implies, may not 'answer the general expectation' (ll. 230–4). For classically initiated auditors, however, the declaration that the play is conceived in the Aristophanic tradition would have created certain expectations. It would have caused speculation about the personal and political nature of the satire, in particular as to the targets of Jonson's satire corresponding to the playwrights, politicians, and civil servants who were the subjects of Aristophanes. Such anticipations are not fully realized in so far as Jonson objectifies the characters and concentrates on their confluence at court. Reputation is the driving obsession of Fastidius Brisk and his protégé Fungoso. Following a scene in which Brisk elaborates on the delights of social recognition through the court, and in particular the attentions of a countess, the Choric dialogue disavows that any direct application of the satire is intended:

> Mitis: Well, I doubt, this last scene will endure some grievous torture.
> Cordatus: How? you fear 'twill be racked, by some hard construction?

Mitis: Do not you?
...

Cordatus: Why (by that proportion) the court might as well take
offence at him we call the courtier, and with much more pretext,
by how much the place transcends, and goes before in dignity
and virtue: but can you imagine that any noble, or true spirit in
court (whose sinowy, and altogether un-affected graces, very
worthily express him a courtier) will make any exception at the
opening of such an empty trunk, as this Brisk is!

(Grex, II. vi. 141–60)

It may be assumed that the mocking tone of the second parenthesis
and its reference to the unaffected graces of the courtier would be
more recognizable as such in performance. Yet, as with later court
allusions in *Cynthia's Revels*, Jonson is at pains to make the distinction between the true and the spurious courtier, a gloss which
makes for ambiguity in the satire. Here, Jonson wraps the dialogue
in a layer of irony. Cordatus's allusion to the dignity and virtue of
the court is disingenuous; if there are no correspondences between
real and representational, the satirist's art is nullified. Whilst the
soothing dialogue is strategically positioned to forestall any accusation of topical satire, it contradicts the initial boast of Asper that he
would expose the follies of the time and Cordatus's own earlier
identification of the play with old comedy.

It is a critical commonplace that Jonson, in contrast with
Shakespeare's disregard of the fixtures of classical comedy, was
transfixed by the classical unities. But in his first comical satire,
Jonson only gestures towards the unities: the action flows freely
between the country, the city, and the court, with the Chorus
announcing the change of location. Jonson stresses rather the flex-
ibility and openness to assimilation of the comic tradition. In the
opening Choric dialogue, Mitis asks whether the laws of comedy
are to be properly observed. Cordatus reels off a catalogue of minor
and major comic writers, including Cratinus, Aristophanes,
Menander, and Plautus, only to claim that 'we should enjoy the
same license, or free power, to illustrate and heighten our invention
as they did' (ll, 266–7). In his adherence to dramatic structure as
prescribed by Donatus in his commentary on Terence, Jonson
reveals himself as the self-conscious classicist. The play calls attention to its structural regularity and the four internal movements:
the prologue, protasis, epitasis, and catastrophe. Following the final

scene located in the country, where Sordido repents of his racketeering, Cordatus announces the transference of the action to the
court, which is given prominence as the location of the epitasis or
'busy part of our subject'. Again, after Donatus, Jonson terms the
final scene, in which the scholar Macilente renounces his envious
humour, the catastrophe. By positioning his play in the canon of
comic writers as understood by Renaissance theory and by con-
ferring such structural conformity, Jonson is both ensuring that his
play has a cultural status denied to the rival romantic comedy and
legitimating the satiric objectives of comedy.

By defining satire against romantic comedy in terms of plot, a
similar dichotomy is achieved. Romantic comedy is represented as
the inferior genre. The commentary on the aesthetics of comedy,
again delivered by the Chorus, follows an inconsequential scene
where the rustic Sogliardo is deceived by the imposter Shift and is
instructed by Carlo Buffone on how to behave as a gallant in a
tavern. Mitis anticipates general objections to the satirical form of
comedy from an audience which would prefer a scenario reminiscent of *Twelfth Night*:

> The argument of his Comedy might have been of some other
> nature, as of a duke to be in love with a countess, and that count-
> ess to be in love with the duke's son, and the son to love the
> lady's waiting maid: some such cross wooing, with a clown to
> their servingman, better than to be thus near, and familiarly
> allied to the time.
>
> (Grex, III. vi. 195–201)

The difference of opinion about the constituents of comedy elicits
an interpretation which seems to come close to Jonson's understanding of the genre. Mitis's anticipation of objection to the
comedy on the grounds that it is 'familiarly allied to the time'
enables a defence of the social relevance of comical satire. Cordatus
comments that only an 'autumn judgement' could prefer hack-
neyed romance formulae and implies that there is a lack of theoretical rigour in the scenario sketched by Mitis. Would a critic
informed only by an experience of such plays be in a position to
answer the question 'Quid sit Comoedia?', which according to
Cordatus, can only be answered by Cicero's definition of comedy
as an imitation of life, a mirror of manners, an image of truth. In
defining his comedy very precisely in opposition to romantic

comedy, Jonson appropriates the familiar dictum from Donatus's commentary on Terence to legitimate the formally ambitious and socially provocative nature of *Every Man Out of His Humour*.

The Mitis/Cordatus Chorus represents an imaginative use and extension of a device found in Attic comedy and praised by Horace. Richard Dutton has commented on its awkwardness and claims that in so lecturing his audience, Jonson is betraying a 'fundamental lack of confidence in the audience's ability to judge for themselves, which in turn perhaps reflects his own lack of confidence in the new style of drama he was experimenting with.'[5] My emphasis would be rather different, in that the Chorus of Old Attic comedy has been adapted for critical ends vital at this moment in Jonson's career. As a pioneering writer of dramatic satire in the unstable political climate of the late 1590s, it was essential for Jonson to defend his art. The role of the Chorus has a dual purpose. First, it sets up a creative tension between Asper, Mitis, and Cordatus about current modes of comedy and, in particular, the nature of contemporary satire. At the same time, the presence and commentary of the Chorus ensure that the audience is one stage removed from the dramatic action. Mitis and Cordatus anticipate criticism and reaction and formulate an appropriate defence. The framing of the scenes by the Chorus's interventions thus serves to distance and contain some of the play's more provocative references.

In spite of the efforts of the Chorus to lend *Every Man Out of His Humour* the authority of the classical tradition, part of the play, namely the Queen's entry in the final court scene, was censored.[6] It is clear from the appendix to the Quarto of 1600, comprising Macilente's eulogy to the Queen, that Jonson's original intention was to represent Elizabeth on the stage in a scene of ritualistic closure. The catastrophe, as Jonson terms it, after Donatus, depicts the final transformation of Macilente out of his envious humour, as taking place miraculously in the Queen's presence. Macilente addresses Elizabeth in terms of high praise, yet with a peroration that manages to hint at the Queen's mortality:

In her dread presence: death himself admire her:
And may her virtues make him to forget
The use of his inevitable hand.
Fly from her age; sleep time before her throne,
Our strongest wall falls down, when she is gone.
(ll. 33–6)

While printing the set speech Jonson alludes to its censorship: 'Many seem'd not to relish it; and therefore 'twas since alter'd.'[7] In his printed defence Jonson employs the language of courtly compliment, claiming that 'If his Imagination had discoursed the whole world over for an object, it could not have met with a more proper, eminent, or worthy figure, than that of her Majesty's: which his election (though boldly, but respectively) used to a moral and mysterious end.'[8] He argues that the Queen's person had been part of the spectacle of city pageants and triumphs and implies that her presence in the drama, affecting the metamorphosis of Macilente, similarly exemplified her quasi-divine power. In his attempt to legitimate the suppressed ending, Jonson is evidently colluding with the mythologizing of the Queen. By 1599, however, it must have been difficult to sustain the myth and, arguably, any attempt to represent the Queen theatrically could only draw attention to the discrepancies between images of immortality and perpetual youth and the reality of the Queen's old age. Whereas it was acceptable to transgress the boundary of stage and audience when the Queen was actually present to receive the compliment, it was not permissible to act the part on the stage of the Globe where representation could contaminate rarefied image and identity. Jonson's panegyric sits uncomfortably beside his words to Drummond that 'Queen Elizabeth never saw herself after she became old in a true glass.'[9] The transformation of the malcontent/scholar wrought merely by the Queen's presence attempts to contain the play's social critiques. It fails because the artful projection of the mystique of royalty was not to be reconciled with stage representation. In the case of the finale of *Every Man Out of His Humour* the representation of the 66-year-old queen, far from enhancing the reality, was seen by authority (and Jonson's cryptic style conceals the impetus of censorship) as dismantling the carefully maintained aura of monarchical power by rendering it accessible and reproducible.[10]

When the Folio text of *Every Man Out of His Humour* was produced in 1616, Jonson was presumably free to revert in print to his original ending. This he chose not to do. Macilente's final speech as it appears in the later text, far from conveying a sense of miraculous transformation, closes with the theatrical convention of the actor's request for a *plaudite*. The suppressed address to the Queen remains as an addition to the Folio version of the play, but it is stripped of Jonson's justification for its inclusion and hence his elaborate praise of the Queen. Moreover, the opening lines of the

original speech have been abandoned, so that the encomium
becomes more muted. Absent in the Folio text are Macilente's
opening lines which greet Elizabeth in fulsome terms:

> Blessed, divine, unblemished, sacred, pure
> Glorious immortal, and indeed immense;
> O that I had a world of attributes,
> To lend or add to this high majesty.[11]

In 1616 such flattery of a monarch, whose reign was receding in the
memory, could only be regarded as embarrassingly redundant.

In *Cynthia's Revels*, performed, two years after *Every Man Out of
His Humour*, at the Blackfriars and at court, Jonson again draws on
the art of courtly compliment. Classical goddesses had been introduced into royal panegyric in the early decades of the reign, but
Cynthia and Diana, as goddesses associated with the moon, became
prominent in the latter part of the reign as the Queen's prospects of
marriage and childbearing waned.[12] Jonson, however, took the pre-
caution of avoiding the unambiguous representation by sublimating
the image of the Queen within that of the mythological Cynthia/
Diana. Instead of an audience being aware of the physical presence
of the Queen, as in the original dénouement of *Every Man Out of His
Humour* and Peele's *The Arraygnment of Paris*, where as Eliza, Queen
of Elisium, she is worshipped by the goddesses and nymphs,
Elizabeth in the *persona* of Queen Perfection is merely viewed by
Cynthia in a crystal ball during the play's closure. In creating
multiple *personae* for Elizabeth whereby she is imaged as Cynthia
and Diana and as the Virgin Queen, ironically presented to Cynthia
by a disguised Cupid, Jonson is following familiar poetic convention. In the work of Spenser, Raleigh, and Chapman there is a proliferation of images associated with the Queen which, as Helen
Hackett has demonstrated, convey both positive suggestions of her
diversity and negative ones of her as a changeable and culpable
woman.[13] But in the context of the court performance of *Cynthia's
Revels* and the reception of *Every Man Out of His Humour*, the
fracturing of the fictional images might be said to constitute more
a strategy of expedience than one of either complaint or critique.

At other moments in this kaleidoscopic drama the identification
of Elizabeth with Diana, goddess of chastity and hunting, is quite
clearly invoked. In the second scene of the play, Mercury, as mes-
senger of the gods, is sent to the nymph Echo, who is still mourning

the metamorphosis of Narcissus, to command her to dwell on earth. Echo is reluctant to leave her celestial abode, which is associated not only with Narcissus, but with the death of Actaeon: 'Here young Actaeon fell, pursued, and torn/ By Cynthia's wrath (more eager, then his hounds)' (1. ii B4r).[14] Later, Cynthia gives the story her own gloss. Addressing the court following the two masques produced by Cupid and Mercury, she revives the episode and strains to exonerate herself for the punishment of Actaeon:

> For so Actaeon, by presuming far,
> Did (to our grief) incur a fatal doom ...
> But are we therefore judged too extreme?
> Seems it no crime to enter sacred bowers,
> And hallowed places with impure aspect,
> Most lewdly to pollute? seems it no crime,
> To brave a deity?
>
> (V. v. L3r–v)

Here the inclusion of one of the most potent myths, that of Diana's revenge upon Actaeon on his discovering the goddess bathing, works to evoke the downfall of the Earl of Essex and, in particular, his unheralded entry into the Queen's private chamber.[15] The allegorical representation of Essex's fateful rebellion permits a degree of freedom in its telling and interpretation. Echo's pity for Actaeon coupled with Cynthia's preoccupation with the event and her resentful awareness that she has been harshly judged conveys an unease at the fate of the Queen's erstwhile favourite.

The inclusion of the Actaeon episode is one indication that Jonson's intervention in the cult of Elizabeth is not an uncritical exercise. The opening Lucianic dialogue between Cupid and Mercury sets the tone of the play as a mixture of satire and uncertain courtly compliment. Like Lyly in his court comedy *Sapho and Phao*, Jonson treats the gods with familiarity and some irreverence. In the first scene, Cupid alludes mockingly to Mercury's thieving:

> *Cupid*: ... you have not a finger, but is as long as my quiver (cousin Mercury) when you please to extend it.
> *Mercury*: Whence derive you all this speech, boy?
> *Cupid*: O! 'tis your best policy to be Ignorant: you did never steal Mars his sword out of the sheath, you? nor Neptune's Trident? nor Apollo's bow? no, not you? Alas, your palms (Jupiter

knows) they are as tender as the foot of a foundred nag, or
lady's face new mercuried, they will touch nothing.
Mercury: Go too (infant) you will be daring still.
Cupid: Daring? O Janus! what a word is there? why, my light
feather-heeled cousse, what are you? any more than my uncle
Jove's pandar, a lackey that runs on errands for him.

(I. i. B1v)

The inspiration comes from Lucian's debunking of myth and
mystic cults in his *Dialogue of the Gods*. In particular, the Cupid/
Mercury dialogue is redolent of the eleventh dialogue between
Hephaestus and Apollo, in which Apollo claims that the infant
Hermes is already a thief.[16] Yet, despite these derogatory impres-
sions which are created in the early scenes of the play, Mercury's
role subsequently changes so that with Criticus and Arete he
becomes part of the plot to unmask the counterfeit courtiers in the
presence of Cynthia. In her final speech Cynthia praises him as 'a
deity, next Jove, beloved of us', such high esteem inviting some
doubt about the supposedly omniscient goddess.

In contrast to the favour shown to Mercury, his companion
Cupid receives only Cynthia's harsh reprobation. There is no place
for the god of love at the court of the chaste Cynthia/Elizabeth. At
the beginning of the play the outlawed Cupid tells Mercury that he
is assuming the habit of a page so that he may practise his arts
upon one of Diana's maids and redeem lost time through 'long and
over-nice proscription of my deity, from their court' (I. i. B2v). The
time-honoured iconic representation of the Queen's chastity is
again mockingly alluded to in a later dialogue between Cupid and
Mercury. Mercury wonders why Cupid is so apparently ineffectual
amongst the self-enamoured courtiers. Cupid replies that he must
be circumspect, 'for if Cynthia heare the twang of my bow, she'll go
near to whip me with the string' (V. v. L2r). Mercury acknowledges
that Cynthia's power is such that it negates the forces of passion:

Marry, all that I fear, is Cynthia's presence; which, with the cold
of her chastity, such an *Antiperistasis* about the place, that no heat
of thine will tarry with the patient.

(V. v. L2r)

Cupid is the presenter of the first masque in honour of Cynthia.
Disguised as Anteros, his identity is ambiguous as the god who

either opposes love or punishes those who do not return love. Cynthia's pleasure in the entertainment does not, however, mitigate her displeasure at discovering his presence in the court and she banishes him:

> Cupid, we must confess this time of mirth
> (Proclaim'd by us) gave opportunity,
> To thy attempts, although no privilege;
> Tempt us no further, we cannot endure
> Thy presence longer: vanish, hence, away
>   (V. v. L4r)

Cynthia's irascible words and her fear of Cupid's temptations present another perspective on the Queen's mystical virginity. Philippa Berry has shown that later courtly conceptions of Elizabeth deliberately effaced her ageing reality, while simultaneously attributing supernatural powers to her.[17] Increasingly, the Queen's virginity was perceived as investing her with such powers, and even as suggesting her immortality. Imagery associated with the Virgin Mary was in the latter decades of the reign re-employed in praise of Elizabeth and her chastity. But in Cynthia's overwrought reaction to Cupid and his subsequent banishment, there is no enhancement of her spiritual image. Chastity has become fetish. This image of Cynthia approximates more to the Elizabeth who dismissed and imprisoned courtiers and ladies in waiting who formed liaisons and entered into marriages against her desire to preside over a celibate court with sexual power wielded only by the Virgin Queen.[18]

Ironically, in a play dedicated to 'the special fountain of manners: the court', it is Cynthia's court which is the object of derision in the play. The conversations of the courtiers and their preoccupations with fashion and self-fashioning are seen as equally facile whether or not they have drunk from the fountain of self-love. Throughout, Cupid and Mercury offer satiric comment on the narcissistic self-absorption of those who congregate on the fringes of the court, waiting to be admitted to the royal presence. When it is announced that Cynthia has postponed the evening's revels, Asotus, who has been practising the arts of courtship under the tutelage of the pretentious Amorphus, expresses his frustration at being thwarted in his courtly ambitions:

What luck is this, that our revels are dashed? Now was I
beginning to glister, in the very high way of preferment.
And Cynthia had but seen me dance a strain, or do but
one trick, I had been kept in court, I should never have
needed to look towards my friends again.

(IV. v. 78–81)

The speech is a neat exposure of a desperate pursuit of patronage,
of which royal patronage is the pinnacle. The court is perceived
accurately as the source of power and favour; but, as with the
passage referring to Actaeon, the lines also carry a more precise
allusion. That Cynthia should favour a courtier because he could
dance elegantly was not so fantastical. It was known that this was
how Sir Christopher Hatton, who became Lord Chancellor, had
first attracted the Queen's attention and had thus earned the
soubriquet of the dancing chancellor.[19]

It is significant that the passage in which Asotus expresses his
hope of attracting Cynthia's attention through his dancing does not
appear in the Quarto text, which is the only edition published
before the 1616 Folio text. Other omissions in the quarto text relate
to the depiction of the female courtiers who are presided over by
Moria, mother of Phantaste. It could be said that the female image
which is physically most representative of the Queen is not Cynthia
but Moria, Folly personified in Erasmus's *Praise of Folly*, and that in
turn she contaminates the image of Cynthia as a female figure of
absolute power. Moria advises the nymphs who wait on her, 'make
much of time, and place, and occasion, and opportunity, and
favourites, and things that belong to them; for I'll ensure you, they
will all relinquish... I was once a reveller myself' (IV. i. 124–9). This
satirical critique of female power is extended in a lengthy conversation which was either removed from the Quarto or was a later addition to the Folio text (IV. i. 134–214). Passing the time before the
arrival of Cynthia, the women fantasize about what they might
become if their identities could be transformed by Juno. Moria has
voyeuristic fantasies of wanting to know 'what were done behind
the arras, what upon the stairs, what i'the garden, what i'the
nymph's chamber, what by the barge, and what by the coach'.
Philantia has monarchical ambitions: 'I would wish ... all the court
were subject to my absolute beck, and all things in it depending in
my look; as if there were no other heaven, but in my smile, nor
other hell, but in my frown.' Phantaste would assume the charac-

ters of women of different social status and experience before becoming the 'richest, fairest, and delicatest in a kingdom, the very centre of wealth and beauty', in which position she would play the unattainable woman toying with her many suitors. The power that the women desire is, of course, that held by the Queen, although here shorn of its glamour. In reducing female power to such trivial dimensions, Jonson, in 1600, would have been running certain risks, not only in exposing the petty ambitions of women with court aspirations, but also in suggesting the frailties of the Queen as the protagonist of absolute female power. This kind of response to the scene may account for its absence in the Elizabethan version of the play.

Ostensibly, then, *Cynthia's Revels* belongs to the genre of courtly pastime and compliment, a cultural formation which has received considerable attention from New Historicist critics, who have emphasized how the crown exploited various cultural symbols, religious and literary, to create a syncretic Elizabethan mythology and iconography.[20] But such an approach tends to demonstrate an inflexible view of court politics and to ignore clear changes in perceptions of Elizabeth. It has been contended, for example, that while in the 1590s the cult of Elizabeth was arguably at its zenith, the years also produced literature which was critical, even iconoclastic, towards the Queen.[21] Jonson's depiction of Cynthia seems to fall into an equivocal category. There is a discrepancy between what we hear and what we see of Cynthia. We are led to believe that Cynthia is morally discriminating and that she recognizes the worth of true courtiers, Arete and Criticus, over that of the spurious court; yet Arete is introduced in the prologue as 'a poor nymph of Cynthia's train, that's scarce able to buy herself a gown, you shall see her play in a black robe anon' (A3r). If Arete and Criticus are held in such estimation, it is curious that they appear as materially unrewarded. In answer to Mercury's question about the status of the nymphs who keep company with Moria, Cupid answers that 'they are in her Court ... but not as starts; these never come in the presence of Cynthia; the nymphs that make her train, are the divine Arete, Time, Phronesis, Thaume, and others of that high sort. These are privately bought in by Moria in this licentious time, against her knowledge and (like so many meteors) will vanish when she appears.' (II.v. E3r). But apart from Arete, Cynthia's true nymphs have no stage presence and this evanescence of the 'licentious' women does not happen in the way Cupid describes; it is Cupid rather than the women whom Cynthia is intent on banishing. Neither is it clear in the final discovery scene, whether or not Cynthia has penetrated the courtiers' disguise before they unmask. Arete informs Criticus that, as a goddess, Cynthia has 'true intelligence' and that the sports she has announced are all part of a strategy to expose and reform the spurious court. But this divine prescience is far from explicit in the actual scene which leads to the unmasking of the courtiers. Cynthia's praise of their solicitude and her expression of gratitude that they, unlike others, have not censured her actions could be read ironically as disclosing a lack of discernment over courtly identities. Moreover, her final act of delegating power to reform the court to Criticus and Arete, while an exaggerated gesture towards Jonson's profession, is far removed from the dynamic creativity associated with the Queen in earlier courtly pastimes.

In *Cynthia's Revels*, by comparison with its dramatic predecessor, there is a relaxation of authorial control of the audience and of the reception of the satire. The apology for satire is more closely integrated into the play proper. The omnipresent Chorus has been replaced by the figure of Criticus (Crites in the Folio): 'one in whom the humours and the elements are peaceably met.' Criticus's role is constructed so that he both participates in the action and stands outside of it registering a revulsion of the persons who hanker after Court preferment. In one scene he recounts at length to Arete several of the worst court practices he has witnessed. In a style reminiscent of formal verse satire, he offers character vignettes comprising 'the strangest pageant, fashioned like a court' (III.iv.4). Significantly, the texts of the Quarto and Folio differ at this point. The early text, the 1601 Quarto, omits the portraits of the 'mincing marmoset/Made all of clothes, and face,' (III. iv. 22–3), of the sycophantic traveller who has 'seen the cringe/Of several courts, and courtiers; knows the time/Of giving titles' (III. iv. 29–31) and of the bribe-taker who accepts 'the coming gold/Of insolent, and base ambition,/That hourly rubs his dry, and itchy palms.' (III. iv. 37–9). The textual discrepancies are interesting in view of the explicit court satire of the scene and in the context of other Quarto omissions which have already been discussed. The missing pages may have been suppressed for Elizabethan performance and publication because of their explicit satirical attack on a court characterized by opportunistic scrambles for rewards and offices or they may have been added at a

later date, prior to the Folio publication, when the Stuart accession made satire of the late regime less dangerously provocative.
Either way, the nature of the difference between the two texts
suggests that in 1601 Jonson felt compelled to moderate his social
critique.

Cynthia's Revels is the most topical of the comical satires, with
Jonson exploiting the mythological cults surrounding Elizabeth for
his own purposes. The mythical location of Gargaphy, the inter-
polation of Echo, Cupid, and Mercury as actors in the drama, the
repeated insistence that 'this nest of spiders' is not the real court
but its travesty, and the classical and humanist material from
Lucian to Erasmus, appear as carefully crafted devices to conceal
the play's contemporary concerns. The fact that the two texts of
Quarto and Folio vary to a considerable extent suggests, however,
the application of either actual censorship or self-censorship, and
reflects an over-stepping of accepted boundaries within which
satirical comedy was constrained.

In *Poetaster* (1601), classical models and material are deployed
more explicitly and more defensively. Tom Cain, commenting on
the uneasy role of the satirist who condemns the court but not the
Queen, has argued that the location of *Poetaster* in the court of
Augustus 'allowed implicit criticism of Elizabeth, contrasted with
the ideal prince, patron of poets who encouraged freedom of
speech'.[22] As Horace points out in his defence of satire, far from
being motivated by envy, the satirist is its victim. Jonson effectively
dramatizes the point by opening the play with Envy as a Prologue
to the Prologue, 'Arising in the midst of the stage' (SD, Induction),
threatening to destroy the play 'With wrestings, comments, applications,/ Spy-like suggestions, privy whisperings' (ll. 24–5). But her
expectations are suddenly defeated when she realizes that the location of the play is Rome, and asks rhetorically how she might 'force
this to the present state' (l. 34). She appeals for help to actors who
might distort and corrupt the author's work. But nobody appears,
apart from an armed Prologue who explains 'this forced defence'
(l. 72) on the grounds that:

> 'tis a dangerous age:
> Wherein who writes, had need present his scenes
> Forty-fold proof against the conjuring means
> Of base detractors and illiterate apes,
>
> (ll. 67–70)

The hostile and the sympathetic prologue in turn reflect the immediate concern of *Poetaster* with the social and cultural role of the
writer and the dangers attendant on producing dramatic satire.
Located in Augustan Rome where Horace, Ovid, and Virgil
freely practise their art , the play nonetheless represents the threat
to poetry from hostile critics, spurious poets, and envious rivals.
Even the Rome of Caesar Augustus seen as a repository of excel-
lence, harbours dangers for the writer of satire. Through the figure
of Horace, Jonson articulates a defence of satire as socially cor-
rective and beneficial to the state. In one scene, Horace is in conversation with the jurist Trebatius about the dangers inherent in the
writing of satire and his determination to persist in that course
(III.v.). Trebatius advises him to turn to other forms: he should
'sing unconquered Caesar's deeds' and praise his fortitude and
justice. But Horace is not attracted by genres of courtly compliment
and royal panegyric: satire is his *métier* and he will write it 'in
spight of fear'. The scene is lifted from the first satire of the second
book of Horace's *Satires*, where the young Horace is counselled by
Trebatius. Jonson, however, contributes an additional, defiant note:
his Horace declares that even the threat of banishment will not
make him compromise his self-elected role as satirist.

Despite the use of familiar antecedents, the play did apparently
elicit complaint from its objects of satire: the legal profession, the
players, and the military. In response, Jonson was evidently keen
to record the details of such accusations and present his defence.
This purpose emerges in the additional material of the Folio text,
principally the 'Apologetical Dialogue' appended to it, in which
Jonson answers 'sundry impotent libels then cast out against me
and the Play' (ll. 4–6). Two new characters are introduced into the
'Apologetical Dialogue', Nastus and Polyposus, who profess not to
have seen the play and so question the author about its scopes and
his intentions. The author denies that he has 'taxed/ The law, and
lawyers, captains, and the players/ By their particular names.'
(ll. 68–70) and he defends his use of satire, which, Polyposus tells
him, some term 'mere railing' (l. 172). In self-justification, he recalls
the tradition as proclaimed by the humanists:

> Ha! If all the salt in the old comedy
> Should be so censured, or the sharper wit
> Of the bold satire, termed scolding rage,
> What age could then compare with those for buffoons?

What should be said of Aristophanes,
Persius? or Juvenal? whose names we now
So glorify in schools, at least pretend it?

(ll. 173–9)

The argument is a neat one. The curricula of the grammar schools prescribed the study and emulation of the classical satiric writers. Jonson queries the genuineness of this reverence: the classical tradition is admired academically and historically, but its transposition and replication is discouraged in contemporary satirical comedy.

The reaction against *Poetaster* and, in so far as certain social sectors protested against the play, the suggestion that its subsequent censorship was not exercised in the face of an unwilling populace, mark a turning point both in Jonson's career and in humanist satirical comedy. At the close of the 'Apologetical Dialogue' Jonson derides the prolific writers who currently serve the 'abused theatres' and announces his departure from comedy: 'And since the Comic Muse/Hath proved so ominous to me, I will try/If Tragedy have a more kind aspect.' (ll. 209–11) Jonson's desire to register the tenor of the times in the forms made available by his humanist education seems to have been prematurely arrested by the harsh reception of the comical satires. When Jonson later returned to comedy with *Eastward Ho* and *Volpone*, the insistent voice of the social satirist had been subsumed under that of the popular entertainer.

In his essay *Of Dramatic Poesy*, Dryden commented on Jonson's appropriations of the classics: 'He has done his robberies so openly, that one may see he fears to be taxed by any law ... he invades authors like a monarch; and what would be theft in other poets, is only victory in him.'[23] The deployment of classical materials and the numerous allusions to celebrated practitioners of satire, dramatic and non-dramatic, are sustained to an unusual degree in Jonson's comical satires. As has been argued, the appeal to such authorities amounts to more than an intellectual display of Jonson's humanist credentials. Nor is the classicism of these early plays grounded entirely in aesthetic judgement. The appeals, explicit and implicit, to classical antecedents were an attempt to afford his experiments in comical satire cultural authority at a time when other forms of comedy predominated. Equally significant, however, is the limited degree of protection offered by the classical precedent of satire as a socially established genre. Imitative poetics, particularly those of classical comedy and courtly pastime, were no watertight defence against accusations of topical satire.[24] Indeed, courtly and social critiques were not legitimated by the extensive classical apparatus of the plays. The anxious deployment of classical materials, the traces of censorship in the texts, and the recorded opposition to Jonson's satiric social commentaries reveal the *fin-de-siècle* constraints on writing satirical comedy. In all three comical satires, the role of social satirist, whether it be occupied by Asper, Criticus, or Horace, is vindicated. This is clearly art triumphing over reality. In co-ordinating comedy and satire, despite all his appeals to erudite traditions, the same freedom did not prevail for Jonson.

Notes

1. See Janet Clare, *Art Made Tongue-Tied by Authority: Elizabethan and Jacobean Dramatic Censorship* (Manchester: Manchester University Press, 1990), pp. 51–5.
2. See Richard A. McCabe, 'Elizabethan Satire and the Bishops' Ban of 1599', *Yearbook of English Studies*, 11 (1981), 188–94.
3. Nicholas Breton, *No Whippinge, nor Trippinge: But a Kinde Friendly Snippinge* (1601), A5r.
4. *Every Man Out of His Humour*, first Chorus, in *Ben Jonson*, ed. by C.H. Herford, Percy and Evelyn Simpson, 11 vols (Oxford: Clarendon Press, 1925–52), III. Henceforth H&S and, unless otherwise stated, all quotations and references are from this edition. Spelling has been modernized.
5. Richard Dutton, *Ben Jonson: To the First Folio* (Cambridge: Cambridge University Press, 1983), p. 41.
6. The suppressed ending and the preface Jonson wrote to accompany it, as they appeared in the quarto of 1600, are reprinted in H&S III, pp. 599–604. The closure in the Folio is quite different.
7. See Appendix X in H&S III, II. 3–4.
8. Ibid., II, 16–20.
9. H&S I, pp. 141–2.
10. My conclusion runs counter to some historicist writing which argues that in the early modern period state power and theatrical power operated on the same principles. See 'Historicism and the Question of Censorship in the Renaissance', *English Literary Renaissance* 27:2 (1997).
11. See H&S III, p. 603.
12. See Helen Hackett, *Virgin Mother, Maiden Queen: Elizabeth I and the Cult of the Virgin Mary* (Basingstoke: Macmillan, 1995), pp. 78–88.
13. Ibid., pp. 176–86.

14. Apart from passages only in the 1616 Folio, all quotations from *Cynthia's Revels* are from the quarto of 1601. Spelling has been modernized and contractions expanded.
15. See, for example, Carole Levin, *The Heart and Stomach of a King: Elizabeth I and the Politics of Sex and Power* (Philadelphia: University of Pennsylvania Press, 1994), p. 154.
16. *Lucian*, ed. by A.M. Harne, 8 vols (London: Heinemann (Loeb), 1913), VII, pp. 293–7.
17. Philippa Berry, *Of Chastity and Power: Elizabethan Literature and the Unmarried Queen* (London: Routledge, 1989).
18. See Christopher Haigh, *Elizabeth I* (London: Longman, 1988), pp. 92–6.
19. See Levin, *The Heart and Stomach of a King*, p. 79; Haigh, *Elizabeth I*, p. 91; and Simon Adams, 'Eliza Enthroned', in *The Reign of Elizabeth I*, ed. by Christopher Haigh (Basingstoke: Macmillan, 1994), p. 70.
20. See Louis Adrian Montrose, 'Eliza, Queene of Shepheardes and the Pastoral of Power', *English Literary Renaissance*, 10 (1980), 153–82, (p. 164).
21. See Hackett, *Virgin Mother*, pp. 180–97.
22. Ben Jonson, *Poetaster*, ed. by Tom Cain (Manchester: Manchester University Press, 1995), Introduction p. 14. All quotations from the play and from the 'Apologetical Dialogue' are from this edition.
23. John Dryden, 'Of Dramatic Poesy: An Essay' (1668), in *Of Dramatic Poesy and Other Critical Essays*, ed. by George Watson, 2 vols (London: Dent, 1962), I, p. 62.
24. Richard Burt has suggested a different emphasis in *Licensed by Authority: Ben Jonson and the Discourses of Censorship* (Ithaca: Cornell University Press, 1993). From the textual details which I have discussed, I would query the assumption that Jonson used an emergent literary criticism, particularly critical theories of imitation, as a mode of critical/censorial regulation.

3

'Satyres, That Girde and Fart at the Time': *Poetaster* and the Essex Rebellion

Tom Cain

There has developed in recent years something approaching a consensus that Jonson's work celebrates an absolutist political ideology. He has been seen as a fairly straightforward spokesman for absolutism in the masques and the poetry of praise, and a more oblique one in such matters as the exultation of monarchy of mind over appetite in many of his plays and poems. In his prescriptive attitudes to language and art, and even in the patriarchal marshalling of his followers as 'Sons', or as a 'Tribe' with him at its head, he seems actively to embrace absolutist attitudes, rather than to be drawn unwillingly into the dominant discourse of power.[1]

Like all such consensuses, this one has a good deal of truth in it, but it is one that needs serious qualification if the debate over reconfiguring Ben Jonson is to have any meaning. For in much of his early work in particular, the satirist is a much more anti-authoritarian figure than his current reputation would suggest, associating with what can reasonably be called a radical circle in the Inns of Court, and challenging the abuse of power even as, in the series of early 'comicall satyres', he seems to offer the absolute monarch as the arbiter of social and moral problems. These early plays become the sites not so much for the containment of subversion as for a contest between contemporary corruption at the centres of power in the Royal Court and the courts of justice, and a vision of ideal rule and ideal justice that is offered less as an alternative to the current state of things, than as a way of illuminating their corruption. Such readings of Jacobean drama as contingent to, or parodic of, contemporary political events have become commonplace in recent years, but partly because of his own frequent disclaimers against a topical application, partly because specific personal and political satire have long been seen as ephemeral, little attention has been given to the contemporary political dimensions of Jonson's early plays, other than *Sejanus*. This paper explores the presence in one of those plays, *Poetaster*, of encoded commentary on the single most dramatic event in domestic politics around the turn of the century: the Essex rebellion of February 1601.

Examination of *Poetaster's* relationship to the events of 1601 must begin with a document written, probably, 15 years later. Jonson's letter of dedication to Richard Martyn in the 1616 folio attributes the play's preservation after its first performance, probably in Michaelmas 1601, to Martyn's interaction with 'the greatest Justice' of the kingdom, that is with Lord Chief Justice Popham:

> I send you this piece of what may live of mine, for whose innocence, as for the Author's, you were once a noble and timely undertaker to the greatest Justice of this kingdom. Enjoy now the delight of your goodness, which is to see that prosper, you preserved; and posterity to owe the reading of that, without offence, to your name, which so much ignorance and malice of the times then conspired to have suppressed.[2]

What this dedication does not make clear is why the play should have run into such serious problems at such a high level. What was there in a comedy set in Augustan Rome which brought it to Popham's attention? What was the 'innocence' Martyn vouched for, and in what quarters did the ignorant and malicious conspiracy to suppress the play originate?

It has usually been assumed that the answer is contained in the 'Apologetical Dialogue' which concludes the play, and which *was* suppressed when it was first printed in 1602, as Jonson was at pains to inform his first readers:

> *HERE (Reader) in place of the Epilogue, was meant to thee an Apology from the Author, with his reasons for the publishing of this booke: but (since he is no less restrain'd, then thou depriv'd of it, by Authoritie) hee praies thee to think charitably of what thou hast read, till thou maist heare him speake what he hath written.*

This Apology must have been substantially the same as the surviving 'Apologetical Dialogue' printed in 1616, when it was described as being 'only once spoken' in 1601–2.[3] Taken together with the epistle to Martyn, the solitary initial performance of the contentious Dialogue (with *Author* possibly played by Jonson himself), the disdainful tone of the quarto's brief note on its omission, and its defiant inclusion in the 1616 folio with an introduction which draws attention to its earlier suppression, constitute a unique sequence of resistance to censorship in this period. The Dialogue defends *Poetaster*'s satire against three groups: lawyers, 'captains', and players. Jonson turns, as often, to his familiar defence from Martial: 'My books have still been taught/ To spare the persons and to speak the vice' (ll. 70–71).[4] He takes refuge in his Roman setting to defend the mockery of lawyers, the most powerful of these groups, invoking historical authenticity by quoting from Ovid:

> First, of the law; indeed, I brought in Ovid,
> Chid by his angry father for neglecting
> The study of their laws for poetry;
> And I am warranted by his own words:
> *Saepe pater dexit, studium quid inutile tentas?*
> *Maeonides nullas ipse reliquit opes.*
> And in far harsher terms elsewhere, as these:
> *Non me verbosas leges ediscere, non me*
> *Ingrato voces prostituisse foro.*
> But how this should relate unto our laws
> Or their just ministers with least abuse,
> I reverence too much to understand.
> ('Apologetical Dialogue', ll. 103–14)

The hurt bewilderment of the scrupulous humanist scholar is clearly disingenuous, however, especially in the light of the long satirical passage in which Tucca and Lupus, both unmistakably citizens of Jonson's London, join Ovid's father in praise of a venal legal career that is clearly an Elizabethan one (I.ii.93–134). This latter passage was also omitted from the 1602 quarto: reconstruction of the printing history of *Poetaster* supports the view that it, and other passages attacking lawyers and players, were in Jonson's original copy, and were therefore probably acted, at least briefly, in 1601, but were dropped from the quarto at a fairly late stage, after it had been cast off for printing.[5] The legal profession was a more influential group to offend than the 'captains', and certainly more than the players. It is entirely possible, therefore, that Jonson's treatment of them was enough to lead to moves to suppress the play, and that the cuts made in the 1602 quarto were a result of Martyn's negotiations with Popham in the latter's role as guardian of the reputation (and *amour propre*) of the English legal profession.[6]

The problem is that on its own, the satire on lawyers hardly seems enough to justify the furore over the play which Jonson's dedication indicates. Lawyers were traditional targets of satire, especially in the 1590s of satire written by and for members of the Inns of Court. Indeed, Martyn himself, on his way to becoming a distinguished barrister, and eventually, if briefly, Recorder of London, takes a similar view to Jonson in his only published work, a speech of welcome to James I in which he looks forward to a reign in which:

Unconscionable Lawiers, and greedie officers shall no longer spinne out the poore mans cause in length to his undoing, and the delay of justice. No more shall bribes blinde the eyes of the wise, nor gold be reputed the common measure of mens worthinesse: Adulterate gold, which can guild a rotten post, make *Balam* a Byshoppe, and *Isachar* as worthy of a iudiciall chaire as *Solomon*, where he may wickedly sell that justice, which he corruptly bought.[7]

Popham, like Martyn a West Country man and a product of Martyn's inn, the Middle Temple, may have been offended, but can hardly have been surprised, at such attacks on the law. As it happens, Popham may also have had strong personal reasons for disliking Jonson's play: his daughter Penelope had married Serjeant Thomas Hanham, a senior Middle Templar and the father of another Middle Templar, Captain Thomas Hanham. It was a 'Capten Hannam' whom Dekker identified as Jonson's model for Captain Tucca in *Poetaster*.[8] To lampoon the grandson (or some other relative) of the Lord Chief Justice may in itself have been enough to call for the intercession of the charismatic Prince D'Amour, the Lord of Misrule of the Middle Temple revels, a role Martyn played for several years.

There may, however, have been larger political issues at stake. It is possible that Martyn interceded to defend Jonson against the much more dangerous accusation that *Poetaster* offered an oblique satirical commentary on the atmosphere, events, and policies leading up to the rebellion and arraignment of the Earl of Essex in February 1601. Such allusion would have to have been oblique in a play performed later in the same year, rendering it all the more difficult to discern now. Chambers long ago expressed the belief (à propos Cynthia's Revels) that no 'Court dramatist would have dared to refer to Essex at all after 25 Feb. 1601'.[9] It may be for this reason that few critics have considered the possibility of such allusion in Poetaster. The latter, however, was not performed at Court: clearly aimed at the Inns of Court, and possibly designed for a performance at the Middle Temple revels of 1601 presided over by Richard Martyn, it is not the work of a 'Court dramatist' but of an 'Inns of Court dramatist'.[10]

Chambers was correct, though, in pointing to government sensitivity over allusions to Essex's rebellion, and not just in 1601. It remained a taboo subject for several years, partly because of its danger as a precedent, partly because James as King of Scotland and aspirant to the English succession had been in close, potentially compromising contact with Essex during the late 1590s.[11] Daniel's Philotas (1604) and Chapman's Byron plays (1608) ran into trouble over Essex allusions some years later, and Troilus and Cressida may have been withdrawn from performance in case of 'application'. Certainly Fulke Greville, an Essexian with more to lose, destroyed his Antony and Cleopatra 'seeing the like instance not poetically, but really fashioned in the Earl of Essex then falling'.[12] Jonson's Blackfriars audience would have been equally sensitive, but on the whole more sympathetic, as I believe the play shows Jonson to be sympathetic. This is especially so for those many members of the audience from the Inns of Court, who had been subjects of the Privy Council's hurried letter on the day of the rebellion to 'the several Innes of Courte' ordering that 'the gentlemen & others might be ready upon all occasions with their armour & weapons, and especially that the younger sorte might be commanded to keepe themselves within the houses to answere all occasions of service'.[13] Essex House was immediately next door to the Middle Temple, and there was a well-founded fear that the 'younger sort' might side with Essex: he was more popular with them than the Cecil–Cobham–Raleigh faction, often for religious as much as political reasons.

Here Jonson's recent conversion to Catholicism is important: many Catholics had looked to Essex for support, his tolerant policy holding together a mixed following of puritans, freethinkers, and Catholics both loyal and disloyal (almost all of the Gunpowder plotters were involved in the Essex rebellion). After his arrest, Essex's Catholic stepfather, Sir Christopher Blount, told his interrogators that 'The Earl did give him assurance that if he came to authority there should be a toleration for religion. He was wont to say that he did not like that any man should be troubled in his religion.'[14] With the exception of Sir John Salusbury (whose cousin, Owen, nevertheless played a prominent part in the rebellion) the sympathies of Jonson's circle at the Inns at this time were probably with Essex and Southampton: the radical sentiments of Martyn and his friends John Hoskyns – Jonson's poetic 'father' – Christopher Brooke and Benjamin Rudyerd, in particular, are close to those of Edwin Sandys, another Middle Templar who was slightly older than this group, but who worked closely with Martyn in the House of Commons, and who was, with Martyn and Brooke, involved with the Earl of Southampton, the other leading figure in the rebellion, in the years immediately following, when all of them were active in the Virginia Company.[15] Chamberlain later mentions Martyn as a lover of Lettice Rich, daughter of Essex's sister Penelope.[16] Donne, another prominent member of this circle, had accompanied Essex on two expeditions, and had the chance to see him at even closer quarters as Egerton's secretary during the period of Essex's house arrest at the Lord Keeper's in 1600. The tone of Donne's letters to Wotton, formerly Essex's own secretary, but now retired to the safety of Bocton Malherbe, remains cautiously sympathetic to Essex during this period, even as he sees the essential weaknesses of Essex's character as a politician, and the hopelessness of his cause.[17] Among other members of the Inns who were close to Jonson and whose sympathies were likely to have been with Essex were Selden, Harington, and Goodyer. At Court, Jonson's patrons, the Earls of Bedford and Rutland, and Lord Monteagle, took a leading if undistinguished part in the rebellion itself. Sir Henry Neville was strongly sympathetic, while the young Earl of Pembroke, a major patron in later years, may already have been helping Jonson at this date: his Sidney connections associated him, too, with the Essex group.[18] All this points to Jonson's sympathy towards Essex, the critical references to Actaeon in *Cynthia's Revels* notwithstanding.[19] Far from being an apologist for the anti-Essex faction, *Poetaster* shows him satirizing the machinations which friends and sympathizers believed had trapped Essex, and mocking as at best an overreaction the accusation of treason.

There is an obvious and unmistakable allusion to one episode in the Essex affair in the interrogation of the actor Histrio by the corrupt tribune Lupus in Act IV scene iv of *Poetaster*. I will consider this in detail later, but I want to begin with the play's title and prologue. The title under which it was performed at the Blackfriars was not *Poetaster*, which was added when it was printed in 1602, but *The Arraignment*. The play opens with Livor (Envy in 1616), the personification of malice and main source of political and social division in the commonwealth, gloating over the promise of the title as he reads it from a board above the tiring house façade:

> What's here? *Th'Arraignment*? Ay, this is it
> That our sunk eyes have waked for all this while:
> Here will be subject for my snakes and me.
>   (Induction, ll. 3–5)

Livor's excitement is understandable, and his expectations of the title are likely to have been shared by many of the audience. *The* arraignment of 1601 – indeed, of the whole decade – had been that of Essex and Southampton the previous February.[20] It is a dramatic treatment of this that Livor seems to expect, but his reasonable assumption that the play will provide occasion for political interpretation, for 'wrestings, comments, applications,/Spy-like assignations, privy whisperings,/And thousand such promoting sleights as these' (Induction, ll. 24–6) is blasted by an inspection of the three locality boards fixed at a lower level: 'the scene is – ha!/'Rome'? 'Rome'? and 'Rome'? (ll. 27–8).

Twentieth-century readers have on the whole followed Livor's directions, and taken the play's location as a signal that they should not 'force [it] to the present state' of England in 1601. In part this desire to keep the play in Rome (and thus to universalize its satire) was an understandable reaction to the excesses of those Victorian scholars who, for a century after the play was resurrected in Gifford's great edition, mined it shamelessly for references not to contemporary politics but contemporary writers. Seeing *Poetaster* exclusively in terms of a highly personalized War of the Theatres, Frederick Fleay *et al.* added to Gifford's quite proper identification of Marston and Dekker ingenious and dubious proofs that Ovid represented Donne, Virgil Shakespeare, and so forth.[21] Critical reaction was predictable: from the early twentieth century onwards emphasis has shifted from the play as part of the War of the Theatres to assessment of it as that entity beloved of the New Criticism, 'a meaningful work in its own right'.[22] The lampooning of individuals being too ephemeral to have any part in the transcendent significance of a meaningful work of art, most twentieth-century critics have ignored the attacks on Marston and Dekker, or pushed them, embarrassed, to one side as a triviality which obscures the universal relevance of the play. With them has gone, all too often, the play's contemporary political reference.[23] It has instead been read either as a satire on Ovidian lust, or an *ars poetica* by Jonson, the first literary statement in English of an Augustan humanist programme (Erskine-Hill's 'Augustan Idea'). Much of this, especially Erskine-Hill's treatment, is a valid correction of emphasis, but Gifford and the maligned Victorians led by Frederick Fleay were surely right to seize on the play's essential contingency to persons and events of 1601. This is, after all, one of those plays deplored by Captain Tucca, that 'girde and fart at the time', and we no longer need to make the idealizing, generalizing aspects of Jonson's Augustan vision and his specificity, his satirizing of recognizable contemporaries and contemporary events, mutually exclusive.

The Roman setting, which seems at first sight to move the play away from contemporary engagement towards that world of universal 'Augustan' values, in fact offered Jonson greater freedom for his political satire. One does not have to take a New Historicist view of the relation of the author to the centre (or competing centres) of political and cultural power to recognize that the satirist's negotiations with authority are likely to have been compromising, especially as Jonson's approach is almost always to insinuate a solidarity between himself and the rulers in pursuit of political virtue. He must have been preoccupied with this difficult relationship at least since his imprisonment over the 'sclanderous matter' of *The Isle of Dogs* in 1597. The controversial ending of *Every Man Out of His Humour* had brought Macilente face to face, late in 1599, with an actor playing the Queen, the mere sight of whom was enough to cure him of his envy. The following year, *Cynthia's Revels* staged the fantasy of a collaboration between a Jonsonian moralist and the Queen in the satiric cleansing of her court. It was hard, however, to avoid the truth that the monarch bore a strong responsibility for the moral ambience of her court. Donne's letter to Wotton, quoted below, makes this point, and the successive changes of character in the courts of the last years of Elizabeth, each of the three succeeding Stuarts, and Cromwell, were to bear him out. In emphasizing Elizabeth's innocence of the corruption of her own court, therefore, Jonson was following an uneasy but necessary convention which Richard Martyn and others of his circle also employed as they attacked monopolies and other doubtful uses of the royal prerogative in the parliament which opened in October 1601, at much the same time as *Poetaster*. Elizabeth's officers, not the Queen herself, were their targets. Donne, though far less outspoken as an MP than his and Jonson's friends, Martyn, Brooke, and Hoskyns, had adopted the same tactic in his fifth satire written two or three years earlier. Having described the corruption of both 'officers' and 'suitors', he asks the important question, and answers it with a simile that, though it seems to exonerate Elizabeth, subverts that exoneration by making her the spring from which the corruption flows:

> Greatest and fairest Empresse, know you this?
> Alas, no more then Thames calme head doth know
> Whose meades her armes drowne, or whose corne o'rflow.[24]

The use of bad counsellors as scapegoats for failures of policy and morality had been used in drama from *Magnificence* onwards, and was fully explored, and exposed, in that play which so interested the Essex conspirators, and Elizabeth herself: *Richard II*. That play, Donne's *Satyre V*, and the inherent self-contradictions of *Every Man Out of His Humour* and *Cynthia's Revels*, all confirm that the role of truth-telling satirist condemning the Court but not the Queen was not sustainable for long, and may, indeed, have been recognized by Jonson's audiences as merely discretion. The move to Augustus's court allowed implicit criticism of Elizabeth, contrasted with the prince who was a patron of poets, who encouraged freedom of speech (Suetonius, *Divus Augustus*, LIV–LVI) and brought peace and prosperity after factionalism, rebellion, and (in Rome, though not yet in England) civil war. Less flattering views of Augustus were available, and their sources were shortly to be used by Jonson in the composition of *Sejanus*. In *Poetaster* the choice of a largely idealized (but historically defensible) version is therefore almost certainly a conscious strategy which helps him to emphasize the distance between the English and Roman rulers. Livor's discomfiture in the Induction as he finds he cannot 'apply' a play set in Rome should not, then, be taken at face value, though it does proclaim a new-found freedom for the satirist.

Jonson's decision to set his play in 'Augustus Caesar's time' when 'wit and arts were at their height in Rome' ('Apologetical Dialogue, ll. 87–8) involved more, however, than making a simple contrast between Augustan Rome and late Elizabethan London. The continuities were equally, if not more, important: even then, 'Virgil, Horace and the rest/ Of those great master spirits did not want/ Detractors' (ll. 90–92). There may be no 'parallel' in merit between himself and Virgil or Horace, but they had their Crispinus and Demetrius as he had his Marston and Dekker. Then, too, there were malicious lawyers with a 'cheverel conscience' which advanced them over 'better men' (I.ii.144–7), actors who appealed to 'all the sinners i'the suburbs' (III.iv.228), genuine poets who betrayed their vocation, poetasters with no idea of a poetic vocation, philistines who regarded poetry as 'idle fruitless studies' (I.ii. 153–4), and courtiers forgetful of their social, moral, and religious obligations. Most important for my purpose here, there were informers and slanderers, corrupt politicians motivated by envy and distraction. Set in Rome, the vices of the play are necessarily Roman as well as English, just as its Roman virtues are at least potentially English ones as well: Jonson's Roman sources and his observation of the contemporary political scene are transmuted into the comic vision of a society which 'hath somewhat in it *moris antiqui*',[25] but in which we also see that nothing changes: the new world imitates the old, but those who comprehend the past imitate it deliberately and discriminatingly, as poets, statesmen, or even monarchs. Those who do not thus use their models as 'guides not commanders',[26] imitate it only by unwittingly repeating its follies and vices.

The first production reinforced this conflation of the two cities: anachronistic clothes and customs infiltrated Jonson's Augustan world. The boys playing Crispinus and Demetrius wore clothes which parodied Marston and Dekker's: Crispinus wears threadbare satin sleeves over a cheap 'rug' undershirt, with 'ample velvet bases' (III.i.77–80), and an 'embroidered hat' with an 'ash coloured feather' (III.iii.2–3). His beard (if he had one: see III.i.31), given the boy actor's age, must have been a comic version of Marston's. Dekker too was probably recognizable in a cloak covering a 'decayed' doubtlet (III.iv.359–60). Tucca has a sword in a velvet scabbard (I.i.27), and a leather 'jerkin' (I.ii.207); Chloe has given up her courtly farthingale for 'bumrolls' and a 'whalebone bodice' (II.i.65–6), and lives in a London merchant's house, with bay windows and a gallery (II.i.121–2, 138). It is probable that all the actors wore contemporary costume; although there is no clue to what Horace, Augustus, Virgil, or Julia wear, Ovid dons the cap and gown of an Elizabethan law student in I.i.6, and the chains which Ovid's father and Maecenas wear are Elizabethan flagon chains (V.iii.38), not Roman *torques*. This is one of the clearest examples during the period of the use of costume for satirical identification, though the strategy was used more often than is normally assumed, and was certainly adopted for some characters in other War of the Theatres productions, as well as in Middleton's *A Game at Chess*.[27] A Roman play acted partially or wholly in English dress would have elicited a powerful synchronic effect, highlighting continuities and differences between the cities. There emerges a timeless city, in which exist simultaneously the ideal moral city of Jonson's Augustanism and the degenerate city which had been linked to satire for generations.[28]

Donne had used the Roman comparison to make a very similar point about the continuity of corruption in looking at the Elizabethan court the year before *Poetaster* was performed. In a letter to Wotton, written, probably, while Essex was a prisoner in Egerton's house, Donne speaks Hamlet-like of the state suffering from an ague whose source is the court:

> for certainly the court hath in it much unnatural heat, and the courts and seats of princes are the hearts of all realms, which taking form from their humours are more or less corrupted as they confine or enlarge their own wills. When I speak of the wills of princes I speak of very unlimited things. Well, whatsoever our diseases are, I must wish that … they may be contagious. My meaning is that I would have other states or neighbours infected with them as well as ourselves, lest within a while there be no history so rich of great errors nor peradventure of great vices as ours. It was an excellent brag of Livy's that the Roman state (whose actions he intended to deliver) was of all other in the world most fertile of good examples. I call it a brag, and so think it. For certainly all times are of one nature, and all courts produce the same effects of envy and distraction, of jealousy and other human weaknesses.[29]

Donne's uncharacteristically candid language indicates a position very close to that of Jonson: envy and detraction are diseases endemic to courts, Roman or Elizabethan, and can be encouraged or suppressed by the prince. The implication is that the Queen herself bears the responsibility for the ague that infects the state. Wotton is invited to 'apply' Donne's metaphor (reminiscent of *Oedipus* as well as *Hamlet*) in blaming her rather than Essex for the state of affairs in 1600. Acts IV and V of *Poetaster* show Augustus, by contrast, on guard against 'the same effects of envy and detraction' which, in the final couplet proper, he too sees as endemic:

Envy will dwell where there is want of merit,
Though the deserving man should crack his spirit.
(V.iii.610–11)

This is followed by a short song, whose last lines are:

Detraction is but baseness varlet
And apes are apes, though clothed in scarlet
(V.iii.615–16)

Whether the scarlet is that of judges, or of pomp in general is not clear, but certainly it is not particularly Roman. Donne's words, *envy* and *detraction* are key words throughout *Poetaster*: after *poet* and its derivatives, *envy*, *spite*, *malice*, and *detraction* with their derivatives occur most often (40 times in all). They motivate the poetasters, Crispinus and Demetrius, but they also motivate the more sinister Lupus, the 'asinine wolf', who successfully informs on Ovid and Julia, and unsuccessfully attempts, backed up by Captain Tucca, to destroy Maecenas and Horace. The difference between the two courts, the Augustan and Elizabethan, is in both the wisdom of the ruler, and the advisers by whom he/she is surrounded. Augustus listens to the poet-counsellors Virgil, Horace, and Maecenas, men who (as Augustus recognizes) tell the truth rather than flatter. They even take physical action when Augustus over-reacts to Ovid's blasphemous banquet by attempting to kill his daughter Julia on the spot. When it comes to Lupus's attack on Horace and Maecenas themselves, Augustus needs no help. Recognizing the wisdom and integrity that are the essential attributes of the good poet he dismisses the libels and slanders immediately, and with them Histrio, Lupus, and Tucca.

Elizabeth's failure similarly to recognize true merit and integrity was, for Essex, central to his predicament in 1600. A concomitant of this view was that the queen was surrounded by far-from-disinterested counsellors, notably Cecil, Cobham, and Raleigh, 'base-born upstarts' who filled her ears with slanders against him, and who produced forgeries that seemed to prove his treasonable intentions. Essex's rash return from Ireland and his unprecedented intrusion into the queen's bedchamber in September 1599 were motivated by the belief that if he could only put his case to her directly all would be well. Part of his defence at his arraignment in 1601 rested on the same agreement, that his intention was to:

> have access to Her majesty's person, there to utter his plaints which he knew were so just that her Majesty upon these allegations which he should urge against his adversaries (the Lord Cobham, Mr Secretary, and Sir Walter Raleigh) would graciously hear him, and immediately she would proceed in disfavour to them.[30]

The 'innocency' which Donne noted as a cause of Essex's inevitable failure, his lack of a key to others' motives and character, could be said to have been displayed here as a fatal confusion of Elizabeth with the type of prince presented in *Poetaster*.

Fulke Greville, though a relative of Essex, is a reliable witness to the fact that Elizabeth did not distinguish so readily as Jonson's Augustus between truth and slander. Greville was loyal (or realistic) enough to command one of the companies that laid siege to Essex House as the rebellion moved to its inglorious conclusion. Despite this, he later wrote sympathetically of Essex being the victim of slander, libel, and innuendo conveyed to a gullible Queen by a faction of 'Pluto's thunder workers' who had first conspired to provoke the great-hearted but equally gullible Essex. In this version, Greville casts himself as the Horace or Maecenas who holds the prince back from unwise action. Essex, he says, was first:

> flattered, tempted and stung by a swarm of sect-animals, whose property was to wound, and fly away and so, by a continual affliction, probably enforce great hearts to turn, and toss for ease; and in those passive postures, perchance to tumble sometimes upon their sovereigns circles./Into which pitfall of theirs, when they had once discerned this earl to be fallen; straight, under the reverend style of *laesa maiestas*, all inferior ministers of justice (they knew) would be justly let loose to work upon him. And

accordingly, under the same cloud, his enemies took audacity to cast libels abroad in his name against the state, made by themselves, set papers upon posts, to bring his innocent friends in question. His power, by the jesuitical craft of rumour, they made infinite, and his ambition more than equal to it. His letters to private men were read openly, by the piercing eyes of an attorney's office, which warrenteth the construction of every line in the worst sense against the writer ... Myself, his kinsman, and while I remained about the Queen, a kind of *remora*, staying the violent course of that fatal ship, and these wind-watching passengers ... abruptly sent away to guard a figurative fleet ... Before which sudden journey, casting mine eyes upon the catching court airs, which I was to part from, I discerned my gracious sovereign to be every way so environed with these, not Jupiter's but Pluto's thunder-workers, as it was impossible for her to see any light that might lead to grace or mercy, but many encouraging meteors of severity, as against an unthankful favourite, and traitorous subject.[31]

The forged 'libels', the papers upon posts incriminating the innocent, the part played by rumour, and the opening of private papers all have their counterparts in *Poetaster*: 'Well, follow me. Thou shalt libel, and I'll cudgel the rascal' says Tucca (IV.vii.13–14), while Lupus's attack in V.iii. is still closer to the machinations Greville describes, involving both the opening of private papers (Horace's emblem has been stolen from his desk) and their malicious misinterpretation in an attempt to deceive the prince, making it 'impossible for [him] to see any light':

Lupus: A libel, Caesar. A dangerous, seditious libel.
    A libel in picture.
Caesar: A libel?
Lupus: Ay, I found it in this Horace his study, in Maecenas his house here. I challenge the penalty of the laws against 'em.
Tucca: Ay, and remember to beg their land betimes, before some of these hungry court-hounds scent it out.

                                 (V.iii.43–9)

The making ridiculous of this sinister and all too dangerous aspect of late-Elizabethan political culture is continued when Crispinus and Demetrius are arraigned under the statute of calumny. In a

form of words that parodies English, not Roman law (and thus
parodies the form of Essex's and Southampton's arraignment) they
are charged that they have 'gone about to deprave and calumniate
the person and writings of Quintus Horatius Flaccus, here present,
poet, and priest to the Muses' (V.iii.218–20) with libels they have
spread against him. Earlier, however, the activities of Lupus and
Histrio are denounced by Horace in a much more serious vein:

> Such as thou,
> They are the moths and scarabs of a state,
> The bane of empires, and the dregs of courts,
> Who, to endear themselves to any employment,
> Care not whose fame they blast, whose life they endanger;
> And under a disguised and cobweb mask
> Of love unto their sovereign, vomit forth
> Their own prodigious malice; and pretending
> To be the props and columns of his safety,
> The guards unto his person and his peace,
> Disturb it most with their false lapwing cries.
>
> (IV.viii.14–24)

In this, and in Virgil's recitation of the passage from the *Aeneid*
dealing with Fame, one can recognize the court that Greville
describes. One is reminded also of Jonas Barish's description of the
parallels found in *Sejanus* between Tacitus's Rome and the England
of the early 1600s: 'a whole nation turning into a race of spies and
eavesdroppers, a situation in which informers were encouraged to
bring charges in hopes of inheriting their victims' property, in
which innocent remarks, half-remarks and non-remarks were made
pretexts for accusations of treason.[32] This needs no modification to
fit the world of *Poetaster*, and the adoption of 'comicall satyre'
rather than Senecan tragedy to display it should not lead us to
agree with Livor that we cannot 'apply' it to 'the present state' of
England in 1601.

It is important to note that Jonson makes Lupus a tribune, a state
official with access (however grudgingly given) to the emperor.
One powerful figure whose role in 1601 invited the character of
Lupus to be 'applied' to him was Henry Brooke, 8th Lord Cobham.
Especially hated by Essex, Cobham had, like Lupus, clashed with
the players for their representation in *Henry IV* of his namesake, Sir
John Oldcastle who after the Brooke family's complaints became Sir

John Falstaff (when Essex was not referring to Cobham as the 'syco-phant' or 'my lord Fool', he and Southampton called him 'Sir John Falstaff').[33] Shakespeare retaliated with 'Mr Brooke' (later 'Mr Broome') in *The Merry Wives of Windsor*, at which point Lupus's complaint 'They will play you or me, the wisest men they can come by still. Me! Only to bring us into contempt with the vulgar, and make us cheap' (I.ii.45–8) becomes Cobham's complaint as well.[34] Other writers showed hostility to Cobham, Nashe and Jonson punning on the 'cob' (either a small herring or the head of a herring) in *Lenten Stuffe* and *Every Man Out of His Humour*. Such punning may even continue in a tortuous form in the epithet 'crop-shin' which Tucca applies to Lupus: this was a headless herring. Cobham was widely believed to have used libels (like Lupus) to influence the Queen. At Essex's arraignment he intervened to make an unnecessarily vehement denial that he had used forged letters, 'neither used he any such means of accusing the Earl to the Queen as the Earl of Essex pretended against him.'[35] Lupus, however, is probably not a straightforward satirical portrait of Cobham or anyone else, so much as a topical presentation of a malicious con-spirator and informer, the danger of his type emphasized by Horace's and Maecenas's warnings against flattery and malice (IV.viii.8–24, 28–31). The 'asinine wolf' is Jonson's version of Sidney's sly wolf, who can 'make justice the cloak of tyranny', and of Spenser's Blatant Beast, itself derived from Virgil's Fame in *Aeneid* IV 160–88, the passage translated by Jonson in *Poetaster* (V.ii.56–97). Elsewhere in *The Faerie Queene* Spenser represents 'malicious *Envie*' riding on 'a ravenous wolfe' (I.iv.30). In the repressive atmosphere of 1601, the threat the wolf represented would have been clear enough.

Most of this has, however, been a matter of suggestive but gener-alized parallels. I want to finish by looking at a particular episode, the interrogation by Lupus of the actor Histrio in Act IV, scene iv, which leads to the discovery of the banquet of the Gods, to the ban-ishment of Ovid, and almost, as we have seen, to Julia's death. This episode must, I believe, allude in a very straightforward way to the interrogation of the actor Augustine Phillips over the special per-formance of *Richard II* on Saturday 7 February, the eve of the Essex rebellion. This interrogation was carried out by 'the greatest Justice of this kingdom', Lord Chief Justice Popham, in the immediate aftermath of the rebellion. Popham played a prominent part in the events of that week, and in the subsequent trial: he was one of the

Privy Councillors who, on the morning of 8 February, went to Essex House and were held as hostages there, making strained conversation with the Countess of Essex and Lady Rich while the rebellion proceeded outside. Popham conducted several interrogations of conspirators in the days that followed, and was one of the court which arraigned Essex and Southampton on 19 February. He also, in what one hopes was a novel procedure for a judge, even an Elizabethan one, gave evidence against Essex. As Lupus interrogates Histrio in search of conspiracy and rebellion, so Popham and his two fellow judges examined Phillips in his role as representative of the Chamberlain's Men:

> He sayeth that on Fryday last was senyght or Thursday, Sr Charles Percy Sr Jostlyne Percy and the L[ord] Montegle wth some thre more spake to some of the players in the presens of this exa[minant] to have the play of the deposyng and kylling of Kyng Rychard the Second to be played the Satedy next promysing to geve them xls more then their ordynary to play yt. Wher this exa[minant] and hys freindes were determyned to have played some other play holdyng that play ... to be so old & so long out of use as that they shold have small or no cumpney at yt. But at their request this exa[minant] played yt accordingly.[36]

Monteagle was a patron of Jonson (see *Epigrams* lx) and, like him, a Catholic; the two Percys were also Catholics, and members of the Middle Temple,[37] a connection that would make the allegory of IV.iv. particularly obvious to Inns members. It would, though, have been available to all those at the Blackfriars who knew of Phillips's interrogation and remembered *Richard II*, a play that had become controversially associated with Essex well before its special performance in 1601.[38] Aspects of Bolingbroke's behaviour as represented by Shakespeare, especially 'his courtship to the common people/ How he did seem to dive into their hearts' (I.iv.24–5), could be (and were) plausibly read as alluding to Essex, who had more overtly been compared to Bolingbroke in John Hayward's dedication of his *First Part of the Life and Reign of Henry IV* to Essex in 1599, where the latter is cryptically but dangerously described as 'magnus et presenti iudicio et futuri temporis expectatione'. In 1600 Essex's treasonous motives were said to have been proved by this dedication, and by 'the Erle himself being so often present at the playing thereof [that is, of *Richard II*], and with great applause giving countenance and liking to the same'. The deposition scene was that which most obviously offended Elizabeth, and it was omitted from the first quarto of 1597, though it is safe to assume that it was included in the special eve-of-rebellion performance. The crucial lines for the Essex conspirators that afternoon must have been those with which Richard gives up the crown and sceptre, the emblems of kingship, to Bolingbroke: 'Now mark me how I will undo myself:/I give this heavy weight from off my head,/And this unwieldy sceptre from my hand' (IV.i.204–5). These lines are ludicrously echoed by Lupus, after Histrio has told him that he and his 'fellow-sharers' have received a letter 'to hire some of our properties, as, a sceptre and a crown for Jove'. 'A crown and a sceptre?' cries Lupus, 'This is good. Rebellion now!' (IV.iv.25–6). This, and his cry of 'Treason, treason' as he leaves with the lictors to head off the rebellion he has invented, indicate Jonson's attitude to the botched revolt: his mockery is not of Essex and his sympathizers, who included so many of his circle, but of the faction that opposed them. The implication of *Poetaster* is that, like Donne and Greville, he saw Essex as a victim of the malice and conspiracy of a corrupt and faction-riven court. In the play, the subversive conspiracy of Lupus and Tucca is contained by the wisdom of Augustus. Its Elizabethan equivalent, the destruction of Essex, was not contained by the Queen, but furthered by her and her ministers of state.

In this context, Augustus's words as he insists on Virgil taking precedence over him to read the newly finished *Aeneid* are doubly significant:

> See then this chair, of purpose set for thee
> To read thy poem in: refuse it not.
> Virtue without presumption place may take
> Above best kings, whom only she should make.
>   (V.ii.24–7)

This episode offers both a symbolic transcendence of the absolute monarch by the vatic poet, guardian of a tradition of wisdom and justice more powerful than Augustus's new sovereignty, and a startling if slightly ambiguous suggestion that kings should be 'made' by virtue: that is, only the virtuous man (or woman) should be invested with regal power. Who does the investing is left for the auditors to consider, but both parts of Augustus's speech involve serious modifications of absolutist ideology: the celebration of

Augustanism in fact becomes a critique of the misapplication of absolutism in Elizabethan England. Seen in this light, *Poetaster* emerges as a play that demands a more prominent place in the Jonson canon than it is normally given. Certainly it is a play that challenged contemporary authority in such a way that Richard Martyn would have needed all his much-praised charm and eloquence to persuade Popham, of all people, of its author's 'innocence'.

Notes

1. One of the most influential formations of this view is by David Norbrook, *Poetry and Politics in the English Renaissance* (London: Routledge, 1984), pp. 16–17, 175–94. See also Peter Womack, *Ben Jonson* (Oxford: Blackwell, 1986): 'in these plays [the comical satires] the *dramatis persona* is problematized within the ideology of absolutism' (p. 58).

2. *Poetaster*, ed. by Tom Cain (Manchester: Manchester University Press, 1995), pp. 62–3. All subsequent references are to this edition.

3. See *Poetaster*, Appendix I, p. 279; cf. E.K. Chambers, *The Elizabethan Stage*, 4 vols (Oxford: Clarendon Press, 1923), III, p. 366; *Ben Jonson*, ed. by C.H. Herford, Percy and Evelyn Simpson, 11 vols (Oxford: Clarendon Press, 1925–52), IV, p. 193, henceforth H&S; and Janet Clare, '*Art Made Tongue-Tied by Authority': Elizabethan and Jacobean Dramatic Censorship* (Manchester: Manchester University Press, 1990), p. 87.

4. '*hunc servare modum nostri novere libelli/ parcere personis, dicere de vitiis.*' Martial, *Epigrams*, ed. by W.C.A. Ker, (London: Heinemann (Loeb Classical Library), 1919), X.xxxii. 9–10. [Full edn notes needed], also quoted in *Poetaster* III. v. 134 and *Epicoene*, 2nd Prologue, 1.4.

5. For a detailed account of the printing of the quarto, see *Poetaster*, Appendix I, pp. 278–82. Other passages dropped included satire on actors as usurers and pimps in III. iv. 307–14.

6. There is no evidence to support the usual assumption that Martyn appeared as an advocate for Jonson in court: though prominent in 1601 as wit, MP, and Prince d'Amour in the Middle Temple, Martyn was not called to the Bar until February 1602: see Charles Henry Hopwood, *Middle Temple Records*, 3 vols (London: Butterworth, 1904), II, p. 419. No legal action against *Poetaster* is known to have been brought, and it is much more likely that Popham acted in his capacity as Privy Councillor and Lord Chief Justice, with Martyn's involvement being unofficial, though perhaps connected with a performance of *Poetaster* at the Middle Temple revels of 1601–2.

7. *A Speech Delivered, to the Kings Most Excellent Maiestie in the Name of the Sherrifes of London and Middlesex, By Maister Richard Martin Temple* (London: for Thomas Thorppe, 1603), B1r, For Martyn's importance in

the literary and political life of the period, see my forthcoming article, 'Donne and Prince D'Amour', in *The John Donne Journal* XIV (1995).

8. *Satiromastix*, 'To the World', in *The Dramatic Works of Thomas Dekker*, ed. by Fredson Bowers, 4 vols (Cambridge: Cambridge University Press, 1953), I, p. 309, II. 32–5. For the various possible Captain Hannams, see *Poetaster*, p. 48–9.

9. E.K. Chambers, *Elizabethan Stage*, III, p. 364.

10. For the argument that *Poetaster* was acted at the Middle Temple revels, see *Poetaster*, p. 29, 44–7.

11. James had sent Essex a secret message which the latter wore in a small black bag round his neck: see Robert Lacey, *Robert Earl of Essex: An Elizabethan Icarus* (London: Weidenfeld and Nicolson, 1970), p. 264.

12. See Chambers, *Elizabethan Stage*, III, pp. 275–6; Clare, 'Art Made Tongue-Tied by Authority', pp. 66–7, 127–31, 143–4. Greville, *The Life of the Renowned Sr. Philip Sidney* (London: for H. Saile, 1652), p. 156 is also cited by E.A.J. Honigmann, *Myriad-Minded Shakespeare* (Basingstoke: Macmillan, 1989), p. 117, where the argument on unintended Essex allusions in *Troilus* is advanced.

13. *Acts of the Privy Council of England*, N.S. XXXI. A.D. 1600–1601, ed. by J.R. Dasent (London: HMSO, 1906), p. 147 (8 Feb. 1601).

14. *Calendar of State Papers, Domestic Series, of the Reign of Elizabeth, 1598–1601*, ed. by M.A.E. Green (London: Longmans, Green and Co., 1889), pp. 578–9 (Vol. CCLXXVIII, 18 Feb. 1601).

15. See, for example, Margot Heinemann, 'Rebel Lords, Popular Playwrights, and Political Culture: Notes on the Political Patronage of the Earl of Southampton', *Yearbook of English Studies*, XXI (1991), 63–86 (p. 66); she notes that Jonson's friend John Selden was arrested and interrogated along with Sandys and Southampton for organizing 'mischievous opposition' in Parliament. For Martyn and the Virginia Company, see Edmund Gosse, *Life and Letters of John Donne*, 2 vols (London: Heinemann, 1899), 1: 240; Hugh Holland's poem on the engraved portrait in John Nichols, *Progresses, Processions, and Magnificent Festivities of Kings James the First*, 4 vols (London: J.B. Nichols, 1828), 1: facing p. 128' Maija Jansson (ed), *Proceedings in Parliament, 1614 (House of Commons)* (Philadelphia: University of Pennsylvania Press, 1988), pp. 275–9; and Susan M. Kingsbury, *The Records of the Virginia Company of London* (Washington: Library of Congress, 1933), III, pp. 68, 80–90.

16. *The Letters of John Chamberlain*, ed. by Norman McLure, 2 vols (Philadelphia, PA: American Philosophical Society, 1939), II. p. 274.

17. For Donne's generally sympathetic, if increasingly critical attitude, see the epigram 'I Earle of Nothing-am', attributed to Donne by Gary A. Stringer in 'Donne's Epigram on the Earl of Nottingham', *John Donne Journal*, 10 (1991), 71–4; and the letter to Wotton of *c.* 1600: 'he [Essex] understood not his age: for it is a naturall weakness of innocency. That such men want lockes for themselves & keyse for others.', 'Burley ms.', Leicestershire Record Office ms. DG. 7/Lit. 2, f. 296v, transcription in Evelyn M. Simpson, *A Study of the Prose Works of John Donne* (Oxford: Clarendon Press, 1948), p. 310.

18. Essex had inherited the allegiances of many of the Leicester/Sidney circle; his mother, Lettice, was Leicester's second wife, while Essex himself married Sidney's widow, Frances Walsingham, as well as inheriting Sidney's best sword. Jonson's letter to Pembroke in 1605 implies the latter's patronage is of some years' standing: 'You have euer been free and Noble to me'; see H&S, I, p. 199.

19. See *Cynthia's Revels*, V.xi. 12–27; the list of contemporary 'wits' in *Discoveries* is more accurately suggestive of Jonson's sympathies: Sidney, Hooker, Essex ('noble and high'), Raleigh, Saville, Sandys, Egerton, and Bacon (H&S, VIII, p. 591). This view is contrary to that of B.N. DeLuna, *Jonson's Romish Plot* (Oxford: Clarendon Press, 1967) that Jonson was an apologist for the anti-Essex faction: see for example p. 8.

20. Expectations of political application in a play were the subject of public speculation that could be commercially exploited by the company, as Jerzy Limon shows in *Dangerous Matter: English Drama and Politics 1623/4* (Cambridge: Cambridge University Press, 1986), pp. 6–7.

21. See for example Robert Cartwright, *Shakespeare and Jonson, Dramatic versus Wit Combats* (London: John Russell Smith, 1864); F.G. Fleay, *A Biographical Chronicle of the English Drama, 1559–1642*, 2 vols (London: Reeves and Turner, 1891); Josiah H. Penniman, *The War of the Theatres* (Philadelphia: University of Pennsylvania Press, 1897), and his combined edition of *'Poetaster'* and *'Satiriomastix'* (Boston and London: D.C. Heath & Co., 1913).

22. Norbert H. Platz, 'Ben Jonson's *Ars Poetica*: An Interpretation of *Poetaster* in its Historical Context', *Salzburg Studies in English Literature*, XII (1973), p. 1.

23. See for example Oscar J. Campbell, *Comicall Satyre and Shakespeare's 'Troilus and Cressida'* (San Marino, CA: Huntington Library Publications, 1938), pp. 109–34, esp. pp. 110–12; Arthur H. King, *The Language of Satirized Characters in 'Poetaster'* (Lund: C.W.K. Gleerup; Williams & Norgate, 1941), pp. 59–60; Ralph W. Berringer, 'Jonson's *Cynthia's Revels* and the War of the Theatres', *Philological Quarterly*, XXII (1943), 1–22; E.W. Talbert, 'The Purpose and Technique of Jonson's *Poetaster*', *Studies in Philology*, XLII (1945), 225–51; Edward B. Patridge, 'Ben Jonson: The Makings of the Dramatist (1596–1602)', in *Elizabethan Theatre, Stratford upon Avon Studies*, IX (London: Edward Arnold, 1966), pp. 221–44; Platz, p. 1; Chambers is, as so often, an exception, noting that the 'Aesop episode' might refer to Augustine Phillips's part on the 'Essex innovation' (*Elizabethan Stage* 1, p. 385), a suggestion briefly followed up by Howard Erskine-Hill, *The Augustan Idea in English Literature* (London: Edward Arnold, 1983), p. 111, and by Richard Dutton, *Mastering the Revels: The Regulation and Censorship of English Renaissance Drama* (London: Macmillan, 1991), pp. 138–9. See also Dutton, 'Ben Jonson and the Master of the Revels', in *Theatre and Government under the Early Stuarts*, ed. by J.R. Mulryne and Margaret Shewring (Cambridge: Cambridge University Press, 1993), pp. 57–86.

24. *The Satires, Epigrams, and Verse Letters*, ed. by W. Milgate (Oxford: Clarendon Press, 1967), p. 23. In *Every Man Out of His Humour*, Jonson seems to recall but reverse Donne's image, making the 'strength and clearenesse of the River [Thames]' in London analogous to the 'ample and unmeasur'd Flood/Of her *Perfections*'; see W. Bang and W.W. Greg (eds), *Ben Jonson's 'Every Man Out of His Humour', Reprinted from Holme's Quarto of 1600* (Louvain: A. Uystpruyst, 1907), p. 127.
25. The phrase is in a covering note sent with the 'Epitaph' on Cecilia Bulstrode in 1609 (Ungathered Verse, ix, in H&S, VIII, p. 372).
26. *Discoveries*, II. 38–9, in H&S, VIII, p. 567.
27. Notably for the 'Jonson' character in *What You Will* and *Satiromastix*. Nashe states that Gabriel Harvey was 'full drawen delineated' in *Pedantius*, and that one of his cloaks was used; see *Works*, ed. by R.B. McKerrow, 4 vols (London: A.H. Bullen, 1904–10), III, p. 80; I. p. 303. The Privy Council complained (10 May 1601) that 'at the Curtaine in Moorefields [players] do represent upon the stage in their interludes the persons of some gentleman of good desert and quality.' Percy Simpson quotes 'a dubious tale' (the more dubious in that he did not wish to believe it) that the Chamberlain's Men stole a suit from Sir Thomas Coningsby in order to portray him as Puntarvolo in *Every Man Out of His Humour* (H&S IX, p. 404, note 2). Chamberlain records that the actor playing the Black Knight in *A Game at Chess* 'had gotten (they say) a cast sute of his apparell for the purpose, and his Lytter, wherein, the world says, lackt nothing but a couple of asses to carrie yt, and Sir G. Peter, or Sir T. Mathew to beare him companie'. (*Letters*, II, p. 577).
28. See for example Earl Miner, 'In Satire's Falling City', in *The Satirist's Art*, ed. by James H. Jensen and Malvin R. Zirker, Jr (Bloomington: Indiana University Press, 1972), pp. 3–27.
29. My modernization: text from Simpson, *Prose Works of John Donne*, p. 308. For a discussion of these letters in the Burley ms., see Claude Summers and Ted-Larry Pebworth, 'Donne's Correspondence with Wotton', *The John Donne Journal*, X (1991), 1–36. They date the letter in 'February or March of 1600' (p. 24).
30. *State Trials Political and Social*, sel. and ed. by H.L. Stephen (London: Duckworth, 1902), III, 39–40.
31. Greville, *The Life of the Renowned Sr. Philip Sidney*, pp. 157–8.
32. *Sejanus*, ed. by Jonas Barish (New Haven: Yale University Press, 1965), p. 16. For the spy network slightly later, see DeLuna. Compare *Poetaster*, V.ii. 40 note and 50–51.
33. Clare, *Art Made Tongue-Tied*, p. 95 n. 43; compare R.B. Sharpe, *The Real War of the Theaters: Shakespeare's Fellows in Rivalry with the Admiral's Men, 1594–1603* (Boston and London: D.C. Heath & Co., and Oxford University Press, 1935), pp. 69–72.
34. The name 'Broome' may not have improved matters: see E.A.J. Honigmann, 'Sir John Oldcastle: Shakespeare's Martyr', *'Fanned and Winnowed Opinions': Shakespearean Essays Presented to Harold Jenkins* (London and New York: Methuen, 1987), pp. 118–32 (pp. 128–9).
35. Stephen, *State Trials, Political and Social*, III, 42.

36. *CSPD Elizabeth*, CCLXXVIII, p. 578, 18 Feb. 1601; text here from the original document, SP 12/278/85.
37. See Wilfred R. Prest, *The Inns of Court under Elizabeth I and the Early Stuarts* (London: Longmans, 1972), p. 179.
38. See Lacey, *Robert, Earl of Essex*, pp. 209–10.

4

Sejanus: Ethics and Politics in the Early Reign of James

Robert C. Evans

Basilikon Doron, written by King James VI of Scotland as a book of advice for his son Prince Henry, was an instant best-seller in the London of 1603–4. The English Queen, Elizabeth, had just died, and her Scottish cousin had now succeeded her as James I. People in England were understandably curious about their new ruler's political, social, and religious ideas, and *Basilikon Doron* more than satisfied such curiosity. At one point, for instance, James instructed Henry about the origins and progress of the Reformation in Scotland. In that country, he noted, the change in ecclesiastical government had not been imposed by order of the prince (as had happened in England and Denmark); instead, it had resulted largely from 'popular tumult and rebellion, of such as blindly were doing the worke of God, but clogged with their owne passions and particular respects ... .'[1] Indeed, 'some fierie spirited men in the ministerie, got such a guiding of the people at that time of confusion, as finding the gust [taste] of gouernment sweete, they begouth [began] to fantasie to themselues a Democraticke forme of gouernment ... .' They 'setled themselves so fast upon that imagined Democracie, as they fed themselves with the hope to become *Tribuni plebis*: and so in a popular gouernment by leading the people by the nose, to beare the sway of all the rule.' (*BD*, p. 23). Some even asserted 'that *all* Kings and Princes were *naturally* enemies to the libertie of the Church, and could *neuer* patiently beare the yoke of Christ: with such sound doctrine fed they their flockes.' (*BD*, p. 23; italics added)[2]

Whether these words accurately describe the Scottish reformers, they do imply a distinction central to my essay – a distinction between private *ethics* and public *politics* (between one's personal moral nature and one's public ideology or philosophy of social

71

organization). In the radical reformers, James believed, ethical lapses (including selfish pride and personal ambition) had fed misguided political principles, thereby producing a compound that was both potent and potentially destructive. James implies that if the radicals had not been so tempted by pride and ambition (ethical failings), they would not have fomented political rebellion. Like many early modern thinkers, James believed that moral sickness (especially pride) was often the root cause of political disease. Indeed, what seems to have bothered him most about the radicals was their willingness to separate politics from ethics – their willingness, that is, to argue that even a king who was a good man should be deposed simply because he was a king. James (like many of his contemporaries) seems to have believed that a king who was personally ethical would be guided by his moral values, including justice, charity, and humility.[3] But the radicals (according to James) were willing to sunder politics from its ideal ethical moorings: 'I was ofttimes calumniated in their populare Sermons, not for any euill or vice in me, but because I was a King, which they thought the highest euill.' (*BD*, p. 23)

Such thinking, James felt, could lead only to ethical and political nightmares – to a world in which a king could be deposed (or killed) simply because he *was* a king, or a Catholic persecuted simply because he *was* a Catholic, or a Protestant victimized merely because she *was* a Protestant, or a poor man oppressed simply because he *was* poor, or a rich person molested simply because she *was* rich. For James and many of his contemporaries, such a world was a grim, unappealing prospect.

The principled belief that one may do to others as one would not wish done to oneself (simply because those others *are* others) is at the heart of the distinction between ethics and politics in the sense used here. How, one might ask, would Ben Jonson, soon to be the new king's favoured poet, have reacted to this distinction? How were 'ethics' and 'politics' related in Jonson's mind? To begin answering such questions, we might well turn to one of the first and most famous of his Jacobean writings.

I

Anyone interested in Ben Jonson's politics must necessarily be interested in *Sejanus*. Few other works by Jonson deal as insistently and explicitly with political themes as this one. Because this play is one of only two surviving tragedies by Jonson, because it comes relatively early in his long career, and because it soon provoked heated reactions (including an official investigation), it is clearly fascinating for anyone trying to understand Jonson's politics. Yet the difficulties of interpreting *Sejanus* are notorious. Just enough evidence survives to tempt us to draw conclusions, but not nearly enough to warrant firm convictions. We cannot say when or where, precisely, the play was first performed; we cannot know how greatly the surviving text differs from the one first composed; we cannot be exactly certain who collaborated with Jonson on the initial text; we cannot be entirely sure why or even when the play provoked the Privy Council to investigate; and we cannot know very certainly either how the play was first received or how, specifically, it was intended to be understood.[4] New evidence may, of course, someday turn up and help resolve such puzzles. In the meantime, though, *Sejanus* is difficult to pin down and thus exemplifies the frustrating limits of most attempts at historical interpretation. Any interpretive approach that relies on relating one text to other texts from the same period will depend crucially on whether such other texts survive, whether they seem relevant, and whether such texts alone can ever provide sufficient clues or evidence for confident interpretation. Our knowledge of the past is inevitably incomplete (as the plethora of competing, often starkly contradictory readings of the past clearly suggests), whether we practise 'old' historicism, 'new' historicism, 'cultural materialism', or some even newer brand of historical criticism.

Given the difficulties just mentioned, it should come as no surprise that *Sejanus* has been read in radically different ways, provoking strikingly different answers to a whole series of intriguing questions. Should the play's Germanican faction be admired or scorned?[5] Is the tragedy a veiled comment on the career of the earl of Essex, or does it instead comment on the fall of Sir Walter Raleigh?[6] Does it satirize the passing reign of Elizabeth or the new regime of James?[7] Does Jonson present stoicism as an effective antidote to tyranny or as an ironic buttress of tyrannical rule?[8] Does the play endorse resistance to, or acceptance of, tyrants? If resistance, resistance to what degree?[9] Are Jonson's sympathies monarchic or republican?[10] Is the play historically reliable, or does it distort history to score political points?[11] Does Jonson favour a specific political programme or ideology, or is his counsel more generally moralistic?[12] These are just a few of the dilemmas raised and confronted by interpreters of the work.

I hardly hope to propose final answers to any of these problems. Rather, I seek to advance several more modest goals. First, I aim to show that fairly specific links can be drawn between *Sejanus* and other works by Jonson written at around the same time. These works – especially the poetic 'Panegyre' and Jonson's *Part of the King's Entertainment in Passing to His Coronation* – have not received much attention in recent criticism. Second, I will demonstrate that many general resemblances exist between the politics of Justus Lipsius (the great neostoic thinker) and the politics implied by *Sejanus*. The relevance of Lipsius to Jonson's own politics has been argued at length elsewhere, and there seems no denying that Jonson found Lipsius's political counsel especially germane during the last decade of his long poetic career.[13] Here, however, I hope to suggest that even so early a work as *Sejanus* already reflects many of the same general political attitudes expressed by Lipsius. These Lipsian views are demonstrably important to Jonson's later writings, but here I seek to show why the man who penned our text of *Sejanus* would also have responded so vigorously, so many years later, to the politics of Lipsius.[14] I hope therefore both to tie *Sejanus* a little more tightly to a particular moment in Jonson's career (a time during the first year or so of James's reign) and to link the play to a larger and essentially moralistic politics – a politics Jonson apparently found congenial throughout his life as a writer.[15]

II

The title-page of the 1616 folio printing of *Sejanus* reports that the play was acted by the King's Men (formerly the Chamberlain's Men). As Philip J. Ayres notes in his extremely helpful edition of the quarto text, the date of the first performance could therefore theoretically have occurred 'between 25 March 1603 and 24 March 1604, the old-style dates for the beginning and end of the year.'[16] However, because the public theatres were closed for much of that period (due firstly to Elizabeth's death in March and then to a summer outbreak of the plague), the play may actually have first been performed at court possibly in December 1603 or January or February 1604. The possibility that Jonson's satire on a corrupt ruler and his corrupt courtiers may first have been staged in the court of the new king, and that it may have been staged with the allowance of the Master of the Revels and the approval of other important officials, is extremely intriguing.

Certainly these possibilities suggest that the original play's satire was not perceived as a direct attack on James (whose rule had only just begun), and the fact that the heavily revised play was printed a few years later and then slightly revised and printed again in 1616 (the year Jonson was granted a royal pension) suggests that James, at least, found little that was personally offensive in those versions of the work. We know, of course, that at some point Jonson was called before the Privy Council, apparently to answer charges levelled by the Earl of Northampton concerning the play's alleged popery and treason, but we do not know precisely when this event took place, whether the charge was motivated by the play as performed or by the later quarto text, what may have motivated Northampton to make such charges, or what, precisely, resulted from them.

All these uncertainties should be kept clearly in mind. Often, for instance, Northampton's role is barely mentioned when the play's reception is discussed. The Earl does seem to have been bothered by the play (for reasons Ayres plausibly explains), but there is little evidence to suggest that the play offended James or 'the court' in general. Even to speak of 'the court' is misleading, for whatever in the play offended Northampton probably pleased other powerful courtiers. 'The court' as such is a mere abstraction; in reality it consisted first and foremost of the king and then of many individuals and factions with competing particular interests.[17] Northampton seems to have been annoyed by *Sejanus*, but there is little reason to think that the same was true of James or of many other highly-placed officials.

In the periods immediately before and after the first staging of *Sejanus*, Jonson's career began to flourish as it never had under Elizabeth. Surely the play was not directly responsible; but neither, apparently, did it stand in his way. *Sejanus* can even be read as a thinly veiled commentary on the dead queen's reign; other works by Jonson written at around the same time in the last years of Elizabeth's reign and the first of James's succession – not least *Cynthia's Revels* and *Poetaster* as we have heard elsewhere in this volume – strongly suggest as much. *Sejanus*, far from being an indictment of Jacobean tyranny, may have been intended (and perceived) as a dark meditation on the reign just ended. James, of course, as a well-read Renaissance monarch, would probably also have seen the play as a warning against tyranny. But much in the play that might seem provocative to us (such as its heavy stress on 'liberty') would probably not have troubled James, who prided himself on being a moral ruler. Indeed, many of the political ideas implied in *Sejanus* closely mirror ideas expressed in print by James in 1603. Examining the king's writings alongside other works written by Jonson in the early months of the new king's rule can help provide a fuller understanding of the politics of *Sejanus*. In some cases the parallels are striking.

III

One of the earliest works Jonson composed during the new reign was the *Entertainment at Althorp*, written for performance before Queen Anne and Prince Henry as they journeyed from Scotland.[18] The work was performed (at least in part) on 25 June 1603 at the estate of Sir Robert Spencer; significantly, it was later printed (in 1604) along with the 'Panegyre' and with Jonson's *Part of the King's Entertainment in Passing to His Coronation*. All three works seem highly relevant to a fuller understanding of *Sejanus*.

Although the Althorp *Entertainment* is much shorter and lighter than the Roman tragedy, it is nonetheless frequently and surprisingly satirical, and also often remarkably specific in its satire. As in *Sejanus*, Jonson here openly attacks both the superficiality of courtiers (*EA* 168) and also their corruption. Such phrasing could just as easily have come from the first scenes of *Sejanus* (for example, I.2., I.29). The intriguing word here is 'lately'; Jonson seems to imply that such corruption flourished in Elizabeth's final years. Similarly, the claim that Spencer now hopes to feel 'safer' when he journeys to court (*EA* 183) parallels all the emphasis in *Sejanus* on the danger at the court of Tiberius (for example: III.482; IV.18–21; IV.301). Curiously, the *Entertainment* takes a quite particular dig at the long-dead Sir Christopher Hatton, who had first attracted Elizabeth's notice by skilful dancing.[19] In the new reign (Jonson claims), no one 'doth hope to come by/Wealth, to build another *Holmby* [Hatton's estate]:/All those dancing days are done,/Men must now have more than one/Grace, to build their fortunes on' (*EA* 261–6). Although lightly delivered, this bit of sarcasm reflects poorly on Elizabeth, implying that her attraction for Hatton was partly sexual. (Sejanus, of course, begins his rise as a male prostitute who serves – and perhaps services – a lecherous prince.)

If 'the court' was offended by Jonson's attack on courts, courtiers, and even the old Queen in the Althorp entertainment, we have no record of it. Instead, the poet was selected to play a pivotal role in the official celebrations of the new king's coronation. Because of the plague, these celebrations were delayed until mid-March 1604 – that is, until after the possible first performance of *Sejanus* at court and perhaps even after Jonson had been called before the Privy Council. The officials who selected the poet to take part in the celebrations, then, seem not to have been bothered by the existence or reception of his Roman play, and in fact two of the works he composed for this occasion have much in common, politically and even verbally, with *Sejanus*. The first – a coronation *Entertainment* – sometimes uses phrasing exactly similar to that used in the 1605 quarto of *Sejanus*. Whether the entertainment echoes the original script of the play, or the revised and printed play echoes the entertainment, both works seem to reflect some common Jonsonian assumptions. Surprisingly, the parallels have not been explored very fully by critics or editors, even though they are very suggestive about Jonson's general political attitudes and about his personal reaction to the new king. Such parallels can help to pin down Jonson's political thinking in the period that produced *Sejanus*.

Jonson's speeches celebrating the king's passage through London on 15 March 1604 were printed that same year in a quarto also containing the 'Panegyre' and the *Entertainment at Althorp*. All three texts, then, would have been widely available, and each has interesting similarities with the recently-performed *Sejanus*. This is particularly true of the *Coronation Entertainment*. It consists not only of the actual speeches but also of elaborate descriptions of the specially designed triumphal arches. Particularly interesting are the speeches and designs for the arch erected at Temple Bar. There James could witness the contrasting figures of 'ELEVTHERIA, or *Libertie*' and 'DOVLOSIS, or *Seruitude*' – figures Jonson explicates by citing Claudian's assertion that 'liberty could never appear more graceful, and lovely, than now under so good a prince' as James (ll. 473–89).[20] Exactly the same phrasing appears in *Sejanus*, when Silius, one of the play's most virtuous characters, comments on the hypocrisy of Tiberius, a flattery-loving ruler whose pretended disdain for sycophants provokes Silius to observe that:

                                   If this man
Had but a mind allied unto his words,
How blest a fate were it to us, and Rome!
We could not think that state for which to change,
Although the aim were our old liberty:
The ghosts of those that fell for that would grieve
Their bodies lived not now, again to serve.
'Men are deceived who think there can be thrall
'Beneath a virtuous prince. *Wished liberty*
'*Ne'er lovelier looks than under such a crown.*'
                              (I.400–9; italics added)

This parallel and many others are not noted by either the Oxford or
Revels editors, though others *have* recently been noticed by Blair
Worden in a fine article on the play.[21] It was not Worden's purpose
to explore these parallels in detail but such exploration does seem
worth pursuing here. Noting the links between *Sejanus* and the
other works by Jonson presented in 1603–4 can help advance not
only our understanding of the play (and those other works) but also
our understanding of Jonson's habits and political assumptions.

    One of Jonson's habits as an artist is to quote himself – reusing
phrases, lines, and even extended passages in different works.
Partly this tendency reflects (as in the present case) his familiarity
with secondary sources such as Claudian; yet, rather than sig-
nifying literary laziness, this practice suggests that he found the
meaning of Claudian's words relevant in both contexts. Moreover,
in the case of this parallel, the similarities amount to more than a
simple echo of a classical predecessor. Both in *Sejanus* and in the
Entertainment Jonson implies that liberty and service need not
conflict: the impulse 'to serve' need not involve 'Servitude'. In these
passages Jonson seems to be echoing not merely Claudian but also
himself. Whether *Sejanus* in its present form preceded or followed
the *Entertainment*, the two works clearly share much the same political ideology, and the verbal parallels are often strikingly exact.

    It is possible of course that such echoes are profoundly ironic: that
Jonson's use of the same words in *Sejanus* and the *Entertainment*
imply that he saw James as another hypocrite, like Tiberius. Such a
reading, however, strikes me as highly implausible for several
reasons, including James's very recent accession, Jonson's praise of
him elsewhere, and the king's apparently positive attitude toward
Jonson. Instead it seems far more likely that Jonson, especially in the

early years of James's reign, saw the king, ideally, an anti-Tiberius –
as a ruler who might actually practise his ideals. I therefore agree
with Worden that what Jonson feared was 'not monarchical power
but its ill administration: not absolute government, which is properly strong but can be healthy, but arbitrary rule'.[22] Jonson
apparently saw no necessary conflict between 'liberty' and the rule
of a *good* king.[23] Jonson's politics, like those he later discovered in
Lipsius, cannot be separated from ethics. He seems to have been
interested less in politics *per se* than in encouraging moral rule –
governance by persons of genuine, selfless virtue.

IV

Many other parallels can be drawn between the *Coronation
Entertainment* and *Sejanus*, so that the attitudes expressed in the
former work can help illuminate the latter. Both texts, for instance,
contrast safety with danger, which is described in both instances
using wolf imagery (*CE* 503; *Sejanus* III.251, 347; IV.298). The
Coronation Entertainment suggests that with the accession of James
'those golden times were returned again, wherein Peace was with
us so advanced, *Rest* received, *Liberty* restored, *Safety* assured, and
all *Blessedness* appearing in every of these virtues her particular
triumph over her opposite evil' (*CE* 524–8). Similarly, *Sejanus* con-
tinually stresses an ideal liberty (I.62, 404; II.312; IV.144) while also
suggesting how the ideal can be perverted, as when the craven sen-
ators, ironically, praise the corrupt Macro by shouting, 'Liberty,
liberty, liberty! Lead on!' (V.758). As Jonson's praise of liberty in
the *Coronation Entertainment* (and in other works addressed to
James) suggests, we need to be careful not to equate such praise
with a distrust of monarchs *per se*. Indeed, Jonson seems to have
believed that the right kind of king could help foster and guarantee
genuine liberty and thereby assure the '*Safety*' and '*Peace*' praised
both in the *Coronation Entertainment* and in *Sejanus* (IV.131; see also
CE 594). James, according to Jonson, 'hath made men see/ Once
more the face of welcome liberty' (*CE* 598), and, as will be seen,
James himself emphasized a good king's necessary commitment to
such an ideal. Modern readers who perceive an inevitable conflict
between liberty and monarchy will probably misperceive the
politics of both Jonson and James.

Jonson's emphasis on liberty recurs in the *Coronation Entertainment* when he praises James as a monarch who:

> hath brought
> Sweet peace to sit in that bright state she ought,
> Unbloody, or untroubled; hath forc'd hence
> All tumults, fears, or other dark portents
> That might invade weak minds; hath made men see
> Once more the face of welcome liberty:
> And doth (in all his present acts) restore
> That first pure world, made of the better ore.
>
> (ll. 595–600)

In this return of the golden age:

> innocence shall cease to be the spoil
> Of ravenous greatness, or to steep the soil
> Of raised peasantry with tears, and blood;
> No more shall rich men (for their little good)
> Suspect to be made guilty; or *vile spies*
> Enjoy the lust of their so *murdering eyes* ... .
>
> (ll. 601–6; italics added)

Interestingly, these last two lines strongly resemble a moment in *Sejanus*, when Sabinus laments the fact that under Tiberius, Romans are made the 'prey to greedy vultures and *vile spies*/ That first transfix us with their *murdering eyes*' (IV.140–1; italics added). The echo suggests once more that the *Coronation Entertainment* may be more relevant to *Sejanus* than scholars have tended to stress, and indeed passages from the *Coronation Entertainment* frequently parallel passages in the play. These include the heavy emphasis on spies (for example: I.64, 259; II.445, 450, 478; III.701; IV.170) and on the dangers of innocence (I.68; III.407, 731; IV.40), as well as the notion that the rich are often a tyrant's favourite victims. Thus at one point in *Sejanus* the virtuous Silius asks:

> What are my crimes? Proclaim them.
> Am I too rich? Too honest for the times?
> Have I or treasure, jewels, land, or houses
> That some informer gapes for?
>
> (III.168–71)

This same emphasis, which will recur in the 'Panegyre', is one of several ways in which Jonson's disdain for tyrants seems to have differed from any commitment to modern egalitarian democracy. Jonson's politics, which seem to have been rooted fundamentally in ethics, would not have made him automatically sympathetic either to the rich or to the poor *per se*: what mattered to him was not how much money one possessed but how much virtue one practised. In this sense Jonson's politics seem not to have been ideological in any simple or knee-jerk fashion: a rich man could be good, a poor man could be bad, and the roles could just as easily be reversed. A tyrant was contemptible not because he held power but because he abused it. Such a ruler was an enemy not only to the aristocracy of virtue Jonson prized but also to aristocracy in general, for tyrants threaten – and feel threatened by – the noble (in both senses of that word). Interestingly, Jonson even reminds James of the fate of one alleged tyrant, Julius Caesar, who was murdered on the very same day – the ides of March – of James's procession (*CE* 629–30; see also *Sejanus* I.95). The poet's hatred of tyrants, however, seems not to have involved any contempt for virtuous monarchs, especially since the very last line of his *Coronation Entertainment* praises the 'lasting glory' of 'Augustus' state' (l. 763; for praise of Augustus in *Sejanus*, see III.417, 426, 432, 436, 484).[24]

Before that ending, however, Jonson once again spells out the qualities of a worthy prince. Thus he prophesies that James will be a king:

> Who[se] so fair
> And wholesome *laws*, in every court, shall strive
> By Equity, and their first innocence to thrive;
> The base and guilty bribes of *guiltier men*
> Shall be thrown back, and Justice look, as when
> She lov'd the earth, and fear'd not to be sold
> For that, which worketh all things to it, gold.
> The dam of other evils, Avarice,
> Shall here lock down her jaws, and that rude vice
> Of ignorant, and pitied greatness, *Pride*,
> Decline with shame; *Ambition* now shall hide
> Her face in dust, as dedicate to sleep,
> That in great portals wont her watch to keep.
> All ills shall fly the light: Thy court be free
> No less from *envy*, than from *flattery*;

> All *tumult, faction, and harsh discord* cease,
> That might perturb the music of thy peace ... .
>   (*CE* 737–53; italics added)

Like much else in the *Coronation Entertainment*, this passage recalls both the general atmosphere and the specific phrasing of *Sejanus*. That play opens, for instance, with a reference to 'guilty men' whose guilt leads to greatness (I.12; compare *CE* 740), and later Tiberius ironically claims that 'we are far from flattering our friend [Sejanus]/ (Let envy know) as from the need to flatter' (I.534–5; compare *CE* 751). Moreover, like this extended passage from the *Coronation Entertainment*, the play in general strongly indicts flattery (I.28, 43, 71, 413, 420, 438), pride (I.57, 473, 572; III.635; V.756), ambition (I.241; V.598, 647), just as it strongly endorses the rule of law (II.314; III.218, 741). These, of course, are precisely the stances Jonson might have been expected to adopt, both in the play and entertainment. And that is the point: the play condemns a tyrant, while the entertainment praises and counsels a good king. *Sejanus*, in other words, seems intended not to imply that James is a tyrant but rather to imply the opposite. James is credited with honouring all the values Sejanus and Tiberius defile.

V

If Jonson felt any optimism when first contemplating James's rule, he would not have been alone. Many English people – bored with, tired of, or disappointed in the old Queen – looked forward to a new era and were grateful for such a bloodless and peaceful transition. Jonson's early works praising James may have seemed less like flattery to his contemporaries than they can seem to modern readers. We, after all, can survey all of James's rule; we know 'what came next' (including the civil wars). Centuries of partisan commentary have shaped an image of James that is not entirely attractive. Although some historians have sought to right the balance,[25] it is still easy to see Jonson as a toady, as a hypocrite, or as a critic whose criticism was necessarily muted or implied. *Sejanus*, in this latter view, is a dark meditation on the tyranny already evident in the new king's conduct.[26]

At the time Jonson wrote *Sejanus*, however, he may have intended it as counsel, not criticism; as advice rather than attack, even as an endorsement of views already expressed by James rather than an indictment of his behaviour. After all, one of the most widely read and praised books in 1603 was James's own *Basilikon Doron*, first published in Edinburgh in 1599 and then regularly reprinted in London between 1603–4.[27] Many of James's pronouncements there about proper rule and godly rulers parallel perfectly ideas implied in *Sejanus*, and Jonson was surely familiar with the monarch's text. Whether or not Jonson intended his drama to endorse views expressed in the *Basilikon Doron*, the latter text suggests why James himself would not have been especially troubled by the play.[28]

James's book and Jonson's play have many points in common. Thus James, like Jonson, stresses the need for a virtuous court (*BD* 33; I.6–19). Both men also strongly condemn flattery (*BD* 32; I.71), praise ethical old Romans (*BD* 42; I.102, 149), and indict favourites (*BD* 33; III.169), endorse temperance (*BD* 37; III.439), and responsibility both to the commonwealth (*BD* 19; V.545ff.) and to God (*BD* 3; V.909). Both stress the common humanity of rulers and ruled (*BD* 41; I.477–8), condemn tyrants (*BD* 19; I.437), and praise rule by law (*BD* 19; III.218). Both emphasize the ruler's public duties (*BD* 3; III.601); and both attack what Jonson terms 'upstart greatness' (*BD* 33; V.465).

Such a list of parallels might easily be extended. Thus James advises a prince always to subject 'his owne private affections and appetites to the weale and standing of his Subjects' (*BD* 18–19; I.482–4); calls parliament 'the honourablest and highest judgement in the land' (*BD* 19; I.391–4); advises his son to 'mixe Justice with Mercie' (*BD* 20; I.514–17); counsels him to practise personal virtue (*BD* 29; I.406–7); reminds him to choose his servants carefully (*BD* 30; III.637–42); urges him to follow the dictates of conscience (*BD* 34; III.742); recommends that he profit from studying history (*BD* 40, 44; III.481–3); entreats him to control his anger (*BD* 41; III.439–41); warns him to avoid suspicion, 'the Tyrants sicknesse' (*BD* 42; IV.9–10); instructs him to use plain language (*BD* 47; II.418–24); and counsels him to promote virtue and the virtuous (*BD* 52; I.70–2). Moreover, just as Jonson's drama depicts the injustice of misinterpreting a writer's words (III.379ff.), so James tries to pre-empt similar misconstruction of his own book (*BD* 9). And, interestingly enough, James seems even more willing than Jonson to speak favourably of revolt against a tyrant. In Jonson's play the virtuous Sabinus declares explicitly that:

No ill should force the subject undertake
Against the sovereign, more than hell should make
The gods do wrong. A good man should and must
Sit rather down with loss, than rise unjust ...

                                        (IV.163–6)

James, on the contrary, warns his son that:

> a Tyrantes miserable and infamous life, armeth in end his own
> Subiects to become his burreux: and although that rebellion be
> ever vnlawfull on their part, yet is the world so wearied of him,
> that his fall is little meaned by the rest of his Subiects, and but
> smiled at by his neighbours. And besides the infamous memorie
> he leaveth behind him here, and the endless paine he sustaineth
> hereafter, it oft falleth out, that the committers not only escape
> unpunished, but farther, the fact will remaine as allowed by the
> Law in diuers ages thereafter.

                                        (*BD* 19)

Such a passage, if penned by Jonson, might lead us to suspect him
of approving regicide. Coming from James, however, it should
remind us how carefully he and many of his contemporaries distinguished between tyrants and true kings. *Sejanus* certainly condemns tyranny; whether it indicts monarchy in general or James in
particular is another question altogether.

If Jonson regarded James as another Tiberius (as a deliberate
hypocrite who mouthed pieties without practising virtue), the parallels between *Sejanus* and *Basilikon Doron* would be deeply ironic
and satirically subversive. The play could then be read as an
implicit, corrosive indictment of a specific ruler and his court.
According to such a view, Jonson would already be expressing
deep and very early scepticism about James's rule, demonstrating
an acute prescience concerning James's failings as a king. He might
even be suggesting the shortcomings of monarchy in general and
might instead be implying the superiority of republican government. He might be suggesting, that is, that specific changes in the
structures of state power could prevent the kinds of corruption and
abuse that his play exposes.

However, another explanation – and one that I find more persuasive – is that Jonson's play expresses a basically moralistic
politics. By this I mean a politics that focuses less on particular

structures of state power than on individual ethics. In this view, a state's particular ideology or specific politics are less significant, in determining its worth, than the moral conduct of its leaders and citizens. Whether a state was monarchical, oligarchical, republican, or democratic would thus matter less than whether its leaders and citizens were ethical. A virtuous monarch surrounded by truly moral aristocrats and supported by honourable citizens would, in this view, be preferable to a republic or democracy whose citizens were driven by self-interest. And, of course, the reverse would also be true. Jonson, I suspect, was less interested in specific ideologies, governmental programmes, or political doctrines, than in the ethical values and behaviour of both rulers and ruled. In other words, merely overthrowing Tiberius and re-establishing a republic would not in itself guarantee a return to good government. Only good citizens – only moral persons willing to act in the best interests of all – would ensure a worthy state. Accordingly, politics *per se* would be far less important than ethics; no amount of structural tinkering could improve a state whose citizens and leaders put private gain above public profit. It is not his role as emperor that makes Tiberius unworthy; rather, it is his personal unworthiness that makes him an unfit prince.[29]

Although to some this ethical (perhaps ultimately religious) view of politics might seem naive, Jonson probably viewed it as profoundly realistic. It takes for granted, for instance, the standard Christian assumption of original sin: the assumption that because all humans are deeply flawed, no mere political system can ever function perfectly or produce an earthly paradise.[30] No simple change in ideology or programmes, that is, can ever set things entirely straight; what is needed, instead, is the slow, difficult cultivation and inculcation of responsible morality in each person, especially in persons who enjoy official power. *Sejanus*, on this view, would be less concerned with broad political 'reform' than with individual moral transformation; only the latter could ultimately help produce the former.

Viewing Jonson's politics as essentially moralistic helps highlight the consistencies in his attitudes over the course of his long career. Doing so helps explain, for instance, how he could loyally serve such kings as James and Charles while also enjoying close ties with leading critics of some of their specific policies. Jonson never seems to have assumed that changing the mere mechanism of state power (replacing a king with a protector; abolishing monarchy and substituting a republic; altering church government in this way or that) would ultimately solve political problems. Partly, of course, those problems seem insoluble; but partly, too, any solutions must depend upon the ethics of millions of individuals.

VI

Late in his career, Jonson showed enormous interest in the 'neo-stoic' political philosophy of the Flemish intellectual Justus Lipsius. His copy of Lipsius's six-book *Politica* is marked extensively, and specific echoes can be found in many of his later works. As it happens, the *Politica* provides a detailed rationale for precisely the kind of moralistic politics outlined above – a politics that emphasizes the priority of general ethics over any particular ideology.[31] Are there, however, any points of contact between this 'Lipsian' view of politics and the politics implied in so early a work as *Sejanus*? Are there, in other words, any reasons to look for continuities between Jonson's later views and the views implied in his early tragedy? It will come as little surprise if I answer 'yes' to both questions. Although I hardly wish to suggest that Lipsius provides any master-key to understanding Jonson's politics (especially the politics of *Sejanus*), I do wish to note some of the many parallels between Jonson's play and Lipsius's political thinking. Doing so may help to explain why the author of *Sejanus* would later show such a striking interest in Lipsius, and why the enthusiast for Lipsius could earlier have written *Sejanus*. Investigating the parallels between Jonson's drama and Lipsius's treatise can perhaps help us see some of the basic assumptions that consistently guided Jonson's political thinking.

Numerous similarities exist between Jonson's play and the passages he marked in Lipsius's *Politica*.[32] Both works, for instance, link private lust to political corruption (I.63; *P* 265). Both stress the crucial importance of virtue (I.119; *P* 160), and both praise rulers who display gravity and greatness (I.129–30; *P* 233) but not disdain. Both censure voluptuousness (I.145; *P* 269); both praise temperance (I.152; *P* 232); both condemn bribery (I.189; *P* 218); and both castigate corrupt favourites (I.217–25; *P* 257). Both works show how corrupt politicians manipulate their followers' greed (I.234–37; *P* 267), and both commend, in contrast, true liberality (I.238; *P* 237). Both works imply that the powerful should champion learning

(I.272; *P* 239); and both remind princes that they are merely men (I.376–7; *P* 232); both commend good monarchs (I.403–4; *P* 195); and both associate virtuous princes with true liberty (I.407–8; *P* 206). Both mock hypocrisy (I.410; *P* 179); both indicate how flattery corrupts a ruler (I.410–18; *P* 204); and both stress the need for princely virtue (I.416; *P* 160). Indeed, in both works such virtue is the key concern.

Both works indicate that the power of a good prince is rooted in his subjects' love (I.447; *P* 221), and both declare that a good king's example is more influential than laws themselves (I.466–7; *P* 212). Both condemn princely pride and ambition (I.472–3; *P* 232); both imply the value of posterity's regard (I.484–9; *P* 273); both suggest that desiring fame can encourage virtue (I.502; *P* 239); and both suggest the evil of disguising anger (I.578–9; *P* 239). Both indicate that virtue should be rewarded (II.8; *P* 271); both extol a prince's faithfulness or fidelity (II.176; *P* 227); both commend a ruler's piety (II.176; *P* 210); and both suggest that a king should uphold religion (II.181; *P* 245). Both approve princely modesty (II.276; *P* 232); both condemn royal cruelty (II.388; *P* 225); and both censure princely fraud (III.209; *P* 229). Both endorse the rule of law (III.218; *P* 156); both suggest that the rich are often the special victims of tyrants (III.169; *P* 252); both extol justice (III.221; *P* 214); both condemn corrupt officers (III.236; *P* 254); and both praise a prince's mercy (III.345; *P* 221). Both works endorse princely restraint (III.359–65); *P* 215–16); both encourage princes to ignore slanders (III.439–41; *P* 239); and just as Jonson has one of his most virtuous characters claim that 'Posterity pays every man his honour' (III.455), so the last marked passage in his copy of Lipsius similarly notes that 'Posterity will give to euery one his due honour' (*P* 273).[33] It is clear from reading *Sejanus* alongside Lipsius's political theory that the two writers were working within a related ethical framework.

Both the play and the treatise, moreover, suggest that severe punishment often backfires (III.475–6; *P* 224); both condemn princely lust (III.601; *P* 206); both indicate an interest in destiny (IV.5–6; *P* 170–71); and both express deep scepticism concerning accusations of treason (IV.342–3; *P* 253). Both imply respect for religion (V.69–70; *P* 245); both show an interest in the prince's majesty (V.570; *P* 235); both prize innocence (V.588; *P* 218); and both affirm that fortune is slippery (V.739; *P* 235). This latter point is reiterated in nearly the final words of Jonson's play (V.900–5; *P* 233), which also warn of the dangers of irreligion (V.908–13; *P* 245). Despite the

Roman setting of *Sejanus*, Jonson's Christian audience would clearly have perceived the relevance of this warning to their own lives, and indeed Jonson's play, like Lipsius's treatise, seems largely designed to emphasize the solid foundation of common ethical wisdom that underlay both classical and Christian culture. If many of the similarities between the two works seem almost platitudinous, that is largely because ethical wisdom is – almost by definition – commonplace, simple, and unoriginal. The golden rule, after all, is quite easy to comprehend (although notoriously difficult to practise). If the links between the ethical politics of Jonson's *Sejanus* and Lipsius's *Politica* can sometimes seem trite, they are nonetheless both numerous and important. Studying the two works side-by-side suggests not only the parallels between them but also the broad continuities that underlay Jonson's politics and ethics, both early and late in his career. Given the parallels between the political and moral assumptions of Jonson and Lipsius, it is not surprising that the author of *Sejanus* could find the *Politica* so fascinating and so relevant so many years after his own play was written.

The links between *Sejanus* and the *Politica* suggest, then, several broad conclusions. First, they imply that Jonson's politics were fundamentally rooted in ethics and emphasized the moral responsibilities of specific individuals rather than the minutiae of competing ideologies or the usefulness of systemic tinkering. Recasting a state's constitution would have little positive effect if a state's citizens were not good persons. Second, the similarities suggest that Jonson, like Lipsius, found much common ground between classical ethical wisdom and traditional Christian morality. Third, the links imply that Jonson's politics did not radically change between the early stages of his career (when he wrote *Sejanus*) and the later stages (when he read, marked, and alluded to Lipsius's *Politica*). Both Jonson and Lipsius, early and late, seem to have taken for granted an assumption that today may seem either simply naive or simply profound; that only moral conduct can ensure a healthy polity. In responding to *Sejanus*, as in assessing Jonson's politics elsewhere, it generally seems worth remembering that ethics, not ideology, is ultimately the bottom line. This is a view he seems to have shared with his great Flemish counterpart and with other 'neo-stoic' thinkers.

Notes

1. For a convenient old-spelling text of James's tract, see *The Political Works of James I*, ed. by Charles Howard McIlwain (Cambridge, MA: Harvard University Press, 1918), pp. 3–52 (p. 23). Henceforth *BD* and page references cited parenthetically within the text.

2. James probably has in mind such men as George Buchanan, his one-time tutor, but this is hardly the place to discuss either the particulars of Buchanan's ideas or the justice of James's charges. On such matters, see, for instance, McIlwain's 'Introduction' to *The Political Works of James I*, esp. pp. xv–xxxiv; J.W. Allen, *A History of Political Thought in the Sixteenth Century* (London: Methuen, 1960), pp. 336–42; the essays by Robert Kingdom and J.H.M. Salmon in *The Cambridge History of Political Thought, 1450–1700*, ed. by J.H. Burns and Mark Goldie (Cambridge: Cambridge University Press, 1991), esp. pp. 215–18; and Jenny Wormald, 'James VI and I, *Basilikon Doron* and *The Trew Law of Free Monarchies*: The Scottish Context and the English Translation', in *The Mental World of the Jacobean Court*, ed. by Linda Levy Peck (Cambridge: Cambridge University Press, 1991), pp. 36–54, esp. pp. 40–46.

3. According to one widely accepted reading of Machiavelli, such assumptions are hopelessly naive. J.W. Allen, for instance, discusses how Machiavelli separated ethics from politics in a different sense from that which I have been discussing here. See his *History of Political Thought in the Sixteenth Century*, esp. pp. 471–84.

4. For a good overview of these basic issues, see the introduction by Philip J. Ayres to his Revels Plays edition of *Sejanus His Fall* (Manchester: Manchester University Press, 1990), pp. 1–36. See also Richard Dutton, *Mastering the Revels: The Regulation of Censorship of English Renaissance Drama* (Basingstoke: Macmillan; Iowa City: University of Iowa Press, 1991), pp. 10–15.

5. On this debate, see, for instance, Marvin L. Vawter, 'The Seeds of Virtue: Political Imperatives in Jonson's *Sejanus*', *Studies in the Literary Imagination*, 6 (1973), 41–60.

6. On the Essex possibility, see Annabel Patterson, '"Roman-Cast Similitude": Ben Jonson and the English Use of Roman History', in *Rome in the Renaissance: The City and the Myth* (Binghamton, NY: Medieval and Renaissance Texts and Studies, 1982), pp. 381–94, esp. p. 385. See also Matthew H. Wikander, '"Queasy To Be Touched": The World of Ben Jonson's *Sejanus*', *Journal of English and Germanic Philology*, 78 (1979), 345–57.

   For a full exploration of the Raleigh possibility, see Philip J. Ayres, 'Jonson, Northampton, and the "Treason" in *Sejanus*', *Modern Philology*, 80 (1983), 356–63.

7. See, for example, Curtis Perry, 'The Crisis of Counsel in Early Jacobean Political Tragedy', *Renaissance Drama*, n.s. 24 (1993), 57–82, esp. pp. 65–6.

8. On this controversy, see Vawter, 'The Seeds of Virtue'; Joseph S.M.J. Chang, '"Of Mighty Opposites": Stoicism and Machiavellianism', *Renaissance Drama*, 9 (1966), 37–57.

9. For two different views, see Perry, p. 69; and Daniel C. Boughner, *The Devil's Disciple: Ben Jonson's Debt to Machiavelli* (New York: Philosophical Library, 1968), pp. 93–4. For extended discussion of such matters, see K.W. Evans, '*Sejanus* and the Ideal Prince Tradition', *Studies in English Literature*, 11 (1971), 249–64.

10. For the former possibility, see Wikander, p. 356. For the latter option, see the chapter on 'Tacitean Republicanism in Jonson's *Sejanus*', in Albert H. Tricomi, *Anticourt Drama in England, 1603–42* (Charlottesville: University of Virginia Press, 1989), pp. 72–9. For a carefully hedged discussion of republican ideas in Jonson's day, see Markku Peltonen, *Classical Humanism and Republicanism in English Political Thought, 1570–1640* (Cambridge: Cambridge University Press, 1995). Interestingly, Peltonen notes that many influential English politicians considered their monarchical state a kind of republic (p. 49). For a thoughtful discussion of Peltonen' arguments, see the lengthy review by Glenn Burgess in the first issue of the electronic journal *Renaissance Forum* (1.1.1996).

11. See Philip J. Ayres, 'The Nature of Jonson's Roman History', *English Literary Renaissance* 16 (1986), 166–81.

12. For the latter view, see for instance, K.M. Burton, 'The Political Tragedies of Chapman and Ben Jonson', *Essays in Criticism* 2 (1952), 397–412, esp. pp. 401–4.

13. See Robert C. Evans, *Jonson, Lipsius, and the Politics of Renaissance Stoicism* (Wakefield, NH: Longwood Academic Press, 1992), and the other studies cited therein.

14. For discussion of Jonson's debt to Lipsius's seminal edition of Tacitus when the playwright was composing *Sejanus*, see Daniel C. Boughner, 'Jonson's Use of Lipsius in *Sejanus*', *Modern Language Notes* 73 (1958), 247–55. See also Ellen M.T. Duffy, 'Ben Jonson's Debt to Renaissance Scholarship in *Sejanus* and *Catiline*', *Modern Language Review* 42 (1947), 24–30. On the more general influence of Tacitus, Seneca, and Lipsius in Jonson's culture, see for instance J.H.M. Salmon, 'Seneca and Tacitus in Jacobean England', in Levy Peck, *Mental World of the Jacobean Court*, pp. 169–88.

15. It would be possible, if space were unlimited, to show the relevance of such a view of politics to the two completed plays (*Cynthia's Revels* and *Poetaster*) that immediately preceded *Sejanus*. Based on the passages Jonson marked in his reading of Thomas More's history of Richard III, it would also be possible to argue that his lost play *Richard Crookback*, on which he was at work just before *Sejanus* may also have had a heavily moralistic (rather than specifically political or ideological) emphasis. For discussion of Jonson's reading of More, see Robert C. Evans, *Habits of Mind: Evidence and Effects of Ben Jonson's Reading* (London: Associated University Presses, 1985), pp. 160–90.

16. Ayres, *Sejanus, His Fall*, p. 9.

17. For a good recent overview of such matters see Malcolm Smuts, 'Cultural Diversity and Cultural Change at the Court of James I', in Levy Peck, *The Mental World of the Jacobean Court*, pp. 99–112 (esp. pp. 108, 111).
18. In quoting from this and other works by Jonson, except *Sejanus*, I will use *Ben Jonson*, ed. by C.H. Herford, Percy and Evelyn Simpson, 11 vols (Oxford: Clarendon Press, 1925–52). I will abbreviate this as H&S. All spellings have been modernized. The *Entertainment* is printed in H&S VII, pp. 119–31. Henceforth abbreviated as *EA* and line numbers cited parenthetically within the text. In quoting from *Sejanus* I will cite the act and line numbers from the Ayres edition, which is based on the 1605 quarto. It is unfortunate that most editions of *Sejanus* do not use quotation marks (as does the 1605 quarto) to set off the numerous passages of sententious wisdom that Jonson highlights in this way. Reproducing those marks would help remind readers of just how much the play originally functioned, like Lipsius's *Politica*, as a collection of wise or memorable sayings.
19. See Janet Clare's essay in this volume.
20. For the full text of the *Coronation Entertainment*, see H&S VII, pp. 67–109. Henceforth *CE* and quotations cited parenthetically within the text.
21. Blair Worden, 'Ben Jonson Among the Historians', in *Culture and Politics in Early Stuart England*, ed. by Kevin Sharpe and Peter Lake (Stanford, CA: Stanford University Press, 1993), pp. 67–90 (esp. p. 84).
22. Ibid., p. 82.
23. For a carefully nuanced discussion of royal 'absolutism', see Glenn Burgess, *Absolute Monarchy and the Stuart Constitution* (New Haven: Yale University Press, 1996).
24. For discussion of Jonson's attitude towards Augustus in the years immediately preceding the composition of *Sejanus*, see, for instance, the Introduction to Tom Cain's edition of *Poetaster* (Manchester: Manchester University Press, 1995), pp. 14–17, 20–23.
25. The most important, of course, is Jenny Wormald, whose forthcoming biography of James should encourage us to reassess his reign; see also, Maurice Lee Jr, *Great Britain's Solomon: James VI and I in His Three Kingdoms* (Urbana: University of Illinois Press, 1990).
26. See for example, K.W. Evans, '*Sejanus* and the Ideal Prince Tradition', p. 258.
27. See Wormald, 'James VI and I', p. 51.
28. In citing examples from *Sejanus*, I am assuming that Jonson frequently endorses an idea by ironically treating its unattractive opposite, or by implying the hypocrisy of insincere speakers. Thus, if Tiberius attacks flattery, I am assuming that Jonson also disdains flattery, even when it is condemned by (the hypocritical Tiberius).
29. For a similar view, see Burton's article on 'The Political Tragedies of Jonson and Chapman', esp. 401–3.
30. We need a much fuller examination than we presently possess of Jonson's religious views. For a start in the right direction, see James

P. Crowley, Jr, 'Honest Ben: Jonson and Religion', Ph.D. Dissertation, University of Delaware Press, 1992.

31. For a detailed discussions of these matters, see Evans, *Jonson, Lipsius, and the Politics of Renaissance Stoicism*, esp. pp. 1–152 and 343–9.

32. I will cite appropriate act and line numbers from *Sejanus* and will cite the page numbers of the William Jones translation of the *Politica* (abbreviated *P*) which is reproduced in Evans, *Jonson, Lipsius, and the Politics of Renaissance Stoicism*, 153–274. In the latter book, photos of the marked pages from Jonson's Latin edition appear on pages 276–338.

    In briefly characterizing the positions expressed in Jonson's *Sejanus*, I have, of course, assumed that he endorses 'worthy' views whether they are expressed by worthy or unworthy characters. For example, the fact that Tiberius endorses virtue so repeatedly is ironic, but the irony reflects negatively on Tiberius, not on the virtues to which he pays lip-service.

33. This echo ultimately comes from Book IV of Tacitus's *Annals*; see Evans, *Jonson, Lipsius, and the Politics of Renaissance Stoicism*, pp. 273–4.

5

'Defacing the Carcass': Anne of Denmark and Jonson's *The Masque of Blackness*

Clare McManus

It is proper ... that not only arms but indeed also the speech of women never be made public; for the speech of a noblewoman can be no less dangerous than the nakedness of her limbs.[1]

So Francesco Barbaro wrote in his early fifteenth-century treatise, *On Wifely Duties*. Although it predates the performance of Jonson's *The Masque of Blackness* by almost two hundred years, this statement remains representative of prevalent attitudes towards women in the early seventeenth century; the danger of the female voice and body is powerfully constant. Barbaro neatly encapsulates the perceived connection between public female speech and a dangerously liberated female sexuality in the open display of the gendered body. Denied access to speech in the court masque, the aspects of the genre which allow the female nobility to perform are also those which simultaneously confine this performative presence to the physical. Yet, as Barbaro's insistence on the danger posed by the female body implies, whether voiced or silent, such a presence constitutes a threat which must be monitored or controlled. From the familiar position of the silenced woman, the noble female masquer finds an expression through the second half of Barbaro's formulation, in the equally expressive and threatening presence of the female body on the masquing stage. In the course of this process, these tools of apparent restraint are themselves rendered ambivalent and liberating.

It is through an examination of the controls exerted over the female masquer that I shall approach Jonson's *The Masque of Blackness* (1605), ascertaining the tensions that exist within this performance as a result of its embodiment of such oppositional energies. Commissioned by Anne of Denmark, wife of King James I, and performed by the queen and 11 of her ladies, *Blackness* has a forceful feminine presence. Jonson's incorporation of this presence within the masque text complicates the primary function of a court festival, the praise of the King as the privileged spectator. Although in theory the performative presence of the noble female upon the masquing stage was unproblematic, male performance exists in an uneasy relationship with the masque genre; its dependency on the social and performative codes of the court, and on its historical and political moment, both demands a feminine presence and lays the masque open to disruption when that presence is a transgressive one. The structure of the court masque, a synthesis of disparate genres of art and performance into a unified whole, leaves it vulnerable to a destabilization which is compounded by Queen Anne's active contribution to the feminine representative strategy and the transgressive form that this takes. Revealed through recent revaluations as a figure of far greater cultural and political engagement and significance than was previously believed, Anne's performance in the social and political form of the masque should also be read in this revisionist light.[2] To this end, I shall offer an evaluation of the nature of female performance and cultural agency as it relates to the demands of the masque form, and of the controversial status of such performance within contemporary society. In particular, I shall consider the manifestation of the tensions which Jonson's accommodations of Anne's active agency, necessary because of her status as patron and his position as commissioned poet and subject, caused in its textual and performative incarnations.

Sir Dudley Carleton's emotive eye-witness account of a night of masquing at the Jacobean court leaves little doubt as to the impact of *Blackness* upon its audience:

> At night we had the Queen's Maske in the Banquetting House, or rather her Pagent ... Their Apparell was rich but too light and Curtizan-like for such great ones. Instead of Vizzards, their Faces, and Arms, up to the Elbows, were painted black, which was Disguise sufficient, for they were hard to be known; *but it*

became them nothing so well as their red and white, and you cannot imagine a more ugly sight than a Troop of lean-cheek'd Moors.[3]

Carleton's comments have proved valuable to critics of the masque, and his violent reaction to the female masquers figures prominently in recent investigations of the discourses of race and empire staged so powerfully in the blackened faces of the noblewomen.[4] I do not intend to focus specifically upon these issues although, given their incorporation into the bodies of the elite female performers, they will inevitably be implicated in my discussion of the masque's gender politics. Instead, I will deal with the dynamics of female performance itself, with the underlying reasons why the women's physical appearance offended against the conventions of the masque form, and with the manifestation of such transgressions in the performance of Jonson's text. Carleton's criticisms of the performance cluster around the transgressive representation of the female masquers, a fact that strongly suggests that the act of female performance is not itself at issue here. I shall discuss the extent to which a feminine presence is indeed necessary and desirable within the masque, and point to the ways in which Anne and her noblewomen overstep the bounds of propriety in the representational strategies adopted in *Blackness*.

I: JONSON AND THE QUEEN'S WILL

Blackness stands in the canon of the court masque as the first collaboration between Ben Jonson and Inigo Jones. It is also, however, the first of several interactions between Jonson and Anne of Denmark, who was herself keenly involved in court entertainments. Anne is deeply implicated in this production; Jonson notes that he had to incorporate her demands within the conceit of the masque, saying that it was 'her majesty's will to have them [the women] blackamores at first.'[5] Given the remark's positioning in a transcript published after the fact of the performance, it is possible that Jonson is attempting to distance himself from the controversy surrounding that conceit, while being seen to have paid the appropriate lipservice to his queen. It is also possible, however, given Anne's previous exposure to performers with blackened skins, in particular in the 1590 royal entry into Edinburgh, that the conceit was indeed hers.[6] Whatever the case may be, this is not Anne's first

contribution to the process of masque creation (in 1604 she commissioned Samuel Daniel's *The Vision of the Twelve Goddesses*), and
her involvement should be read in the light of her ongoing engagement with the masquing performances of the Jacobean court.
Blackness is neither Anne's first nor last masque performance; it
stands at the head of a performative masquing career that stretches
until 1611 and in which Jonson figures prominently, scripting all
but two of the masques in which the queen performs.[7] I would
suggest that, through the power of patronage and the exploitation
of her elite status as queen consort, Anne directly influences the
stage representation of the female, offering what could be read as a
distinct process of feminine self-fashioning and the manipulation
of the performance of power.

The masque genre is one in which the concept of performance
itself and in particular that of women, so anomalous in its time, is
foregrounded. Against the background of Renaissance England's
rejection of the female dramatic performer, noblewomen are permitted performative expression within the masque. The synthesis
of apparent oppositions extends beyond the masque's structure to
its participants; members of royalty appear alongside those actors
categorized in the statute of 1572 with vagabonds and beggars, and
aristocratic women perform alongside male actors playing female
roles. Such an emergence of the female performer is only possible
amongst the elite of the age because, as I shall make clear, this performance is dependent upon the courtly norms and regulations of
aristocratic behaviour. Elite female performance, by definition,
involves the intersection of class and gender issues which circulate
within the masque and find a specific site of expression in the performing female body. Any feminine corporeal transgression is compounded by its performance against the background of the stricter
controls that operate on the female rather than the male body. The
gendered bodily decorum of Jacobean society as manifested in the
masque will be examined, establishing the different restrictions
such a gendering places on the male and female courtier and the
extent to which a feminine expression is achieved through, rather
than in spite of, these restrictions.

Commissioned by his queen to script a performance expressly
avoiding female speech, Jonson is himself both confronted by and
strongly implicated in the restrictions surrounding a feminine presence in this masque. The published text of *Blackness* lays out the
poet's polarized categorization of the disparate aspects that the

masque form sought to synthesize: scenery, dance, and costume he refers to as the 'carcass' and text and allegorical significance as 'spirit' (l. 7). He writes of the elite audience of the masque, whose privilege it was to 'deface their carcasses' (that is to tear down the enormously expensive scenery), and his fear that if he were not to immortalize the masque through the process of writing and publication the 'spirits' would also perish. This same concern, expressed in similar terms, is also found in the preface to the 1606 masque *Hymenaei*, often read as Jonson's definitive statement on the masque genre: 'So short lived are the bodies of all things in comparison of their souls.'[8] Just as tensions exist within the masque form, so too are they manifest in the relationship between masque performances and published text; Jonson's framing statement offers a theorization of the masque not available in performance, but in the end it is one directly engaged with the representational strategies used to depict the female masquer on stage. Denied access to spoken text, the female masquer appears to be aligned only with the carcass, with the physical aspects of the masque. This carcass is that which has no textual representation: music for which no text survives, the movement of the body, both danced and unchoreographed, scenic design and costume (the designs of which were not initially included in Jonson's transcripts). The female masquers were granted access to expression only through the media of make-up, costume, dance, and gesture; through the physicality of the body within which they were confined.

Jonson's concern with the relationship of soul and body pervades *Blackness*, recurring in Niger's commentary on the mingling of 'the immortal souls of creatures mortal/... with their bodies' (ll. 101–2). The poet's choice of terminology carries with it a value-judgement; the apparent inferiority of the body of the masque is in turn communicated to the female performers associated with that carcass. The alignment of the feminine with the physical is a commonplace of the early modern period. Contemporary Aristotelian theories of conception evoke the essential passivity of the female, whose bodily matter, aligned with the elements of earth and water, receives the stamp of the celestial masculine energy of fire and air. Just as in the act of creation the female supposedly receives the imprint of the actively creative male, so in dramatic creation female performers are burdened with significance according to the Renaissance taste for allegory. Connected intrinsically with the body and the bodily, the female is considered the bearer, not

the creator of allegorical significance. Jonathan Sawday has
described dissection (a literal 'de-facing') as the marker of sovereign power through the interpretation of the transgressive subject's
body.[9] It is just this passivity that I will suggest is challenged in
Blackness. In what at first sight appears to be a further assertion of
the monarch's centrality within the masque, these noblewomen
take to the stage in order to be symbolically opened to interpretation; yet the act of interpretation reveals a feminine corporeality
which posits an alternative ideology to that of the court's dominant
faction. This is an argument I shall develop further in my discussion of the relationship between the female performer and the
linguistic dynamics of *Blackness*. I hope to demonstrate that the
alignment of the feminine with the corporeal actually provides
opportunities for a measure of female expression and autonomy
within the masque, primarily since it is this very confinement of
the female to the physical which allows women to masque. Furthermore, I would propose that although the female masquer does
remain within a silent corporeality, the physical expression of
costume and make-up destabilizes the restrictions placed upon her
and subverts a reading of the masque which sees it merely as a
panegyric to James. Apparently constrained to submission within
this physicality, the masquers in fact occupy an ambiguous, liminal
position, transforming apparent tools of constraint into the means
for near-autonomous self-fashioning.

II: THE FEMALE BODY: A NECESSARY PRESENCE

The court masque is a form of elite social ritual rather than public
drama and it derives its performance conventions from its social
environment. During the non-dramatic main masque, the stage is
imaginatively and physically continuous with the body of the audi-
torium and noble masquers are unified with noble spectators.
Noble men and women are judged on the masquing stage as they
would be were they watching instead of participating. It is the
social nature of the masque genre that offers female nobles access to
the masquing stage; although this is complicated by the theatrical-
ized nature of the ideologies of courtly behaviour, which themselves demand their own concealment, masquing is postulated
simply as participation in court society rather than as performance.
Citing the court's social order as the motivating factor behind

female performance in a society in which the conceptualization of the male and female directly results in the exclusion of women from the more usual theatrical performance may seem perverse. It will become clear, however, that women achieve performance within the masque not through a lessening of social restrictions, but rather through a strict, class-engendered imposition of controls upon both male and female nobility, which sets the otherwise strictly gendered aristocracy upon a more even footing.

Neither noblewomen nor noblemen were permitted to speak in the masque; as silent participators, Anne and her gentlewomen can be more fruitfully considered as dancers rather than actors. When speech was required, as in the dramatic antimasque which works in opposition to the essentially non-dramatic masque proper, these roles were taken by professional actors hired for the purpose. While, as we shall see, to dance is the privilege of the nobility, Stephen Orgel points out that acting – which he defines as the adoption of an identity not one's own – was considered detrimental to the status of the courtier, something made clear in the condemnatory response to the later role-playing of George Villiers, the Earl of Buckingham.[10] It is extremely significant that there exists within the masque an equivalency of attitudes to the performance of men and women of the elite social class not found in other theatrical forms within this period. Noblemen and women are surrounded by the same limitations, the same restrictions. This equivalency of attitudes, the overpowering of gender definition by class concerns, may at one level have worked towards allowing female access to the masquing stage. Male silence actually creates the possibility of female performance; the masque's class-consciousness creates a level starting point for the performance of the gendered aristocracy through the defusing of the perceived threat of the garrulous woman.

Just as the masque is firmly based on the ideology and decorum of courtly society, so too is dance. Andrew Sabol defines dance as the *'raison d'être* of the typical Stuart masque.'[11] The masque dances, including both the performative dances of the main and antimasque (although the last category is not applicable to *Blackness*) and the social dances of the revels, are perhaps the genre's primary component. Stephen Orgel regards this assertion as 'tendentious' because the masque was always 'a mixed genre, and its inventors and its participants always saw it differently'.[12] What can be said is that the sheer length of the revels and their performative inclusion of the audience means that dance, despite its scanty representation within the transcripts, is the most substantial of the masque's performative aspects. Open and available to all members of the Jacobean court, both male and female, dance is the defining influence upon female involvement, and its importance as the noblewoman's primary point of entry to the masque form itself cannot be overestimated.

The early modern European court enshrines the dance as a necessary attribute of the courtly elite. Stephen Orgel states that it 'was permissible for masquers to be dancers, because dancing is the prerogative of every lady and gentlemen'.[13] Skill in dance, attained through long years of training from an early age, defines what it is to be an aristocrat; it opposes the courtly against the non-courtly in an expression of elite community. Though voices of Puritan dissent from beyond court circles branded dance as an incitement to lust, it is ranked alongside other courtly attributes in early modern educationalist handbooks, such as Sir Thomas Elyot's *The Book Named the Governor*, as a comely and decorous activity.[14] Although pre-dating the cultural production of the Jacobean court, Elyot's text gives an insight into the theorization of the dance at a time so crucial to the masque's development. The specific necessity of a feminine participation is made clearer in his conceptualization of the dance as an image of the gendered order of the social hierarchy; dance represents the Aristotelian ethical mean between the extremes of gendered characteristics: 'Wherefore, when we behold a man and a woman dancing together, let us suppose there to be a concord of all the said qualities ... .'[15] The dance's social nature opens it to the female performer and seeks to mark her as an acquiescent member of courtly society; dance training forms part of the literal incorporation into the individual of the controls exerted upon the noble body. The noblewoman's danced participation is intrinsic to the masque genre (at the very least within the revels) for it to offer the social affirmation necessary to its existence as state ritual.

Female participation is therefore necessary, and is made inevitable by the essential theatricality of these governing codes of aristocratic behaviour. Mark Franko, in his analysis of the codes of the aristocratic body in dance and society, remarks that the Renaissance term 'grace' in fact refers to a kind of theatricality.[16] The masque dances are predicated upon a performative code of bodily display intended to win the praise or regard of a watching audience. This code is one in which virtue is defined as the creation of its appearance; the theatrical core of courtly behaviour entails the creation of identity through performance.[17] The dynamics and tensions of this correspondence between physical appearance and inner being will be significant later in my analysis of the feminine relationship to discourse in *Blackness*. At this point in my discussion, however, what is important is that the dance of the female masquers is to some extent theatrical, a performance of their identities. Recognition of the identity of the noble performer is an intrinsic aspect of the masque form and one of the most important influences on female participation. The concept of masquing differs radically from that of acting, demanding neither the effacement of self nor the adoption of an alternative identity. Instead, the theatricality at the core of the courtier's identity, regularly enacted within the daily life of the court, is now performed upon the masquing stage. The body of the Renaissance aristocrat is itself a space of theatrical play – the leap from the performance of a courtly identity to a staged participation in the masque is not so great as it first appears.

Within this apparent parity of attitudes, there do, however, exist further distinctions in the conceptualization of the gendered body in performance. Even within their shared silence, male and female courtiers are differentiated on a specifically corporeal level through the same ideologies of dance that grant them access to the masquing stage. Just as restrictions are imposed upon the speech of both male and female nobles within the masque, so conformity to the codes of courtly grace is imposed upon both genders. These constraints are, however, gendered ones; they differ in their details and in the nature of the limits they impose upon the male and female noble dancer. Any transgression in the corporeal realm, involving motion or not, is performed against the background of the stricter controls that operate on the female body.

One of the clearest theoretical statements of the gendering of the dancing body is made by Elyot in a continuation of his remarks cited above:

> Wherefore, when we behold a man and a woman dancing together, let us suppose there to be a concord of all the said qualities ... And the moving of the man would be more vehement, of the woman more delicate, and with less advancing of the body, signifying the courage and strength that ought to be in a man, and the pleasant soberness that should be in a woman.[18]

This description, in line with contemporary corporeal codes, implies an unproblematic correspondence between gender-determined kinesis and internal being – gender is imaged as ethical essence rather than as created construct. Elyot's theoretical statements seem to correspond fairly well to the actual practice of the dance, as documented in contemporary dance treatises.[19] The specific detail of dance steps reveals the gendering of the body's movement, perhaps most clearly in the galliard, which entails a peacock-like male display in contrast with a more restrained female role. This is demonstrated in the dance which Fabritio Caroso entitles the *Nido d'Amore* and describes in his dance treatise, the *Nobiltà di Dame* (1600), a text available to the English court. In this dance the specifics of gendered movement become clear: the male performs galliard leaps and capers while the female dances a less showy tordion version, the tordion being a more solemn and weighty version of the galliard.[20]

A specific example of the operation and intersection of such codes of class and gender can be found within the performance of *Blackness*. Carleton implicitly praises the Spanish ambassador for leading Anne to dance in the social dances of the revels despite the shocking nature of her appearance. His remark has an interesting context, however, in his comparison of the ambassador's dancing in a previous masque to that of 'a lusty old Gallant with his Country Woman', hardly the description of courtly grace.[21] In this case it is possible either that the skill of the individual dancer failed him, or that the mode of Spanish courtly dance differs from that of England. What is clear, though, is that non-conformity to the demands of the courtly dance acts as a marker of alien status: the discourse of courtesy defines the dancer's social identity. Within the performance, commentary, and social context of *Blackness*, the groups categorized are those who do not conform to the ideologies of the masculine courtly elite, namely women and foreigners. Queen Anne, of course, was both. The dance of the ambassador with the black-faced queen reflects the liminal positions of the foreigner and the female; this dance is a nexus of class and gender issues circulating within the masque. These women are presented as members of another, specifically alien, community through the transgression of the physical norms of appearance. Although the lack of comment suggests that no transgression of the norms of the dance occurred, the codes governing movement and appearance are closely interrelated. Having gained access to the masquing stage through the physicality of the body in confirmation of the ideology of court society, female transgression against those controls is staged in that same body.

In the court masque, therefore, Jonson is engaging with a performative genre which simultaneously demands female participation and the control of the representation of the female during her performance. It is clear that the codes of social and gendered order and the court's demands of corporeal decorum and aristocratic community propel the female into the masque, yet on her arrival on stage as a masquer she is trammelled by these very same codes of social convention and limitation. Yet, as I shall now discuss, these tools of control are also a means of expression for the masquing noblewoman. The performative strategies of costume and face-paint oppose the requirements of court decorum, highlighting the ineffectual nature of feminine containment and emphasizing the pre-existent tensions within the structure and form of this masque.

III: MOORS AND COURTESANS: THE CONTROVERSY OF PERFORMANCE

A major issue that surfaces in the performance of *Blackness* is its non-adherence to either the conventions of the masque form or the aristocratic code of corporeal grace. Such non-conformity is symptomatic of the divergent energies of this masquing occasion, of the tensions caused by Anne's transgressive presence and demands, and of the need for the masque to be offered as a panegyric to James I. The breaking of the restrictions of genre and decorum goes hand in hand with the radically subversive nature of the black-painted faces of the queen and her women. Contemporary reaction to the costuming and make-up of the women was violent, as instanced in Carleton's description of the 'ugly sight' of the 'Troop of lean-cheek'd Moors'. In order to fully understand the ramifications of Jonson's accommodation of Anne's wish that the women's faces be blackened, an awareness of contemporary connotations of race and colour is necessary.

The aesthetic sensibilities of the Renaissance held 'black' to be synonymous with 'ugly'. Niger's assertion that his black-skinned daughters are beautiful would, for the contemporary audience versed in the traditions of the black-faced devils of the mystery plays and the association of tanned skin with outdoor and menial labour, be a paradox. Importantly, both this blackness and the act of face-painting itself were also held to imply a certain sexual voracity. Such an admission of sexuality complements that found in the masquers' bare limbs, which Jacobean decorum decreed should remain covered and which Barbaro's statement classifies as dangerously expressive. Anne, six months pregnant with her daughter Mary at the time of the masque, her face and arms burnt by the heat of the imperial sun of James, is an embodiment of consummated sexual passion. Carleton and the audience were, therefore, watching their queen perform in a garb of ugliness and sexual indecorum.

Carleton's emotional violence does not however stem so much from the sight of aesthetically displeasing females as from the demeaning impact such a displeasure has on the status of the queen. For Carleton, it is extremely offensive that his queen cannot be recognized, that her body is de-faced. The black face paint removes Anne's identity and status during the enactment of the very ritual of courtly power intended to confirm it. Still more offensive is the fact that her royal status is neglected even to the extent that she is not distinguished from her masquing companions. Jonson, in the transcript of the masque, describes the nymphs' costumes as 'alike in all, without difference' (l. 56). As a communal form, the masque should reflect the hierarchies of the creating society. A great deal, though probably not all, of Carleton's aversion at this open display of sexuality arises from the link between that sexuality and the social indecorum of such a display in royalty. The blackened skins of the performers, acceptable for the non-courtly male performers of the Edinburgh entry, are damaging to Anne's status as a queen and performer. Stephen Orgel sums up the masque's essential tensions when he says that it 'fulfils the requirements of the queen but does not, in any deeper sense, take into account that fact that she *is* the queen'.[22]

Carleton's criticisms are not aimed at Anne's presence on the stage, rather he is attacking her physical appearance. Anne's indecorum manifests itself in her body; her fault is to be seen as a woman whose sexuality, although necessary to produce heirs, does not accord with the model demanded by the court. The make-up that blackens the faces of the noblewomen operates in a paradoxical manner. While painting over the facial markers of the performers' individuality transforms them into examples of the indistinguishable, generic 'Woman' and so offends court hierarchies, it does focus attention upon the transgressive nature of this physicality; in setting the women beyond the bounds of accepted decorum and aligning them with a subversively open and fulfilled sexuality, it affirms their independence from the court's structures. Placing the noblewomen beyond the constraints of court decorum, this strategy establishes them in a position of liminality and so attributes to them a new source of power and influence. The masque form, intended as an enactment of the power of the monarch and of the queen and noblewomen through their association with the king, is destabilized through this insistence on a display of non-conformity. The black face-paint is to those watching a failure to take into account the performers' status, but it is also a liberating expression of female sexuality.

That tensions are felt between the neo-Platonic feminine ideal and the masquers' transgression is evident within the masque text itself. The sexuality embodied in the noblewomen's appearance, in their bare limbs and blackened skin, is swiftly countered by the establishment of the positive ideal of James I's bleaching power, banishing such transgressive traits. In this masque, white is pure. A fair complexion is offered as a sign of chastity and sexual conformity in a motif which is a vindication of the social order. James is depicted as a figure whose power marginalizes the disruptive effect of a liberated female sexuality. As his light is to blanch the nymphs' shocking blackness so he, with the power of the absolute monarch, is to constrain and transmute their sexuality into a more acceptable form of femininity. This is, of course, strongly undermined by the fact that it remains incomplete within *Blackness*; the white skin sought by the nymphs and promised by the monarch remains just that – an unfulfilled promise. The court must wait for Jonson's *The Masque of Beauty* (the complement to *Blackness* performed, after some delay, in 1608) for the delivery of the sun-bleached nymphs. The true dramatic action of *Blackness* does not take place on stage but in the court's lived experience of the controversy found in the years between the masques and in its resolution as Anne and her ladies appear from the outset of the second masque with white skins and decorous costumes. As a result of this lack of closure, *Blackness* suffers from serious formal flaws; Anne's presence and the demands she places upon the masque's content are problematic and unsettling.

IV: MUTE HIEROGLYPHS AND PAINTED WORDS: THE PHYSICALITY OF DISCOURSE

The pervasive physicalization of the feminine within *Blackness*
extends even to the forms of language with which the masquers
were associated. The tension and stresses created by the presence of
the female performers as cultural agents are forcefully present
within the discursive dynamics of this masque. Jonson describes
the moment when the masquers began their dance:

> Here the tritons sounded, and they danced on the shore, every
> couple as they advanced severally presenting their fans, in one of
> which were inscribed their mixed names, in the other a mute
> hieroglyph expressing their mixed qualities. (Which manner of
> symbol I rather chose than imprese, as well for strangeness as
> relishing of antiquity, and more applying to that original
> doctrine of sculpture which the Egyptians are said first to have
> brought from the Ethiopians.)
>
> (ll. 236–42)

Twelve silent women approach their peers holding painted words
and symbols and purporting to capture and identify their very
essences. Striking as this image of the dislocation of the female
masquer from speech is, and however much it highlights the
enforced silence of the noblewomen, it does not represent the end-
point of feminine discursive dynamics in this masque. Denied
verbal expression, the women are granted a physical medium of
communication which is aligned with their constraint within the
corporeal. The language of the masque is itself physical; it has
become pictorial – the painted word and the painted hieroglyph.

Jonson's explicit choice of the hieroglyph over the *imprese* is more
than just an appeal to the cultural authority of antiquity; in light of
contemporary emblem theory it is extremely pertinent to the depiction of the female performer. Michael Bath cites Bacon's discussion
of the hieroglyph in *The Advancement of Learning*:

> hieroglyphics, (things of ancient use, and embraced chiefly by the
> Egyptians, one of the most ancient nations) ... are but as con-
> tinued impreses and emblems. And as for gestures, they are as
> transitory hieroglyphics, and are to hieroglyphics as words spoken

are to words written, in that they abide not; but they have ever-more, as well as the other, an affinity with the thing signified ... .[23]

Bacon's alignment of gesture and hieroglyphs as physicalized forms of language is revealing; the physicality of the female masquing body exists on the same imaginative and discursive level as that of the hieroglyph – both participate in the creation of significance. Within the very discourse that attempts to constrain the significance of the female through confinement to the physical is a recognition of the corporeal creation of meaning which offers the female masquer expressive possibilities.

Even more striking is Bacon's assertion of the hieroglyph's 'affinity' with its referent. In contrast to the context-dependent imprese, emphatically rejected by Jonson, for which the association with the referent is felt to be merely conventional, the hieroglyph is thought to have a natural, single, and readily available significance. The hieroglyph is seen to erase the gap between sign and signifier and offer what Bath terms a 'natural, Adamic language'.[24] Similarly, Jonson's alliance of hieroglyphs and sculpture resonates within the dynamics of the physical confinement of the female and the ready availability of meaning within *Blackness*. In line with the neo-Platonic embodiment of the ideal within the physical and with Renaissance theories of sculpture which saw the artefact as pre-existent within the sculptural medium, the use of this physicalized discourse is an attempt to define the essence of the female mas-quers. The use of hieroglyphs – of linguistic sculpture – is an attempt to constrain the female to single, predetermined and readily available authorial meaning, and to further limit the gen-eration of significance through an apparently clear and available representation of what is defined as the feminine essence.

Against this conceptual background, I would suggest that the structure and performance of *Blackness* complicates the straightfor-ward interpretation of significance. The masque's fundamental conceit is the attempt to bleach the archetypal Moor, found in both Alciati and Whitney as an emblem of 'futile labour'.[25] Jonson cuts this free from its original context of canonical textual authority by establishing its seemingly impossible fulfilment as the marker of James I's royal authority. This in turn means that, in a challenge to the interpretative authority of the emblem books, it is the failure to fulfil this proverbial impossibility that disappoints audience expec-tations. In much the same way, the apparently unproblematic correspondence of the names and hieroglyphs to a single meaning is destabilized; their juxtaposition with the openly sexual bodies of the female masquers dislocates them from conventions of interpretative authority and opens them to a more various reading. The depiction of Anne and her partner, Lucy, Countess of Bedford, is a prominent example of this process. They carry between them the hieroglyph of 'A golden tree laden with fruit' (l. 245). The names painted on the second fan were 'Euphoris' and 'Aglaia' which, according to the studies carried out by D.J. Gordon, refer to the quality of fertility and to the first of the three Graces, herself associated with the fertility and abundance of the earth.[26] Gordon suggests one overall interpretation as being the representation of spiritual beauty fertilizing the earth. His analysis also associates the theme of purity with these nymphs and with several of the other masquers' names and hieroglyphs. Yet the figures of the women holding these symbols of pure fertility are ones whose bodies are markers of a dangerous and open sexuality, destabilizing the simplistic assumptions accompanying such emblems of purity and fertility. While the masquers, in particular the pregnant queen, are indeed fertile, and while they do represent a form of feminine grace and beauty, once again it is not a form acceptable to the Jacobean court. Qualities of grace and fertility, and spiritual beauty are represented through feminine corporeality, yet this does not accord with the interpretations imposed upon the openly displayed female body by the dominant ideology.

The association of the hieroglyph with the female masquer is not an isolated occurrence but can also be detected in an earlier masque of the Jacobean court which involved Anne and others of her ladies, Samuel Daniel's *The Vision of the Twelve Goddesses*. In his dedicatory letter to the Countess of Bedford, herself a participant in *Blackness*, Daniel writes of the roles taken by the female masquers:

> though these images gave oftentimes divers significations, yet it being not our purpose to represent them with all those curious and superfluous observations, we took them only to serve as hieroglyphs for our present intention, according to some property that fitted our present occasion … .[27]

Again it would seem that the very choice of hieroglyphic expression is itself an attempt to limit the potential significances of women within the masque to that desired by the author, to a single and predetermined statement of meaning. Yet Daniel's strategy of containment fails; it results not in the creation of readily available significances in the bodies of the female performers, but rather in the explanatory text of the letter itself which further opens the masque to the very kind of analysis and interpretative multiplicity that was to have been avoided. Visual and written or spoken text operate on similar levels of indeterminacy and the attempt to constrain one with the other fails.

Such a failure points to the problematic status of the correspondence between inner essence and outer representation, the dynamics of which resonate throughout *Blackness*. As my analysis has shown, the codes of noble behaviour, the gendering of the aristocratic body, and the discursive dynamics of this masque all operate in accordance with the notion of the unproblematic correspondence. Yet, as examination of the performative actuality of the strategies of female representation shows, this certainty is challenged by the female masquers' non-conformity, a departure which points up the constructed nature of these strategies. The female masquer's body is the nexus of issues of gender, discourse, the social conception and control of the body, and performance; all seek to control the feminine creation of significance by constraining her to the physical and seeking to simplify that physicality, and all fail. Gender, discourse, and the grace of courtly behaviour are instead shown to operate through convention and consensus; they have no actual connection with that to which they gesture. More positively, the status of the female body as a powerful signifier becomes clear; despite the loss of a prelapsarian immediacy, the female body is not merely the passive bearer of significance but its active creator.

The masque audience would, therefore, have been witness to a problematic conjunction of the physical bodies of the female masquers and the physicalized language of the hieroglyphs which communicate two varying significances and which are forced together in the composite image of the women holding the painted words. The women, garbed in sexuality and danger, advance holding meekly conformist symbols which purport to 'speak' their natures to those watching. This uncomfortable meeting of a physicalized language which seeks (but fails) to be clearly available and the unsettling force of an openly consummated female sexuality would appear to ironize a straightforward reading of both the figures of the women and the nature of the discourse within this masque. In their enforced physicality, the female masquers themselves become emblematic; the women's bodies themselves become part of the discursive system of meaning-creation. Their presence is a disruptive one, however, exerting pressure upon the fractures already existent within the previously apparently stable linguistic system. The emblems exist in a reciprocal position of ironic commentary over the disruptive women, a position which also allows the transgressive female figure to commentate upon the canonical female ideal and upon the effort to constrain the abundance of significance – both gendered and discursive – to a single, one might say absolutist, meaning.

As Anne's commissioned poet, Jonson was faced with the need to synthesize the demands of both his queen and the social conventions of the masque genre with which they conflicted. The energies of female performance and cultural engagement circulate within the performance of *Blackness*, destabilizing its nature as a straightforward panegyric to James I. Pre-existent tensions are further compounded within *Blackness* since it contains not only a female masquing presence but also the assumption of a degree of cultural agency in Anne's demands for the specific content of the masque.

The prohibition of female speech is a constraint of the female within her corporeality. Aristocratic women enter the masque through dance and are seen as physical beings, visions of beauty or shame robed in luxurious costumes. The performative status of dance as a substantial aspect of the masque means that the only form of subversion open to the female courtier – that of the physical – is one which is very close to the heart of the masque form itself. Tools of apparent constraint can be used to destabilize a simple acceptance of significance and are themselves rendered increasingly ambiguous; the physicality which seems to enclose and inhibit the women itself provides an outlet for their expression. The open sexuality which shocked Carleton can be interpreted as an assertion of female sexual and political autonomy; twisted away from the simplistic flattery of the King to a statement of female agency, *Blackness* finds no favour with its courtly audience. Costume and dance may be the only means of female expression and are undoubtedly hedged around with strict conventions of female physical decorum. However, while masculine control can be instanced in the regulation of female bodily appearance, female rebellion against such restraints also takes a physical form – the indecorum of bare and blackened limbs.

Notes

I would like to thank Kate Chedgzoy, Stephen Orgel, J.R. Mulryne, and Margaret Shewring for their help and comments on earlier versions of this article.

1. Cited in Peter Stallybrass, 'Patriarchal Territories: The Body Enclosed', in *Rewriting the Renaissance: The Discourses of Sexual Difference in Early Modern Europe*, ed. by Margaret W. Ferguson, Maureen Quillingan and Nancy J. Vickers (Chicago: University of Chicago Press, 1986), pp. 123–42 (p. 127).
2. See Barbara Kiefer Lewalski, *Writing Women in Jacobean England* (London and Cambridge, MA: Harvard University Press, 1993); Leeds Barroll, 'The Court of the First Stuart Queen', in *The Mental World of the Jacobean Court*, ed. by Linda Levy Peck (Cambridge: Cambridge University Press, 1991), pp. 191–208.
3. C.H. Herford, Percy and Evelyn Simpson (eds), *Ben Jonson* 11 vols (Oxford: Clarendon Press, 1925–52), I, p. 448. Henceforth H&S.
4. See, in particular, Hardin Aasand, '"To Blanch an Ethiop, and Revive a Corse": Queen Anne and *The Masque of Blackness*', *Studies in English Literature, 1500–1900*, 32 (1992), 271–85; Kim F. Hall, 'Sexual Politics and Cultural Identity in *The Masque of Blackness*' in *The Performance of Power: Theatrical Discourse and Politics*, ed. by Sue-Ellen Case and Janelle Reinelt (Iowa City: University of Iowa Press, 1991), pp. 3–18; Marion Wynne-Davies, 'The Queen's Masque: Renaissance Women and the Seventeenth-Century Court Masque', in *Gloriana's Face: Women, Public and Private, in the English Renaissance*, ed. by S.P. Cerasano and Marion Wynne-Davies (Hemel Hempstead: Harvester Wheatsheaf, 1992), pp. 79–104. Although Carleton's comments are not mentioned, also relevant to the discussion of race in *The Masque of Blackness* is Yumna Siddiqi, 'Dark Incontinents: The Discourse of Race and Gender in Three Renaissance Masques', *Renaissance Drama*, 23 (1992), 139–63.
5. Ben Jonson, *The Masque of Blackness*, in *Ben Jonson: The Complete Masques*, ed. by Stephen Orgel (London and New Haven: Yale University Press, 1975), p. 48, l. 18. All further references to this edition will appear in parentheses within the text.
6. *The Receiving of King James the Sixth and His Queene, at Lyeth*, in *Papers Relative to the Marriage of James the Sixth of Scotland, with the Princess Anna of Denmark: AD MDLXXXIX and the form and manner of Her Majesty's Coronation at Holyrood House*, ed. by J.T. Gibson Craig (Edinburgh: Ballantyne Club, 1828), pp. 38–42 (p. 40).
7. Anne's final appearance as a conventional masquer was in the 1611 masque *Love Freed from Ignorance and Folly*. She did, however, appear briefly in Campion's *Somerset Masque* in 1614, but not as a conventional masquer; rather she appeared alone, precipitating the masque's main action by plucking a golden bough from a tree and freeing the male masquers from imprisonment. See Thomas Campion, *The Somerset Masque*, in *The Works of Thomas Campion*, ed. by Walter R. Davies (London: Faber and Faber, 1969), pp. 263–84.

8. Ben Jonson, *Hymenaei*, in Orgel, *Complete Masques*, p. 75, ll. 4–5.
9. Jonathan Sawday, *The Body Emblazoned: Dissection and the Human Body in Renaissance Culture* (London and New York: Routledge, 1995), p. 189.
10. Orgel, *Complete Masques*, p. 5. In 1626 Buckingham and two other prominent male courtiers took part in the Rabelaisian antimasque of an unidentified masque 'which many thought too histrionical to become him; when in the presence of king, queen, ambassadors, and the flower of the court, he acted as a master of the fence'; a letter to the Rev. Joseph Mead, 3 December 1626, in Stephen Orgel and Roy Strong (eds), *Inigo Jones and the Theatre of the Stuart Court* (London: Sotheby Parke Bernet, 1973), I, p. 389.
11. Andrew J. Sabol, *Four Hundred Songs and Dances from the Stuart Court Masque* (London: University Press of New England for Brown University Press, 1982), p. 21.
12. Stephen Orgel, 'Review of Andrew Sabol, *Four Hundred Songs and Dances from the Stuart Court Masque*', *Criticism, a Quarterly for Literature and the Arts* 21 (1979), 362–5, (p. 365).
13. Orgel, *Complete Masques*, p. 5.
14. Sir Thomas Elyot, *The Book Named the Governor*, ed. by S.E. Lehmberg (London: Everyman, 1962), Books XIX–XXV, pp. 69–88. Further evidence of the high regard for dance within the European court tradition in Baldesar Castiglione, *The Book of the Courtier*, ed. by George Bull (Harmondsworth: Penguin, 1976), pp. 66–9. Bacon's condemnation of the masque in the 1625 essay 'Of Masques and Triumphs' smacks of bitterness after his own involvement, prior to his fall from grace, in the production of masques performed for the King by the Inns of Court, such as Francis Beaumont's *Masque of the Inner Temple and Gray's Inn*. See Frances Bacon, 'Of Masques and Triumphs', in *Essays* (London: Everyman, Dent, 1994), pp. 99–100.
15. Elyot, I, *The Book Named the Governor*, pp. 77–8.
16. Mark Franko, 'Renaissance Conduct Literature and the Basse Dance: The Kinesis of Bonne Grace', in *Persons in Groups: Social Behaviour as Identity Formation in Medieval and Renaissance Europe*, ed. by Richard C. Trexler (Binghamton, NY: Medieval and Renaissance Texts and Studies, 1985), pp. 55–66 (p. 55).
17. Mark Franko, *The Dancing Body in Renaissance Choreography (c. 1416–1589)* (Birmingham, AL: Summa Publications, 1986), p. 38.
18. Elyot, I, *The Book Named the Governor*, pp. 77–8.
19. It should be mentioned that, as in so many dealings with the court masque, the nature of the evidence found in dance treatises is unstable; the reconstruction of the dance from text is methodologically flawed and the texts themselves are open to the suspicion of being utopian rather than practical representations of dance practice. See Franko, *The Dancing Body*, p. 7.
20. The availability of this text is demonstrated by Judy Smith and Ian Gatiss, 'What Did Prince Henry Do with His Feet on Sunday 19 August 1604?', *Early Music*, 14 (1986), 204–7 (p. 201). The description

of the dance is to be found in Fabritio Caroso, *Nobiltà di Dame*, trans. by Julia Sutton (Oxford: Oxford University Press, 1986), pp. 266–9.

21. Carleton's letter can be found in H&S X, p. 448. They identify the masque in question as that for the marriage of Lady Susan de Vere and Sir Philip Herbert.

22. Stephen Orgel, *The Jonsonian Masque* (New York: Columbia University Press, 1981), p. 69.

23. Francis Bacon, *The Advancement of Learning*, II. xvi. 3, cited in Michael Bath, *Speaking Pictures: English Emblem Books and Renaissance Culture* (London: Longman, 1994), p. 51.

24. Bath, *Speaking Pictures*, p. 52.

25. This emblem is number 59 in Peter Daly and Simon Cutter (eds), *Andreas Alciati 2: Emblems in Transition* (London: University of Toronto Press, 1985). Geoffrey Whitney, *A Choice of Emblems*, intro. by John Manning (Aldershot: Scolar Press, 1989), p. 57.

26. D.J. Gordon, 'The Imagery of Ben Jonson's *The Masque of Blackness* and *The Masque of Beautie*', *Journal of the Warburg and Courtauld Institutes*, 6 (1943), 122–41.

27. Samuel Daniel, *The Vision of the Twelve Goddesses*, in *A Book of Masques in Honour of Allardyce Nicol*, ed. by T.J.B. Spencer and Stanley Wells (Cambridge: Cambridge University Press, 1967), ll. 31–5.

6

The Lone Wolf: Jonson's Epistle to *Volpone*

Richard Dutton

Ben Johnson, I think, had all the critical learning to himself; and till of late years England was as free from critics, as it is from wolves.

(Thomas Rymer, 1674)

The Epistle to *Volpone* (1607) was the earliest free-standing critical treatise by Jonson to see print. There are, to be sure, a number of critical pronouncements in earlier works by Jonson, such as Lorenzo Jr's encomium on poetry in *Every Man In His Humour* (printed in 1601), the various Grexes in *Every Man Out Of His Humour* (1600), and incidental commentary on those parts of *The Magnificent Entertainment* (1604) for which Jonson had been responsible. There are also relatively brief prefaces to the printed texts of *Sejanus* (1605) and the masque *Hymenaei* (1606). But all of these relate very specifically to the works in which they appear, even if the neoclassical and humanist vocabularies they deploy connect them readily enough with wider socio-aesthetic agendas.

The Epistle to *Volpone* very conspicuously addresses a wider context than the play it introduces. It does glance at one feature of the play itself – an ending which flouts 'the strict rigour of comic law' – but only in the context of a much broader *apologia*, touching on many features of contemporary theatre and its audiences. Jonson had in fact written an earlier self-contained critical discourse, an 'Apologetical Dialogue' which he had intended to append to the quarto text of *Poetaster* (printed 1602). But that was suppressed by some unnamed authority after it 'was only once spoken upon the stage' and was not printed until the 1616 Folio of Jonson's *Works* which incensed some influential people. Jonson may also by this time have written a treatise relating to his own translation of Horace's *Ars Poetica* to which, as we shall see, he refers in the course of the Epistle. But that was never printed at all, and the manuscript was lost in the fire that destroyed his library in 1623.[1]

So the Epistle to *Volpone* was in many ways a landmark in Jonson's career, a distinctive statement of principles which (partly because it was invariably reprinted with one of his most enduring plays) rapidly acquired authoritative status. I have already written on the Epistle's place in Jonson's evolving relationship with the Master of the Revels, the censor of plays whose post Jonson almost acquired himself in his later years, and it will be necessary to rehearse some of that material here.[2] But I want to go beyond that to explore the intense ambivalence of this supposedly 'authoritative' document, and how this ambivalence has been overlooked – one might even say deliberately ignored – by later commentators. This is in good part a matter of exploring the very particular resonances that the text carried when it was first printed in 1607, and seeing how it subsequently lost many of these – a process to which Jonson himself gave impetus when he revised the text for its inclusion in the 1616 *Works*.[3]

The resonances to which I refer all relate to events in Jonson's career in the years immediately preceding *Volpone*'s publication. As I shall argue, the precise formulation of the Epistle owes a good deal to what were in fact intensely traumatic experiences in those years, though he only touches on them briefly and obliquely. The most striking instance occurs in the Epistle's rousing conclusion, where he envisages how poetry, turning on her detractors:

> shall out of just rage incite her servants ... to spout ink in their faces, that shall eat, farther than their marrow, into their fames; and not Cinnamus the barber, with his art, shall be able to take out the brands, but they shall live, and be read, till the wretches die, as things worst deserving of themselves in chief, and then of all mankind.'[4]

Cinnamus is celebrated in Martial (VI.lxiv.24–6) for his skill in removing brands.

This cannot but have reminded Jonson's original readers of his own branding. In 1598 he had killed his fellow actor, Gabriel Spencer, in a duel, and only escaped hanging by claiming benefit of clergy – that is, by proving his ability to read from the Bible, an archaic exemption from due process of law which reflected the reverence of an earlier age for the literacy of holy orders. Jonson nevertheless forfeited all his possessions and had to submit to the 'deep and public brand' of Tyburn 'T' at the base of his thumb – an ineradicable sign that his life was forfeit to the state if he transgressed again. He had intended to air this matter in the suppressed 'Apologetical Dialogue' to *Poetaster*, where his 'Author' turns back charges that he has libelled people by claiming that he *could* himself, if he chose, repay those who have libelled *him* over his play:

> I could stamp
> Their foreheads with those deep, and public brands,
> That the whole company of Barber-Surgeons
> Should not take off, with all their art, and plasters.
> And these my prints should last, still to be read
> In their pale fronts when what they write 'gainst me
> Shall, like a figure drawn in water, fleet
> (H&S, IV, p. 322)

This is a striking inversion of Jonson's own subjection to authority. Following classical precedent, he turns a graphic image of the state's authority over himself into a metaphor for his own powers as a writer (however much the state may attempt to circumscribe them). We may suppose that the forfeiture and branding was even more charged for Jonson than it would otherwise have been, because it was 'then took he his religion [Roman Catholicism] by trust of a priest who visited him in prison. Thereafter he was twelve years a papist' (*Conversations*, 249–51), a dangerous change of allegiance at a time of intense Counter-Reformation pressures.[5] The spirit of the poet resisted the authority of the state, even as the state literally imposed that authority upon his body.

Nevertheless, between the 'Apologetical Dialogue' (1601/2) and *Volpone*, the state again came close to imprinting its authority upon Jonson's person. During the imprisonment which both he and Chapman suffered as a consequence of the unlicensed performance of *Eastward Ho*, 'the report was that they should then have their ears cut & noses' (*Conversations*, 276–7). The reference to judicial mutilation in the Epistle is thus doubly charged for Jonson himself and for those who know what he has gone through. In the 'Apologetical

Dialogue' he had reserved the threat of branding for those who had libelled his own writing. In the Epistle he claims more generally for poetry (a term he has consistently and exclusively identified with his own works) the right to inflict public mutilation upon all its detractors – a right which the state had so recently threatened to exercise a second time upon his own person. In the prologue to *Volpone* (where, as he wryly remarks, 'From no needful rule he swerveth', l. 32) Jonson promises to forgo that right, exercising the prerogative of mercy which, in the end, had been extended to Chapman and himself. The key issue is that of authority: the authority of the state and of the poet, and of the relationship between them. This public flourishing of his own branding in the Epistle – for the first time, as far as the reading public was concerned – emphasizes the paradox of Jonson's position, the subject refashioned as authority.

Part of the claim to authority which Jonson seeks to establish throughout this document depends upon his establishing his own 'innocence', a tall order given all the official wrath his works had incurred hitherto. One tactic he deploys to this end is a brief, parenthetical distinction between plays written solely by himself and those written in collaboration, implying that others have been less scrupulous than himself but that he has been tarred with the same brush – 'I speak of those that are entirely mine' (ll. 54–5). This specifically relates to the question of 'allowance' by the licensers and so primarily alludes to *Eastward Ho*, where this was a critical issue. But for those with long memories – and I shall shortly suggest that Robert Cecil, Earl of Salisbury, was one of these – it would also evoke Jonson's imprisonment over the scandalous *Isle of Dogs* which he co-authored with Thomas Nashe.

It might also evoke memories of *Sejanus*, for the Earl of Northampton had him 'called before the Council for his *Sejanus*, and accused both of popery and treason by him' (*Conversations*, ll. 326–7). The precise circumstances of these accusations are far from easy to establish, and we do not know if it was the play as staged (1603), which was co-authored, or the printed text (1605), which Jonson wrote alone, which elicited them.[6] But Jonson seems to allude again to *Sejanus* – his most recent play in print – in the Epistle when he wryly observes that 'not my youngest infant but hath come into the world with all his teeth' (ll. 49–50), rebutting the charge of 'sharpness'. In such ways he tries to encircle himself with 'innocence', by distancing himself both from malicious accusations and unfortunate collaborations. In the process, however, he cannot help reiterating the traumas to which he has been subjected.

This is even more fundamentally true of the *Eastward Ho* affair than I have so far suggested, since while he was imprisoned over that Jonson wrote a string of letters to people of influence. Passages from one of these, to the king's chief minister, the Earl of Salisbury, reappeared *verbatim* in the Epistle to *Volpone*. He composed the letter with the utmost care – it exists both in an early draft and in the holograph Salisbury actually received – partly, no doubt, because of its recipient's importance, but also because Jonson had had dealings with Sir Robert Cecil (as he then was) as early as the *Isle of Dogs* affair. Cecil had handled the correspondence over that business for the Privy Council. It was probably politic of Jonson, therefore, to acknowledge it in the letter as a genuine 'error' on his part – but one from which he had learned his lesson, insisting on his 'innocence', his compliance with authority, ever since: 'I protest to your Honour, and call God to testimony (since my first error, which (yet) is punished in me more with my shame, than it was then with my bondage) I have so attempered my style, that I have given no cause to any good man of grief.'[7] In the Epistle, as we have seen, he disingenuously glosses over *any* admission of guilt by dissociating himself from all works not 'entirely mine'. He also makes no mention of any 'error'.

The first passage to be reproduced in the Epistle (like so much else in Jonson's criticism) is based on Martial, and specifically the preface to his *Epigrams*: 'My noble Lord, they deal not charitably, who are too witty in another man's works, and utter, sometimes, their own malicious meanings, under our words' (p. 221). This reappears in the Epistle as: 'there are that profess to have a key for the deciphering of everything: but let wise and noble persons take heed how they be too credulous, or give leave to these invading interpreters, to be over-familiar with their fames, who cunningly, and often, utter their own virulent malice, under other men's simplest meanings' (ll. 65–70). The second passage is this:

> let me be examined, both all my works past, and this present … whether, I have ever (in any thing I have written private, or public) given offence to a nation, to any public order or state, or any person of honour, or authority, but have equally laboured to keep their dignity, as mine own person safe.
>
> (p. 221)

This reappears in the Epistle as:

> howsoever I cannot escape, from some, the imputation of sharp-
> ness … I would ask of these supercilious politics, what nation,
> society, or general order, or state I have provoked? what public
> person? whether I have not (in all these) preserved their dignity,
> as mine own person, safe?
>
> (ll. 47–54)

In both contexts, this passage leads to a very particular pay-off.
In the letter to Salisbury, Jonson immediately protests: 'If others
have transgressed, let not me be entitled to their follies.' This was
not in the early draft of the letter, and is clearly a careful after-
thought. Jonson is hinting at something made much more explicit
in a letter sent by Chapman to the king over his and Jonson's joint
predicament: 'our chief offences are but two clauses, and both of
them not our own' (*ed. cit.*, p. 218). Two particular passages in
Eastward Ho had apparently caused offence, rather than the play as
a whole. The usual construction of Jonson's and Chapman's letters
is that they were both implicitly blaming Marston (who apparently
contrived to avoid imprisonment) for these 'clauses', though it is
equally possible that they meant that they were interpolations by
actors. Whereas Chapman effectively admits that an offence has
been committed (though he and Jonson are not guilty of it), Jonson
himself turns the issue towards his own rectitude; he does not enter
into the question of the other persons' guilt, but insists upon his
own *consistent* innocence: he has not 'transgressed' but respected
'authority'.

This, in more general terms, is the issue he also takes up at the
parallel point in the Epistle to *Volpone*: 'My works are read, allowed
… look into them' (ll. 54–5). His own works submit themselves to
the licensing required by authority, both for performance and for
publication. Tongue-tied by authority in the publication of
Poetaster, he could only beseech his reader there to 'think charitably
of what thou hast read' – which the Earl of Northampton, who
challenged *Sejanus*, and Sir James Murray, who denounced
Eastward Ho, conspicuously had not done. Here, in the Epistle,
Jonson recognizes that 'nothing can be so innocently writ, or
carried, but may be made obnoxious to construction', though he
continues to protest his 'innocence' (ll. 62–3, 64). But this acknowledgement of the process of 'allowance' whereby the Master of the

Revels licensed a play for performance and the Bishop of London's licensers gave it another for print points to a degree of control over what *other* readers could legitimately find in his writing. By acquiescing to a form of policing which he had previously found irksome, Jonson paradoxically acquires a power to determine (delimit) the meaning of what he writes (and so his integrity as an author) which he had never enjoyed before. But it is a telling fact that this public submission to the general authority of state censorship follows on – literally and directly – from a private submission to the most powerful man in the state, after the king, and from the state's renewed threat of physical mutilation.

One further trauma, not directly linked to his writing, certainly also left its mark on the Epistle, that is the Gunpowder Plot and its aftermath. The first we know of Jonson, after his release (unharmed) from imprisonment over *Eastward Ho*, was that he attended a party in the Strand, on or about 9 October 1605. This was given by Robert Catesby, leader of the Gunpowder Plot conspiracy, whose 'providential discovery was less than a month away; several of the other conspirators were there too.[8] Immediately after that discovery (7 November) Jonson was summoned by the Privy Council to act as a go-between in their efforts to contact a certain Roman Catholic priest 'that offered to do good service to the state'; they provided him with a warrant to demonstrate both his and their own honourable intentions. Despite Jonson's earnest endeavours, conducted initially via the chaplain of the Venetian ambassador, 'the party will not be found', as he reported the next day to Salisbury personally, protesting 'May it please your Lordship to understand that there hath been no want in me either of labour or sincerity in the discharge of this business.' He regretted his inability to resolve matters 'to the satisfaction of your Lordship and the state.'[9] As a Catholic convert Jonson may have had ready access to Catesby and the other conspirators, as well as to the Catholic priesthood. The question is whether, knowing this, Salisbury only used Jonson in the aftermath of the affair – or whether he had been using him throughout, as a double agent.[10] His imprisonment, and threats of worse, over *Eastward Ho* would have made him all the more plausible a companion for his desperate co-religionists.

Volpone was apparently staged in February or March 1606. If Jonson's claim that 'five weeks fully penned it' (Prologue, l.16) is true, he must have written the play immediately in the wake of the Gunpowder Plot and at a time when some of those implicated in the plot (like the Jesuit, Father Henry Garnet) were paying the ghastly penalty. Jonson's personal tension could only have increased when, in the crack-down on known Catholics after the Plot, he was 'presented' for 'correction' that January in the Consistory Court of London. He was accused of failing to take communion in the Church of England, which was required by law and deliberate omission could be construed as treason. The charge sheet dryly noted Jonson to be a 'poet', who was reported 'by fame a seducer of youth to the Popish religion' (H&S I, pp. 220–22). The charges were first heard in April, and subsequent hearings dragged on through the early summer. Jonson acknowledged his failure to take communion, over religious scruples, but pointed out that he had regularly worshipped at his local Anglican church for the past six months – in effect, since the Plot. He denied the rumour about his being a 'seducer of youth' and challenged the court to present proper evidence, which it was apparently unable to do. Jonson was required to submit his scruples to the consideration of one of a number of notable Anglican clergy, including the Dean of St Paul's and the Archbishop of Canterbury; he was to choose one of these and attend twice a week for spiritual guidance, under which terms the charges were 'stayed under seal' but not formally dismissed.

This, then, is the context in which the Epistle to *Volpone* was composed: a whole sequence of traumas and confrontations with authority, dating back to the *Isle of Dogs* affair, including conviction and branding for killing Gabriel Spencer, conversion to Roman Catholicism, problems over the ending of *Every Man Out of His Humour* (where Jonson originally brought onstage a boy actor impersonating Queen Elizabeth), examination over *Poetaster* and the staying by authority of its 'Apologetical Dialogue', examination by the Privy Council over *Sejanus*, imprisonment and threat of mutilation over *Eastward Ho*, implication in possible government manipulation of the Gunpowder Plot, and prosecution for recusancy in the aftermath of the Plot itself. These are all addressed, implicitly or directly, in the Epistle itself or the documents upon which it demonstrably draws: the 'Apologetical Dialogue' and the letter to Salisbury.

Once that is perceived, we are better placed to appreciate the strategy of the Epistle as a whole. The dedication of the play to those 'most learned ARBITRESSES', the universities, can be seen – like the invocation to classical authorities (notably, here, Strabo, Martial, and Horace) – as an appeal to timeless, apolitical values, placing art in a transcendent framework of disinterested scholarship, abstracted from the social and political conditions of its own composition. But this is belied by the manner and location of the Epistle itself. In the quarto text, the portentous capitals of the dedication stand over the laconic invitation: 'There follows an *Epistle*, if you dare venture on the length' and the document itself is subscribed 'From my house in the Blackfriars this 11 of February 1607', locating it very specifically in a world of writers and readers, time and place (H&S IV, fn., p. 16). Quite apart from anything else, it is a very fashionable address for someone who had been stripped of all his goods less than ten years before: a man much in demand to write royal masques and entertainments has done well for himself materially, whatever other difficulties he may have faced.

The universities themselves, invoked as judges, were no more outside the structure of authority than those other courts – civil, criminal, and ecclesiastical – which Jonson so regularly confronted, even if he more readily concurred with their judgement on *Volpone*. Indeed, their leading luminaries were key names in Jonson's history: the Chancellor of Cambridge was Salisbury; its High Steward was Lord Chamberlain Suffolk (whose missing licence was such a key element in the *Eastward Ho* affair though he also seems to have been the person responsible for effecting the release of Jonson and Chapman).[11] The Chancellor of Oxford was Thomas Sackville, Earl of Dorset, the Lord Treasurer, who in his youth had part-authored *Gorboduc*. He would be a very plausible candidate for the unnamed lord of the third in the sequence of Jonson's letters from prison over *Eastward Ho*, the more so in that Jonson is supposed to have declared: 'I laid the plot of my *Volpone*, and wrote most of it, after a present of ten dozen of palm sack from my very good Lord Treasurer' (H&S I, p. 188). As we have seen, the composition of *Volpone* certainly followed hard on his release from prison, and such a gift would have befitted the occasion.

Whatever we make of specific occasions and personalities, it remains inescapable that a dedication to the universities was inevitably also a dedication to the powerbrokers in the Privy Council. The invocation of the 'equal sisters' as 'arbitresses' in literary matters should perhaps be put alongside the performance of the Court of Avocatori within *Volpone* itself as judges in civil and criminal ones. The burden of the Epistle is very much that of the 'Apologetical Dialogue', to justify Jonson's claim that he properly fulfils 'the offices, and function of a Poet' (l. 21) in contradistinction to 'the too-much licence of poetasters, in this time' (l. 14). But Jonson lifts the argument into a different frame of reference by linking his definition of 'a poet' with Strabo's 'universal' dictum about the impossibility of any man's being the good Poet, without first being a good man' (ll. 22–3).[12] At a time when Jonson was still formally under investigation for failing to conform to the state religion, and when the virtuous intentions of his last three plays had all been impugned in one context or another, the question of his 'goodness' is a challenging one: by whom, and in what court, is this to be determined? Jonson immediately follows this with a broad encomium of 'a poet', beginning: 'He that is said to be able to inform young-men to all good disciplines' and latterly including among his accomplishments, 'a teacher of things divine, no less than human' (1.28). This might almost be taken to parody the charge he had faced in the Consistory Court: 'a poet, and by fame a seducer of youth to the Popish religion'. But if anyone had challenged Jonson for mocking authority here he could (as with the annotations in the quarto of Sejanus) have cited the chapter and verse of the innocent derivation of the whole passage: Minturno's De Poeta (1559), (p. 8).

From such equivocal foundations, Jonson launches out against 'this bold adventure for hell' (l. 42), which is how he characterizes much current 'dramatic, or (as they term it) stage-poetry' (ll. 36–7) and from which he is determined to distinguish his own writing. Denying that he has ever engaged in 'prophaneness' (an issue of particular topicality, since in 1606 Parliament had passed an Act of Abuses to prevent blasphemy and profanity on public stages) or 'bawdry' (ll. 45, 46), it is here that he addresses 'the imputation of sharpness', drawing on the classical precedents of Horace and Martial, as reworked in the 'Apologetical Dialogue' and the letter to Salisbury, to deny that he has ever been 'particular' or 'provoked' any 'nation' or 'public person'. Those of his works 'that are entirely mine' are 'read, allowed', conforming to the requirements of authority. He insists that 'it is not rumour can make men guilty, much less entitle me to other men's crimes' (ll. 60–2) – picking up the theme of unwarranted 'fame' or 'rumour' that runs from the 'Apologetical Dialogue', through the letters from prison, to the trial for recusancy, hammering home his point in attacking 'these invading interpreters' (who, he warns 'wise and noble persons', may also be 'over-familiar with *their* fames': my emphasis) and a breed of satiric writers who 'care not whose living faces they entrench, with their petulant styles' (ll. 67–8, 74–5) to gain notice and popularity: he declines 'so preposterous a fame'. Jonson's implicit claim to be himself a good man and a true poet is thus advanced on two fronts: dissociation from three forms of contamination – from the company of 'poetasters', from misreadings (malicious and otherwise) and from guilt-by-association with what other writers have done – and a protestation of 'mine own innocence', the authority for which he cannot generate himself but must derive from being 'allowed'. His private intentions are guaranteed by a very public subjectivity.

Jonson then turns the terms of the argument from intention and interpretation, towards dramatic form, sympathizing with 'those severe, and wiser patriots' (ll. 77–8) who would prefer a return to older, unsophisticated styles of drama (with fools and devils) rather than be subjected to the lampoons and state satires of the current stage. He ascribes to a 'lust in liberty' the vogue for 'misc'line interludes [variety entertainments] ... where nothing but the filth of the time is utter'd, and that with such impropriety of phrase, such plenty of solecisms, such dearth of sense, so bold prolepses, so racked metaphors' (ll. 86–91). It is to rebut such examples, and to restore poetry to its former dignity 'that were wont to be the care of kings, and happiest monarchs' (as depicted in *Poetaster*), that Jonson claims he has laboured in *Volpone* 'to reduce [bring back], not only the ancient forms, but manners of the scene, the easiness, the propriety, the innocence, and last the doctrine, which is the principal end of poesy, to inform men in the best reason of living.' (ll. 99–109).

All of this he reiterates in the Prologue to the play, where he promises 'rhyme, not empty of reason' (l. 4), and 'no eggs are broken;/Nor quaking custards with fierce teeth affrighted' (ll. 20–1) in an example of 'quick comedy, refined,/As best critics have designed' (ll. 29–30); he invokes Horace in the ambition 'To mix profit with your pleasure' (l. 8) and Aristotle in his claim 'The laws of time, place, persons he observeth' (l. 31) as he distances himself from the tasteless lawlessness of the 'misc'line interludes' elsewhere on the contemporary stage. He acknowledges in the Epistle that his 'catastrophe' may be criticized for being over-severe (with Mosca consigned to the galleys and Volpone to a lingering mortification in the hospital for incurables) but points out that it was deliberate policy not slip-shod work, that it was done to give the lie to those 'that cry out, we never punish vice in our interludes' (l. 116), and that he could find classical precedent for it anyway:

'fitly, it being the office of a comic-Poet, to imitate justice, and to instruct to life, as well as purity of language, or stir up gentle affections' (ll. 121–3). This might readily be construed as an ironic reading of the 'catastrophe' of *Volpone* itself, where the 'justice' meted out is hard to distinguish from the revenge of a self-seeking, hoodwinked court.

But the ironies of the legal discourse of both the Epistle and the play are compounded several times over if we recall that, only weeks before the latter was staged, the author had written to the king's chief minister (in a letter from which he was now borrowing passages), complaining of being 'un-examined, or unheard, committed to a vile prison' (to Salisbury, p. 221) and contemplating worse penalties yet. Furthermore, around the time he wrote the play itself, he was subject to another court's investigation into his religious and political orthodoxy. To 'imitate justice' and to 'instruct to life' may not be coterminous exercises for 'a poet'. Jonson does not, however, enforce any of these contextual ironies as he consigns his copy to the printer from his house in Blackfriars in February 1607, merely promising (in the quarto text): 'To which, upon my next opportunity toward the examining and digesting of my notes, I shall speak more wealthily, and pay the world a debt' (notes to ll. 123–4). This is presumably the long-promised 'observations upon Horace', later described as 'Apology for *Bartholomew Fair*', whose failure to find print is one of the great enigmas of Jonson's career.[13] If it actually had more to say about the proper functions of the poet, the relationship between his intentions and his reception, or the proper balance between his own liberty and the authority of the state, it is one of the major losses of English literature.

Jonson rounds the Epistle off with a final obeisance to the universities, a promise to 'raise the despised head of poetry again', and a fierce, final denunciation of those who 'keep her in contempt', for the terms of which – as we have seen – he returns to the theme of branding first explored in the 'Apologetical Dialogue'. James D. Redwine Jr has observed that: 'The importance of the *Volpone* criticism ... can scarcely be stressed too often – it marks a turning point in the development of Jonson's critical theory. Up to the time he wrote *Volpone*, his attitude toward the so-called laws would seem to be one of respectful independence.' He cites a dialogue between Cordatus and Mitis in the Induction to *Every Man Out of His Humour* as evidence of Jonson's indulgent earlier view of the 'licence' or 'liberty' that may be properly exercised by modern poets. But:

> from *Volpone* onward ... 'licence, or free power to illustrate and heighten our invention' is more likely to be attacked as a dangerous tendency of an illiterate age than to be defended on the grounds of classical precedent ... Throughout [the Epistle to *Volpone*] it is the 'liberty' or 'licence' of contemporary poetry that he attacks most bitterly. And in the *Volpone* prologue, three of Mitis's 'too nice observations' are brought forth as necessary elements ('needful rules') of 'quick comedy'.[14]

I suggest, however, that it is a mistake to treat the *Volpone* material in this way, as a defining watershed in Jonson's critical thinking, though I agree that it most forcefully represents one end of the spectrum of his thinking about the 'licence' or 'liberty' of poetry. For one thing, Redwine underplays the extent to which some of Jonson's libertarian observations on the freedom of poets were written much later in his career; take, for example, the much-quoted passage in *Discoveries* (which was put together after the 1623 fire, even if passages from it may have been survivals from earlier):

> For to all the observations of the ancients, we have our own experience: which, if we will use and apply, we have better means to pronounce. It is true they open'd the gates and made the way, that went before us; but as guides not commanders: *non domini nostri, sed duces fuere*. Truth lies open to us all; it is no man's several.[15]

More importantly, Redwine completely ignores the very specific historical context within which the *Volpone* material was written, and which it has been my main concern to trace here. These circumstances placed enormous pressures on Jonson, and he responded to them very provocatively by running together the 'rules' of poetry and the 'laws' of the state. Once that is appreciated, we can see that his entire vocabulary – of law and arbitration, innocence and branding, allowance and mulcting, liberty and licence – is, if not positively ironic, ambivalent and double-edged. His own subjective 'innocence' (for which we might substitute the term 'honesty') is not defined by the laws of the state, any more than it is by authority of the ancients, but these are useful markers when the alternative is to be misread, misconstrued, misreported in a world where reception is governed by the lowest common denominators of ignorance, spite, and the suspiciousness of those with power.

We may relate these ambivalences to what Martin Elsky observes about Jonson's inheritance from the humanist tradition, and its acknowledgement of the ultimate authority of the monarch: 'his authority, to comment on social matters stems from the King ... Like Ascham and Elyot, Jonson points to the monarch as the guarantor of his word, though he does not go to the extreme of seeing his entire poetic as being constituted by the authority of the king.'[16] The final reservation here tacitly marks a difference between Elsky's position (and my own) and that of Jonathan Goldberg in *James I and the Politics of English Literature*, who argues with Foucauldian pessimism that Jonson's entire identity as an author is subsumed in the ideological authority of the King: intention is beside the point in a world where language writes us (rather than *vice-versa*) and meaning is entirely defined by the power which sanctions that language.[17] This is an elegant post-structuralist double-bind, but it is one which needs to be confronted with the equal and opposite deconstructionist proposition, deriving from the supposedly arbitrary processes of signification, and rendered with deliberate crudity by Stanley Fish when he propounds that 'there are no determinate meanings and ... the stability of the text is an illusion.'[18]

It is not monarchs, writers, or texts which generate or sanction meaning: but readers, in all their perplexing variety. In the Epistle to *Volpone* Jonson was, in effect mediating between the Scylla of Goldberg and the Charybdis of Fish, the tyranny of royal 'allowance' or authority and the terror of endless misreading. If he settles, in this instance, more for the former than the latter, he does so in a context where the very fact of mediation preserves a separate authority for the writer, a distinct identity for the author, though (as we shall see) this can easily by overlooked.

These are matters of moment, because what Redwine views simply as a change in Jonson's critical priorities can be construed as symptomatic of a much more fundamental reorientation of his career. Put at its crudest, it could be said that he was turning his back on the rebellious 'liberty' which had been such a hallmark of his early life and writing, and becoming a creature of the state. My own reading of the Epistle to *Volpone*, in the context of all the confrontations with authority from which it derives and to which it refers, has stressed the ironic transpositions involved, Jonson appropriating to himself the language of law and authority which had so repeatedly and until so recently been applied to his own person and writings: words that had helped gain his release after 'transgressing' in his last work (*Eastward Ho*) here celebrate the 'authoritative' reception of his new one. As such, it is *potentially* a very subversive document indeed: mocking those who would seek to restrain his art (as they had repeatedly restrained his body) just as much as he reviles those who denigrate or misconstrue it, while at the same time appearing to accept the terms and conditions they set for him to continue writing.

Yet there is no doubt that Jonson's career actually took a more establishment turn from this point. His brushes with authority diminished in number and severity, and by the time he received a royal pension in 1616 he was in all but name Poet Laureate, regularly polishing the court's self-image with his masques. What was this if not selling out? Jonson had concluded his letter to Salisbury with the hope that he 'will be the most honoured cause of our liberty, where freeing us from one prison, you shall remove us to another, which is eternally to bind us and our Muses, to the thankful honouring of you and yours to posterity; as your own virtues have by many descents of ancestors ennobled you to time. Your Honor's most devoted in heart as words./Ben. Jonson' (p. 222). Is this Jonson's offer, in the most literal of terms, to become Salisbury's poet, as perhaps he also had to agree to be his spy? If so, it truly freed Jonson from one prison to remove him to another, and may explain the bitterness with which – when Salisbury was dead, and he was free to do so – Jonson berated his muse for betraying him 'to a worthless lord', in a context which makes it perfectly plain that it was Salisbury he had in mind.[19] We do not know if Jonson felt it necessary to consult Salisbury before reproducing in public parts of the letter he had written him, but at the very least he could hardly have reused that material without being conscious of his dependence on a whole structure of institutionalized power, with Salisbury at the centre of it.

But in a sense Jonson's view of what he was doing in the Epistle to *Volpone*, and how he felt about whatever trade-offs lie behind its earnest protestations, have long since ceased to matter. As that document articulates only too clearly, we lose control of the meaning of a text as soon as we release it to a readership. And that is exactly what happened to the Epistle, which became a chapter – an important chapter, because of its priority and because of its association with such a powerful play – in the larger document of Jonson's own career. As David Riggs observes, 'Since his career coincides with the rise of the literary profession in England, his personal success story takes on the characteristics of a cultural phenomenon: in following his rise we are also witnessing the emergence of authorship as a full-time vocation.'[20] And for the Caroline sons of Ben, and the Restoration grandsons, that cultural phenomenon was overwhelmingly one of royalism and critical conservatism. The tensions and conflicts of the first decade of his career – still so apparent in a historical reading of the Epistle – disappear in the massive authority of the 1616 and 1640 folios.

The ambivalences of the Epistle ceased to resonate and it was, so to speak, only the 'establishment' side of the equation – the law-abiding author/citizen – which later generations acknowledged, as the modern concepts both of responsible authorship and of literary criticism emerged alongside it. Jonson himself doubtless furthered the process in the text's subsequent manifestations: the self-deprecatory reference to the Epistle's length, and its dating and placement from the Blackfriars in 1607, disappeared from the 1616 folio version, immediately casting it as a more 'authoritative', out-of-time document. And, because of the respect the *Works* enjoyed, this is the version best known to posterity (taking precedence, for example, in the great Herford and Simpson edition and in most modern editions of *Volpone*). The promise, referring to 'the office of a comic-Poet' that 'upon my next opportunity toward the examining and digesting of my notes, I shall speak more wealthily, and pay the world a debt' is toned down to a bland 'To which, I shall take the occasion elsewhere to speak.' As we have observed, Jonson never did so speak in public. The 'observations on Horace his *Art of Poesy*' apparently burned in the fire, and with them the last chance that Jonson might have spoken more conclusively or radically about his own authority as a writer; in this respect, it is a loss as tantalizing as that of Aristotle's treatise on comedy, which absorbed Umberto Eco so entertainingly in *The Name of the Rose*. In its absence, Jonson has branded himself to posterity as a keeper of the laws, an 'allowed' poet, more thoroughly than the authorities could ever have done: 'and not Cinnamus the barber, with his art, shall be able to take out the brands'.

Jonson's Restoration successors did not trouble to scrutinize the brands, because it entirely suited their purposes to take them at face value. As Richard C. Newton observes, 'Of this Ben Jonson ... the first English classic author, virtually all subsequent English authors claim some degree of paternity.'[21] Dryden claimed more of that paternity than most, though it was a claim shot through with Oedipal tensions.[22] When it suited him, Jonson was a model to follow, an authority to invoke, as he was for many writers in the Restoration. As Jennifer Brady has recently shown, many Restoration literary quarrels in effect revolved around competing appropriations of Jonson; behind Dryden's 'MacFlecknoe', for example, Richard Flecknoe, Thomas Shadwell, and Dryden himself all laid claim to be heirs of Jonson, and the issue becomes one of establishing primacy or greatest authenticity.[23] Brady quotes Dryden's dedication to *The Assignation*: 'I am made a Detractor from my Predecessors, whom I confess to have been my Masters in the art ... I will be no more mistaken for my good meaning: I know I honour Ben Johnson more than my little critiques, because without vanity I may own, I understand him better'.[24] She points to the key term 'understand', which is so central to Jonson's critical vocabulary, as Dryden's demonstration of his fitness to be heir; she might also have pointed to the theme of being 'mistaken for my good meaning', which is such an important issue in the Epistle to *Volpone*.

What mattered most for Restoration writers was that Jonson was inescapably *there*, a native English base line on which they could build, a position with which they could negotiate, an 'authority'. Edward Howard knew Jonson was so familiar (both visually and by reputation) that he wrote for his play *The Women's Conquest* (1671) 'The Second Prologue personated like Ben Johnson rising from below':

Did I instruct you (well near half an age)
To understand the grandeur of the stage,
With the exactest rules of comedy ... .[25]

It suited them that this authority should be solid and unambivalent. And, in constituting him as such, what Dryden and the others could not see, or chose to ignore, were the tensions and internal contradictions which ran through that achievement, making its outcome less assured. (It is striking how often, for example, they ignored the unique spelling of the name, his bid for distinctive self-construction not seen before the 1604 *Magnificent Entertainment* which met King James's ceremonial entry into London). Jonson's own example only *belatedly* resolved (or could be construed by his successors as resolving) the problematics of authorship with which he himself always had to wrestle.

By 1674 Thomas Rymer could facetiously write about him as a lone wolf of a critic, in the words that stand as an epigraph to this essay. In his usual insensitive way, he seems to have given no thought to what it might be like to be a lone wolf in such a context. Jeremy Collier, too, seems to treat Jonson (as he does most Elizabethan/Jacobean dramatists) with a degree of condescension in his *A Short View of the Immorality, and Profaneness of the English Stage* (1698): 'Ben Johnson shall speak for himself afterwards in the character of a Critic.'[26] To be fair, we must acknowledge that Jonson wished some of this on himself. The two monumental folios that confronted the world as his legacy after 1640 inevitably engendered resentment as well as respect. And his career after the 1616 folio was almost calculated to inspire filial loyalty and Oedipal resentment in equal measure; his eminence translated him (how willingly or deliberately is not clear) into the Father of a 'tribe' or 'sons' of Ben, who congregated in the Apollo Room of the 'Devil' tavern, admonished by Jonson's own *Leges Conviviales*, rules for tavern conduct. That father-figure role inspired not only 'sealed members' of the tribe but a younger generation as a whole to think in terms of 'our acknowledged master, learned Jonson' (James Shirley, in his dedication of *The Grateful Servant*, 1629), his longevity doubtless enhancing the effect. And there are moments when Jonson actively connives in his own myth, as in his commendatory poem to Richard Brome's *The Northern Lass*, where he stressed 'observation of those comic laws/Which I, your master, first did teach the age' (*Uncollected Verse* 38, ll. 7–8). As William Winstanley observed in 1687, 'he may be truly said to be the first reformer of the English stage, as he himself more truly than modestly writes in his commendatory verses of his servant's Richard Broom's comedy of *The Northern Lass*.'[27]

This is only one instance of what is a sadly common phenomenon: Jonson's own words being refracted into a posthumous – and not always very attractive – reputation. This may have been a price he was bound to pay for latterly acquiring what, despite his own pretence to the contrary, he never securely held in his own lifetime:

the status of a classic author. Succeeding generations could not ignore that status, but appropriated or belittled it, as suited their own situations. In the process, they elided into a single magisterial (and essentially *safe*) figure the complex, combative and shifting personalities which had built up the first lone wolf of English criticism – an elision that continued to define our view of Jonson well into this century, lying behind (for example) James Redwine's comments on the *Volpone* criticism, quoted earlier.

It has been my purpose here to rediscover in the Epistle to *Volpone* something less monolithic, less self-assured, less safe – elements that Jonson himself was the first to try to disguise. In doing so I have re-demonstrated the central truth that Jonson attempted to confront and contain these: that once a text finds readers they alone possess its meaning.

Notes

1. See Richard Dutton, *Ben Jonson: Authority: Criticism* (Basingstoke: Macmillan; New York: St Martin's Press, 1996), pp. 13–19. The present article is largely a reworking of parts of this book.
2. See Richard Dutton, 'Ben Jonson and the Master of the Revels', in *Theatre and Government under the Early Stuarts*, ed. by J.R. Mulryne and Margaret Shewring (Cambridge: Cambridge University Press, 1993), pp. 57–86, esp. pp. 64–7.
3. See Kate McLuskie's essay in this volume on 'the self-fashioning success of Jonson's own publicity'.
4. Lines 138–46. References to all of Jonson's works are to the edition by C.H. Herford, Percy and Evelyn Simpson, 11 vols (Oxford: Oxford University Press, 1925–52) – hereafter H&S – though the texts are silently modernized. The Epistle to *Volpone* is in H&S IV, pp. 16–21; references will normally be to H&S's line-numbering, cited parenthetically within the text. It will sometimes be necessary to refer to their critical apparatus in order to recover quarto readings.
5. References to Jonson's *Conversations with William Drummond of Hawthornden* are to the version in H&S I, Appendix I, pp. 128–78, cited by line-numbers within the text.
6. See Richard Dutton, *Mastering the Revels: The Regulation and Censorship of English Renaissance Drama* (Basingstoke: Macmillan, 1991), pp. 10–15.
7. The letter to the Earl of Salisbury is quoted from the Revels Plays *Eastward Ho*, ed. by R.W. Van Fossen (Manchester: Manchester University Press, 1979), Appendix 2, 218–25, pp. 220–21. References to Jonson's other letters (and Chapman's) over the *Eastward Ho* affair are to these versions (modernized), cited by page number within the text.

8. See Rosalind Miles, *Ben Jonson: His Life and Work* (London: Routledge, 1986), p. 100.
9. Ibid., p. 102.
10. See John Archer, *Sovereignty and Intelligence: Spying and Court Culture in English Renaissance Writing* (Stanford. CA: Stanford University Press, 1993).
11. See Chapman's second letter to him, *ed. cit.*, p. 219.
12. Strabo, *Geographica*, I.ii.5.
13. See Dutton, *Ben Jonson: Authority: Criticism*, pp. 13–19.
14. *Ben Jonson's Literary Criticism*, ed. by James D. Redwine Jr (Lincoln: University of Nebraska Press, 1970), p. xv.
15. *Discoveries*, H&S VIII, pp. 555–649, ll. 134–40.
16. Martin Elsky, *Authorizing Words: Speech, Writing, and Print in the English Renaissance* (Ithaca and London: Cornell University Press, 1989), pp. 87–8.
17. See Jonathan Goldberg, *James I and the Politics of English Literature* (Baltimore, MD: Johns Hopkins University Press, 1983), esp. pp. 219–30.
18. Stanley Fish, *Is There a Text in This Class?* (Cambridge, MA and London: Harvard University Press, 1980), p. 312.
19. See Dutton, *Ben Jonson: Authority: Criticism*, pp. 62–3.
20. David Riggs, *Ben Jonson: A Life* (Cambridge, MA and London: Harvard University Press, 1989), p. 3.
21. Richard C. Newton, 'Jonson and the (Re-)Invention of the Book' in *Classic and Cavalier: Essays of Jonson and the Sons of Ben*, ed. by Claude J. Summers and Ted-Larry Pebworth (Pittsburg, PA: University of Pittsburg Press, 1982), pp. 31–58, p. 46.
22. See J.F. Bradley and J.O. Adams (eds), *The Jonson Allusion Book* (New Haven: Yale University Press, 1922), for a collection of Dryden's references to Jonson, Index, pp. 456–7. He could be very positive, as in 'I prefer the *Silent Woman* before all other plays, I think justly, as I do its author, in judgement, above all other poets' (p. 346); but he is best remembered for putting him in Shakespeare's critical shade: 'I must acknowledge him the more correct poet, but Shakespeare the greater wit ... I admire him, but I love Shakespeare' (p. 344); and his dismissal of Jonson's verses to the memory of Shakespeare as 'an insolent, sparing, and invidious panegyric' (p. 442) and of his last plays as 'but his dotages' (p. 343) had a serious long-term effect on his reputation.
23. Jennifer Brady, 'Collaborating with the Forebear: Dryden's Reception of Ben Jonson', *Modern Language Quarterly*, 54 (1993), 344–69.
24. Ibid., p. 350.
25. Edward Howard's 'Second Prologue' to *The Women's Conquest* is quoted from H&S XI, p. 532.
26. Thomas Rymer, Preface to Rapin's *Reflections on Aristotle's Treatise of Poesie*, quoted in *Ben Jonson: The Critical Heritage*, ed. by D.H. Craig (London and New York: Routledge, 1990), p. 331. Jeremy Collier's *A Short View of the Immorality and Profaneness of the English Stage* is quoted from H&S XI, p. 551.
27. Quoted in Bradley and Adams, *The Jonson Allusion Book*, p. 412.

7

Making and Buying: Ben Jonson and the Commercial Theatre Audience

Kate McLuskie

In the second act of *The Alchemist*, Don Surly interrupts Sir Epicure Mammon's exuberant celebration of the riches which the philosopher's stone will bring him:

> Why, I have heard, he must be *homo frugi*,
> A pious, holy, and religious man,
> One free from mortal sin, a very virgin.

Sir Epicure is completely unfazed by this reminder of the supposed conditions for the stone's production:

> That makes it, sir, he is so. But I buy it.
> (II.ii.97–100)[1]

Mammon's triumphant distinction between production and consumption, making and buying, epitomizes the social relations of commercial culture. In a move which is liberating as well as alienating, commercialization severs the links between those who make and those who buy, connecting them only temporarily in the transactions of exchange.

The disturbing social impact of these changing relations was noted as early as 1573 when the Merchant Taylor's court books record how:

> at our common playes and such lyke exercises which be commonly exposed to be seane for money ev'ry lewed persone thinketh him selfe (for his penny) worthy of the chief and most

comodious place without respecte of any other either for age or
estimacion in the common weale.[2]

Similar changes in the social relations of theatrical production were
widely noted by contemporaries[3] and provide ample evidence to
support Bordieu's summarizing contention that 'the mode of
expression characteristic of a cultural production always depends
on the laws of the market in which it is offered'.[4]

This connection between the theatre and the market has become
a commonplace of recent criticism. As Bruster asserts:

> As businesses, playhouses operated with a logic of profit and
> loss: it is to such a logic, I believe, that we should look in order to
> understand their place in the cultural dynamics of Renaissance
> London.[5]

The ensuing analyses, however, seldom engage in questions of economics: the day-to-day manoeuvrings of companies, the *processes* of
theatrical production, the often nit-picking and complicated negotiations between companies and scriptwriters, payment for apparel
and properties as well as texts. They offer instead a *poetics* of the
market[6] in which the discursive connections between images and
metaphors of markets and marketing can be satisfyingly traced
within a discursive (rather than a material) context. The focus on
the manifest content of plays, even when it involves subtle and
complex readings, assumes a stable theatrical market in which the
'logic of profit and loss' offered a firm foundation for the activity of
playmaking. This kind of analysis glosses over the problems of a
theatrical market in which the primary commodity itself was highly
unstable. A play could exist in a variety of forms: it might be paid
for in instalments, sold in book form to readers and in script form
to other playing companies and its market value varied according
to whether it was sold to a playing company, performed at court, or
produced in a public or private theatre company.

The problem of keeping both the poetics and the economics of
the market in the same focus is particularly acute when we attempt
to view early modern culture through the lenses of Ben Jonson's
plays. The sheer range and quality of his work, the fact that he
wrote plays for public and private theatres, masques for the court,
poetry and epigrams on real and identifiable people, letters to
lords, formal learned analysis in *Discoveries*, and was recorded in

revealingly relaxed conversations with Drummond of Hawthornden, allows his work to be read as a paradigm of the form and pressure of the early modern world. His own dominating presence within this work – psychologically complex, tormented, needing patronage but scornfully independent, above all wittily articulate and learned too – also contributes to the attraction of working with a figure who provides (as Virginia Woolf said of women)[7] the mirror in which modern academics can see themselves mirrored at twice their size. Ben Jonson's witty and acute negotiation of the tension between taste and value, his formulation of the boundaries between popular and elite culture, his apparent contempt for commerce, and his desperate desire to do the state some service, all are echoed in the position of the liberal academic in late twentieth-century commercialized education. Praise for Ben Jonson is an expression of admiration for the intellectual whose integrity is not compromised by patronage[8] and whose higher learning never desensitizes his common touch:

> Jonson who was the friend of Selden and Camden and who proved his classical learning in detailed footnotes to his plays was also author of that most brilliant evocation of popular culture, *Bartholomew Fair*.[9]

I

This celebration of Jonson shows the extent to which modern historians are inclined to concur with Jonson's presentation of himself. Jonson's preoccupation with the terms and conditions in which his art was practised provided a language to express the conflict between patronage and commerce which would recur in succeeding culture. His formulation of the terms of that conflict was particularly persuasive because of the subtlety with which he distinguished between satire, calumny, and abuse, between folly and crimes, and above all between poetry and the hack work of commercializing culture. These critical views were, of course, shared by many of his contemporaries and expressed the commonplaces of contemporary critical theory in both discursive and dramatic form. However, Jonson's expression of these views gained a particular edge from his direct involvement with a range of pressures on artistic production. Elsewhere in this volume, Richard Dutton has

discussed the relations between Jonson's criticism and his negotiations with state authority. A similar complexity attends Jonson's
vexed relations with commercial culture. The prologues and epi-
logues to his plays instruct his audience to view the poet as above
the calculations of commerce and as contrasted with those other
poets who were content to work within them. In the prologue to
the Folio version of *Every Man In His Humour*, for example, he distinguishes himself clearly from poets who are driven by 'need' for
commercial reward and makes clear his refusal to 'purchase' the
audience's 'delight':

> Though need make many Poets, and some such
> As art, and nature have bettered much;
> Yet ours, for want, hath not so loved the stage,
> As he dare serve th'ill customs of the age:
> Or purchase your delight at such a rate,
> As, for it, he himself must justly hate.[10]

In this prologue, the rhetorical rejection of a commercial relationship with his audiences slips into a comic travesty of old-fashioned
theatre in which the players:

> ... make a child, now swaddled, to proceed
> Man, and then shoot up, in one beard and weed,
> Past threescore years.
>
> (Prologue, ll. 7–9)

The theatrical delight which Jonson had to offer was no more or
less commercial, the audience paid for their seats and the dramatists were paid for their plays, but the association between commerce and hack work was firmly, if rhetorically, established.

In the Induction to *Bartholomew Fair*, this rhetorical opposition
between good taste and commercial relations is rendered more
complex by being turned into drama. The stage keeper who deni-
grates the poet's ignorance of 'the humors ... the Bartholomew-
birds' (ll. 12–13) can easily be dismissed as both tasteless and old
fashioned for he 'kept the Stage in Master Tarleton's time' (ll. 36–7).
However old-fashioned, taste is no longer dismissed as merely
commercial, for the Induction goes on to address head-on the
complex relationship between taste, judgement, and the commercial relations between poet and audience. The contract between the

poet and the audience acknowledges the audience's right to demand pleasure in return for money paid and offers substitute entertainment for those missed by the stage keeper. However the contract also imposes limits on the audience, in the requirement that each member of the audience judge independently and consistently, in the terms established by the play's conventions, without looking for hidden meaning and above all with the agreement that:

> his place get not above his wit. And if he pay for half a dozen, he may censure for them all too, so that he will undertake that they shall be silent.
>
> (Induction, ll. 90–93)

By dressing up this discussion of taste and money in the dramatic encounter between Scrivener, Bookholder, and Stage Keeper, Jonson is able to be heavily ironic about a reductive, commercialized idea of taste, without ever solving the conundrum of judgement, pleasure, and money or even touching on the real roles of stage keeper, book holder, and scrivener in the production of theatrical pleasure.

The complexity of these addresses to the audience, the ironic placing of both the audience's taste and the poet's own relation to it, involved both rhetorical and conceptual juggling. The difficulty of keeping the audience's pleasure and the poet's higher aims in balance is particularly pronounced in the prologue to *Poetaster*. There the Prologue declares that he is armed because it is a dangerous age:

> Wherein, who writes, had need present his Scenes
> Forty-fold proof against the conjuring means
> Of base detractors, and illiterate apes.
>
> (Prologue, ll. 68–70)[11]

Clearly, no-one in the audience would want to identify with the base detractors and illiterate apes, and yet the pleasures of scurrilous satire need to be acknowledged if the play as a whole is to be successful. Jonson solves this conundrum by offering these pleasures via the ambiguous figure of Envy. Envy has been fomenting the poison of her hate for the fifteen weeks that the author has been writing the play: she wants to offer her snakes to the audience (in the curiously sexual image of 'stick down in your deep throats') so that they can damn the author. But this envy of the author will only be one pleasure. Envy will also:

> ... blast your pleasures, and destroy your sports,
> With wrestings, comments, applications,
> Spy-like suggestions, privy whisperings,
> And thousand such promoting sleights as these.
>
> (Prologue, ll. 23–6)

The audience are admired as too bright to fall for Envy's stratagem, warned against the pleasurable possibility of particular applications and yet, because they are watching Envy, need not deny themselves the further pleasures of squeezing envy through their black jaws. For the greatest comic pleasures of this play are not those of restrained moral superiority. They are the much more directly vicious humiliations of Jonson's enemies such as the scene where Crispinus is purged of his poetic affectations or the contemptuous representation of Lupus as the bone-headed bureaucrat, too stupid to distinguish between theatrical convention and a threat to the state.[12]

These theatrical pleasures are in some tension with the ideal view of the role of the satirist which Jonson offers in the scenes with Virgil and Augustus. Augustus is a shadowy figure, much more readily characterized by poetic descriptions of him than by his action and therefore theatrically very dull. Jonson seems to have recognized the tension between the pleasures of poetry and the responsibilities of the public poet. He has Horace discuss them in an extra scene, interpolated into the folio text of the play. Horace is frank about what he sees as a weakness in his writing, his inability:

> To paint the horrid troops of armed men;
> The lances burst, in Gallia's slaughtered forces;
> Or wounded Parthians, tumbled from their horses:
>
> (III.v.21–24)

However, the audience in the theatre, with their own pleasure in mind, may have been glad that Jonson recognized the incompatibility of 'the old state and splendour of Dramatic Poems, with the preservation of any popular delight'.[13]

What Jonson achieved instead in *Poetaster* was the representation of a set of theatrical values around which an audience could cohere.

They could sneer at the upstart affectation of the poetasters, not only because they were exposed in the finale but because they were associated with the taste of the empty-headed Chloe. Chloe's naiveté produces some of the funniest lines in the play – 'a man may be a poet and yet not change his hair' (II.ii.78–9) – but she fulfils the role taken by all the female aspirants to high culture from the Grocer's wife in Beaumont's *The Knight of the Burning Pestle* to the heroine of Willie Russell's *Educating Rita*. She dramatizes the boundary separating true from false art and places the sophisticated male audience on the correct side.

The players themselves occupy a curiously ambiguous position on this boundary. Characters such as Ovid and his friends who get too close to them risk becoming:

> a stager ... an ingle for players, a gull, a rook, a shot-clog,
> to make suppers, and be laughed at.
>
> (I.ii.15–17)

Ovid's father, who denounces his son in these terms, is not the most reliable judge of the fit role for poetry but Ovid's eventual fate shows the dangers of poetic talent which is misused merely for social pleasure. Players who will do anything for money, it is suggested, deserve no better than to be exploited by Tucca who strikes the harder bargain in a deal in which they can perform in his name but will have to 'buy your own cloth' and give him 'two shares for my countenance.' (III.iv.356–7).

II

Ben Jonson's translation of classical criticism into theatrical pleasure allowed his audience to identify themselves as sophisticated men, rich enough to buy the pleasures of theatre but properly sceptical about the limits of the connection between taste and wealth. In order to understand the plays, this audience was supposed to recognize the virtues of the high moral position but have enough sense of humour to enjoy the vitality of Chloe or Tucca and to recognize the attractions of art as pleasure even as they acknowledged the dangers this uncontrolled artistic licence presented to the virtuous state. They were capable of a sophistication which would enable them both to rise above the simple-minded analogizing of a 'state decipherer or politic picklock' while at the same time being sufficiently in the know to pick up the play's topicality.

This ideal audience was, of course, a fiction, a fiction which was the satisfying mirror image of the ideal satirist. However, Jonson's view of his own position in the culture was not shared by all his professional colleagues. Dekker's remorseless mockery of Jonson in *Satiromastix* consisted partly of direct insults about his complexion 'punched full of eyelet-holes, like the cover of a warming pan' (V.ii.258–9).[14] It was also directed, with particular irritation, at Jonson's presumption to be above the market. When Horace, the Jonson figure in the play, is interrupted in the throes of composing an epithalamium for his patron's wedding, he hilariously plays on the evident commercial nature of the undertaking by reversing the commonplace metaphoric connection between coins and heavenly visitors:

> I no sooner opened his letter, but there appeared to me
> three glorious Angels, whom I adored, as subjects do their
> Sovereigns: the honest knight angles for my acquaintance,
> with such golden baits.
>
> (I.ii.108–11)

The exposure of Horace in the final scenes of Dekker's play explicitly connects Jonson's affectation over money to the theatre, insisting that the playwright acknowledge his need for the players and the importance of their contribution to theatrical success. Horace is made to swear:

> you shall not sit in a Gallery, when your comedies and
> interludes have entered their actions, and there make vile
> and bad faces at every line, to make gentlemen have an
> eye to you, and to make players afraid to take your part.
>
> (V.ii.298–301)

Jonson was, of course, equally quick to pre-empt and answer criticism by personal imputation. In *Poetaster*, he has his Dekker figure, Demetrius Fannius, explain petulantly that his critique came from no more than childish envy:

> no great cause ... I must confess, but that he kept better
> company for the most part than I, and that better men

loved him than loved me, and that his writings thrived
better than mine and were better liked and graced.
Nothing else.

(V.iii.441–5)

In purging Crispinus, humiliating Demetrius Fannius, and sneer-
ing at Lupus, Jonson was creating a new kind of consumer for the
theatre, one of a smart, self-reinforcing male circle for whom a
rather brutal wit was as important as moral or social standing.

The terms of this quarrel offer an interesting insight into the
social relations which developed in a competitive commercial
theatre. In 1600 Jonson and Dekker could not so easily have been
assigned to different cultural camps as their modern reputations
might suggest. They had collaborated on plays for Henslowe in
1597–98 and Marston, the other antagonist in the Poetomachia, may
have worked with them there too.[15] Both Dekker and Jonson were
involved in the commission for the speeches for James's coronation
entry into the City of London and though Dekker permitted
himself a sarcastic aside about writers who put in too many pretentious classical references, there was no suggestion that one
writer was more commercially involved than the other. Like
Jonson, Dekker seized the new commercial opportunity offered by
the reopening of the boy player companies and, with Webster,
placed *Westward Ho* with Paul's boys, but he soon moved back to
the adult companies, working with Middleton in *The Honest Whore*
to adapt the new style for sexy city comedy to the larger theatres.
Moreover, although Dekker was more grateful to the players who
saved his work from oblivion,[16] the prologues to his plays constructed an audience who would appreciate the sophisticated new
drama much as Jonson's did. In other words the distinction
between Dekker the envious hack and Jonson the high-minded
poet was one of the illusions created by Jonson's self-fashioning
and articulated by the distinction between art and commerce,
between high culture and low entertainment which was increasingly dominating theatrical commentary. It was an illusion, moreover, which was reinforced by Jonson's greater facility in following
the most successful of the new theatrical ventures.

Jonson's move from Langley's Swan to Henslowe, to Burbage's
Chamberlain's Men and then to the Children of the Queen's Revels
at Blackfriars may have been part of a restless search for a fit audience: it was also a set of moves which followed in the increasing

power of the theatre owners and theatrical entrepreneurs over the players.[17] Langley had attached very stringent conditions to the provisions of playing space and apparel he made for the players at the Swan and in disentangling them from Langley's clutches after the *Isle of Dogs* débâcle, Henslowe also put their relationship with him on a more formal contractual footing.[18] The men who managed the boys' companies had the most power of all since their players were children, apprenticed and occasionally pressganged into service. The most recent edition of *Poetaster* is right to insist that the quarrel between Jonson and Dekker 'was not purely a matter of gaining publicity for rival theatrical companies'.[19] Nevertheless, the commercial context in which the debates about poetry, and Jonson's self-fashioning within them, took place had the effect of altering the terms in which 'true poetry' and the mode of its reception was to be seen.

The proliferation of theatre companies at the turn of the century \ made it necessary for them to create new markets and the differentiation of kinds of plays was one of the means which was used for that effect. Jonson's efforts to position his audience in *Poetaster* were repeated in numerous inductions and prologues and prefaces to the reader.[20] In particular, the playwrights who wrote for the boy player companies seemed anxious to create a market niche for the new ventures, taking their 'choise selected influence' and assuring them they were too sophisticated for 'the mouldy fopperies of stale poetry.'[21] There was a certain disingenuousness in this rejection of the plays of the last age. Paul's Boys opened with a repertory consisting mainly of revivals of Lyly and *The Spanish Tragedy*, which later became a byword for the old-fashioned drama, was stolen by \ a boy player company from the adult players who retaliated with the theft of *The Malcontent*.[22] The mockery of *The Spanish Tragedy* in *Poetaster* and in *Eastward Ho* was picked up again in *Bartholomew Fair* when the Scrivener's contract agrees that:

> He that will swear, Hieronimo, or Andronicus, are the best plays, yet, shall pass unexcepted at, here, as a man whose Judgement shows it is constant, and hath stood still, these five and twenty, or thirty years.
>
> (Induction, ll. 106–9)

For the spectator with a long memory, part of the special pleasure in that reference may have consisted in the knowledge that Jonson himself had been involved in bringing Hieronimo back to the stage a decade or so before.

III

These discursive manoeuvrings around the concepts of taste, commerce, and theatre were rendered even more intricate when the question of court patronage entered into the discussion. Once again, *Bartholomew Fair* offers a particularly interesting case because the poet made an explicit distinction between the court and commercial audience by offering a prologue and epilogue to the King which was quite different from the Induction for the audience at the Hope. The transfer of plays from the professional theatre repertory to the court was commonplace. However, in the case of *Bartholomew Fair*, the speed of the transfer has encouraged some critics to believe that the play was specifically destined for a royal, as opposed to a common, audience. Keith Sturgess included the play in his discussion of *Jacobean Private Theatre*, insisting that: 'The key performance, then, is that at Whitehall, and the play may even have been a kind of royal commission.' His key argument is 'the sheer unlikelihood of Jonson ever compromising his artistic integrity' together with the inference that 'the content of the play, with its enthusiastically anti-Puritan stance, would be especially congenial to James'.[23]

The tradition that the play had a special association with the Jacobean court began with Aubrey who wrote that 'King James made him write against the Puritans who began to be troublesome in his time.'[24] Aubrey offers no more evidence for this statement than he does for his other famous assertion of direct royal involvement, that Shakespeare wrote *The Merry Wives of Windsor* so that Queen Elizabeth could see Falstaff in love. However, Aubrey's observation does reiterate Jonson's prologue to the play which identifies the players and the author with the King's side in the opposition to 'your land's faction'[25] and the connection between this gloss on the play and James's handling of the Puritan opposition has generated persuasive thematic readings. Leah Marcus has shown how the play's treatment of issues of law and licence, including theatrical licence, was echoed both in contemporary writing and in the contemporary regulation of both the theatres and *Bartholomew Fair* itself. She makes a persuasive case for

Jonson's commitment to the King's position on issues of prerogative and shows how the fair exposes the hypocrisy and incom-
petence of the City's attempt to regulate its own affairs.[26] This view
is certainly borne out by the Epilogue to the court performance in
which the King's judgement is presented as the only one worth
having. It is contrasted with 'the envy of a few' (l. 10) and the epilogue concludes, 'We value less what their dislike can bring/ If it so
happy be t'have pleased the King.' (ll. 11–12).

The addresses to the king are, in their own way, just as seductive
as the address to the urbane city audience. For the modern critic
who eagerly takes up the position of judicious sophisticate offered
by the Induction to the public theatre performance, the prospect of
agreeing with a king might seem even more attractive. Thus these
critics happily endorse the playwrights' own assertions that they
were happiest and richest and most influential when their audience
was the king. Leah Marcus, for example, suggests that the Scrivener's
insistence on no-one judging more than they had paid for offered
sly support to the monarch since 'James was far and away the most
lavish supporter of the drama.'[27]

This was certainly the ideological position which had under-
pinned the development of the professional theatre in London. In
their conflict with the city authorities, the players had frequently
taken refuge in the myth that their public performances were mere
rehearsals for court performances. Moreover there was some commercial foundation for the myth. The reorganized Revels Office
under Edmund Tylney had found it significantly cheaper to buy in
professional players than to maintain the necessary level of provision to organize royal entertainments in-house and the patronage
of playing companies involved provided him with a lucrative side-
line in licence fees and other sweeteners.[28] Under James and
Charles significantly more was spent on the in-house entertainments of masques but plays from all the professional companies
provided a regular supply of court entertainment. However there is
no evidence to suggest that performance at court involved any
direct relationship with the king at all. In the case of *Bartholomew
Fair*, Nathan Field, 'in behalf of himself and the rest of his fellowes',
was paid £10 for the performance, the standard fee.[29] In addition,
the Revels Office accounts also include a payment for 'Canvas for
the Boothes and other necessaries for a play called *Bartholomew
Faire*'.[30] However in the same season, the Prince's Men offered six
plays, the Palsgrave's men, 'two … before the Kinges matie and one

before the Prince,' and the King's Men played no less than eight. There is no evidence to suppose that Jonson's play had the special status of a royal commission among these entertainments or that the payment for canvas for the booths was anything more than a routine expense in the making ready of rooms for plays.[31] Nor could such expenditure be regarded as egregious for the office which oversaw the production costs of masques and spent £159 3s and 9d on them in the season when *Bartholomew Fair* was performed.[32] The prologue to the court performance, of course, occludes any consideration of the real relations of production and consumption of plays in the elegant fiction which welcomes James to the fair and offers him 'for a fairing, true delight'. (l. 12).

In the case of the Lady Elizabeth's Men, who performed *Bartholomew Fair* at both the Hope and the Court, the gap between the free exchange of fairings and the commercial relations of the theatre was more than usually wide, and questions of the contracts which governed their financial health and independence were particularly pressing. The Lady Elizabeth's Men had been licensed by a patent of 1611 to play (formulaically):

> in and about our Cittie of London in such vsuall howses as themselues shall prouide. And alsoe within anie Towne halles, mootehalles, Guyld-halles, Schoolehowses or other convenient place, etc. etc.[33]

The 'Towne-halles, mootehalles, Guyld-halles' were easy to find since they were available in the towns on the established touring routes and permission to play in them was a matter of negotiation with the local authority. The Lady Elizabeth's Men is first located playing – no doubt with their pumps full of gravel[34] – across the breadth of the country (Bath in 1610 and Ipswich in 1611). However, since the legislation controlling playing in London,[35] a playing venue in the city – 'such vsuall howses as themselues shall prouide' – could only be found by entering into a bond with a playhouse owner, in this case, the ubiquitous Henslowe. And this the company duly did in August 1611 for £500.

The Lady Elizabeth's Men was made up of a motley assortment of players from the Admiral's, the King's, and the Duke of York's company[36] but at least one player came from the former Queen's Revels Company, the group of boys which had played *Epicoene* and *Poetaster* and *Eastward Ho*. By 1613 the company had been filled out with others from the former Queen's Revels Company (including Nathan Field) and Henslowe was in partnership with Rosseter who had taken on the Queen's Revels in 1609 and moved them to the Whitefriars.

Ensuing relations between Henslowe and the company did not suggest the easy cooperation implied by playing 'in and about our Cittie of London in such usuall howses as themselves shall provide'. In 1615, the players of the Lady Elizabeth's Men put together a document outlining their grievances against Henslowe over the years from the spring of 1613. According to their account, Henslowe had so complicated the relations of debt to him and so confused the combination of commodities, apparel, playbooks, and cash which formed their financial dealings with him as to put their continued viability as a playing company entirely at his disposal. One of Henslowe's ploys was to take:

> all boundes [bonds] or our hired men in his owne name, whose wages though wee have truely paid yet att his pleasure hee hath taken them a waye, and turned them over to others to the breaking of our Companie. For lending of vi li to p[ay] them theire wages, hee made vs enter bond to give him the profitt of a warraunt of tenn poundes due to vs att Court.[37]

This ten pounds so sadly earned with one act and lost immediately with another may not have been the payment for *Bartholomew Fair* – the Lady Elizabeth's company played three times at court in the Christmas season 1612–13. However, its location in a discussion of complicated and acrimonious financial dealing illustrates the layers of commercial and practical activity which surrounded offering a fairing to a king.

The conflict between Henslowe and the Lady Elizabeth's Men also locates the play more firmly in a particular moment of commercial development. For the companies which had established this new sophisticated audience, which had given the drama the new direction of satirical comedy, which had tempted the censor with defiant treatments of dangerous matter, depended for their financial strength on the labour of children. The fiction that they were training singers had been exposed by the Clifton case in 1601 when a gentleman took the Queen's Revels company to court for abducting his son.[38] As Hillebrand points out, they were 'after 1600, commercial companies hiring their dramatists and guided no longer by a single singing master but by a board of directors banded together in accordance with strictly business principles.'[39] It is important not to be sentimental about the fate of the exploited youngsters, for they received an education and careers in return for profits they made for the entrepreneurs who controlled them.[40] However, the organizations which controlled them did seem to herald a new kind of commercialism in the theatre. The companies which emerged after the collapse of the boy players seem to have operated a much clearer division and more exploitative relations between the men who financed them and those who put on the plays, with more complaints about contracts and more sense of companies being made or broken by those who controlled their assets. Those commercial principles did not in every case produce commercial success: a key feature of theatrical investment at the turn of the century was the greedily high expectations of profit which lay behind the lawsuits and in some cases the companies' collapse.[41]

IV

This changed relationship between entrepreneurs and companies, a fundamental change in the conditions of play production, was not directly acknowledged in the playtexts but it did alter the ways in which plays connected to the occasions for their performance. The Lady Elizabeth's Men's articles of grievance against Henslowe show that the company's playbooks, together with their costumes, were one of their most important assets. After the amalgamation with the Queen's Revels, the Lady Elizabeth's Men complained of Henslowe that 'wee have paid him for plaie bookes 200 li or thereabouts and yet hee denies to give us the Coppies of any one of them.'[42] Nevertheless, in spite of this disagreement over the ownership of the plays, the Lady Elizabeth's Men were able to reuse the plays from the boys' company to build up their repertory and among the plays they recycled was Jonson's *Eastward Ho*. In August 1613, Daborne wrote to Henslowe suggesting that *Eastward Ho* be used as a stopgap in the repertory for one of his plays which was not yet complete; on 25 January 1614, the Lady Elizabeth's Men played Jonson's play at court.[43]

The court performance of *Eastward Ho* passed off without incident. Joseph Taylor 'and the reste of his fellowes servaunts to the

Lady Eliz her grace', were paid £6.13s and 4d by the Council's warrant and 'by way of his Majesty's reward 66 shillings and 8d'. The two sums together come, of course, to £10, the standard court payment for a play.[44] The King's favour, noted in these records and not, as it happened, in the record for *Bartholomew Fair*, was clearly an accounting formula. If it had any substance, the King's reward would have been surprising, given the scandal which the play had caused in the first phase of its performance history in 1605. Its casual reproduction as a repertory stopgap might highlight the relationship between political meaning and commercial performance.

The meaning read into *Eastward Ho* in 1605 seems to have come as a surprise and an embarrassment to the writers themselves, as the squirming parentheses of Jonson's letter to Salisbury show:

The Cause (would I could name some worthier) though I wishe we had known none worthy our Imprisonment) is (the word irks me that our Fortune hath necessitated us to so despised a Course) a Play, my Lord.[45]

Jonson's insistence that he had no intention to offend seems disingenuous but it can illuminatingly be placed in the context of the commercial games played by many of the boy company playwrights in the new commercial milieu.

The discursive construction of an appropriate audience involved addressing their auditors as politically as well as aesthetically alert. A number of the boy company plays flirt quite openly with the possibility of censorship, adding political audacity to the theatrical pleasures of the sophisticated audience. Day's *Isle of Gulls*, for example, with its story of homosexuality and cross-dressing even now seems breathtakingly pointed in its representation of a corrupt court. Day was committed to Bridewell for his part in the play but was released unmutilated and the children's company, in spite of threats, continued to play.[46] The Induction to Beaumont's *The Woman Hater* teases the informer in the audience looking for 'fit matter to feede his malice on' and ends with a cheeky double bluff about the need to 'please Auditors so, as hee may be an auditor himself hereafter, and not purchase them with the deare losse of his eares.'[47] However this was no call to political opposition; the audience in the theatre is not addressed in terms of faction or as occupying a group within the structures of power but as a group constituted in aesthetic terms; appreciating innovation, able to take a joke against themselves, ready to collude with the author for the sake of theatrical pleasure.

That aesthetics and good judgement were at issue as much as *realpolitik* was evident from Jonson's reaction when things went wrong. His letter to an unnamed lady, probably the Countess of Bedford, about the *Eastward Ho* affair bristles with contempt for the stupidity of his accusers. He claims that the play was 'so mistaken, so misapplied, as I do wonder whether their Ignorance, or Impudence be most, who are our adversaries'.[48] The longer-winded 'Apologetical Dialogue' to *Poetaster*, occasioned by the furore that that play aroused, similarly took a high tone of scorn for his opponents' literal mindedness and the conclusions that those stung by his satire deserved to be so:

> ... all the rest might have sat still, unquestioned,
> Had they but had the wit, or conscience,
> To think well of themselves.
>
> (ll. 130–32)

Jonson's high-minded location of himself above the melée and in the tradition of the equally misunderstood classical satirists is a familiar aspect of his self-fashioning. However his position is endorsed by recent readings of the periodic scandals which brought theatrical activity to official attention. Richard Dutton, for example, in a scrupulously thorough account of the *Eastward Ho* affair, shows that Jonson and Chapman's imprisonment was caused by a temporary slip in the delicate balance of understanding 'among those who shared power' which 'depended in turn upon a general sense of security within the power-structure'.[49] He also suggests that the significance of episodes and references in the play depend on the surrounding context for particular applications and shows how plays which may have aroused no comment at first production, become topical when major scandals, like the Essex affair, swamp the whole culture with meaning. The case of *Eastward Ho*'s 1613 revival offers the opposite and corollary case of the play which seems to have had an overplus of meaning, at least for one trouble-making member of the audience, Sir James Murray, at a particular performance in 1605. However, its continued commercial existence seems to have been able to empty that meaning out.[50]

In the world of commercial theatre it may be that there was a similar balance of understanding to be established between the companies, the playwrights, and the audience for the plays: the trick was to retain enough meaning in a play to keep an audience engaged while avoiding the particularity which might separate off individuals or influential groups. It was to create an illusion of coherence out of a disparate group of people whose only connection was the ability to pay. Achieving that balance in the new theatre conditions of the turn of the century seems to have required constant intervention, explaining the terms in which this style was to be appreciated and by whom. Those interventions used the language of a politics of culture, of a relationship between status and taste and the social significance of good judgement. However, in doing so, they reiterated older views of culture which took little cognizance of the changing conditions in which performances were seen and in effect forced open the gap between economic and cultural relations which informs cultural ideology today. The politicized criticism of the last decade or so has in a variety of ways attempted to close that gap, to suggest the importance of the social work, the circulation of political ideology, effected by early modern theatre.[51] To suggest that the political relations of early modern theatre with its surrounding culture may have been compromised and dispersed by the commercial relations of production through which they were disseminated is not to deny that a relationship exists. It was not that the players had sold their influence for a mess of commercial pottage,[52] nor that the playwrights were naive or disingenuous in their expectation of a judicious audience. However an entertainment for sale sets up rather different relations with its audience than an entertainment offered as a tribute or even a 'fairing'. In attempting to establish the relations between commerce and culture we need to investigate the ways in which the players acquired the plays and the ways in which they purveyed them to their audience in economic as well as discursive terms.

Notes

1. C.H. Herford, Percy and Evelyn Simpson (eds), *Ben Jonson*, 11 vols (Oxford: Clarendon Press, 1925–52), V (1937). All quotations from Ben Jonson's plays are from this edition, unless otherwise cited. Henceforth H&S. Spellings modernized.
2. Merchant Taylor's Court Books, i. 699: *A Calendar of Dramatic Records in the Books of the Livery Companies of London, 1485–1640*, ed. by Jean

Robertson and D.J. Gordon (Oxford: Malone Society Collections III, 1954), p. 140.

3. See, for example, comments by Samuel Cox; Robert Greene; Henry Crosse; and J. Cocke in E.K. Chambers, *The Elizabethan Stage*, 4 vols (Oxford: Clarendon Press, 1923), IV, Appendix C: 'Documents of Criticism', pp. 185–259.

4. Pierre Bordieu, *Distinction: A Social Critique of the Judgement of Taste*, trans. by Richard Nice (London: Routledge and Kegan Paul, 1984), p. xiii.

5. Douglas Bruster, *Drama and the Market in the Age of Shakespeare* (Cambridge: Cambridge University Press, 1992), p. 27. See also Jean Christophe Agnew, *Worlds Apart: The Theatre and the Market in Anglo-American Thought* (Cambridge: Cambridge University Press, 1986).

6. See Bruster, *Drama and the Market in the Age of Shakespeare*, p. 11.

7. Virginia Woolf, *A Room of One's Own* (New York: Harcourt, Brace, Jovanovitch, 1969), p. 35.

8. See, for example, Martin Butler's recent Chatterton lecture (1995) at the British Academy whose title echoed Jonson's self-description, 'Servant not Slave'.

9. Kevin Sharpe and Peter Lake (eds), *Culture and Politics in Early Stuart England* (Basingstoke: Macmillan, 1994), Introduction, p. 12.

10. H&S III, Folio Version of *Every Man In His Humour*, Prologue, ll. 1–6. Henceforth cited parenthetically within the text.

11. Ben Jonson, *Poetaster*, ed. by Tom Cain (Manchester: Manchester University Press, 1995), Prologue, ll. 68–70. All quotations from *Poetaster* are from this edition and henceforth cited parenthetically within the text.

12. See *Poetaster*, V.iii. On the connection between Lupus and those who interrogated the players after the Essex rebellion, see Introduction, pp. 40–44.

13. Preface 'To the Readers' of *Sejanus*, H&S IV, p. 350.

14. Thomas Dekker, *Satiromastix*, in *The Dramatic Works of Thomas Dekker*, ed. by Fredson Bowers, 4 vols (Cambridge: Cambridge University Press, 1962), I. Spellings modernized.

15. David Riggs, *Ben Jonson: A Life* (Cambridge, MA: Harvard University Press, 1989), pp. 78–9; Cain, *Poetaster*, Introduction, p. 31 and note 60.

16. See, for example, Dekker's dedication of *If This Be Not a Good Play, the Devil Is In It* to the Queen's Men, who performed it at the Red Bull when it seems to have been rejected by the Prince's Men at the Fortune. Bowers, *Dekker*, III, p. 119.

17. See Kathleen E. McLuskie, 'Patronage and the Economics of Theatrical Production', in *A New History of Early English Drama*, ed. by John D. Cox and David Scott Kastan (New York: Columbia University Press, forthcoming).

18. On Langley's contracts with the players, see William Ingram, *A London Life in the Brazen Age: Francis Langley 1548–1602* (Cambridge, MA: Harvard University Press, 1978), pp. 155–6; on Henslowe's use of contracts, see Carol Chillington Rutter (ed.) *Documents of the Rose Playhouse* (Manchester: Manchester University Press, 1984), p. 119.

19. Cain, *Poetaster*, Introduction, p. 30.
20. See, for example, Webster's Preface 'To the Reader' of *The White Devil*; Beaumont's Induction to *The Knight of the Burning Pestle*; Dekker's Prologue to *If This Be Not a Good Play, the Devil Is In It*; Middleton's Preface 'To the Comicke Play-Readers' of *The Roaring Girl*.
21. John Marston, 'Prologue' to *Jack Drum's Entertainment*, quoted in Andrew Gurr, *Playgoing in Shakespeare's London* (Cambridge: Cambridge University Press, 1987), p. 215.
22. See John Marston, *The Malcontent*, ed. by G.K. Hunter (London: Methuen, 1975), Introduction, pp. xxiii–xxxviii. For a discussion of the importance of *The Spanish Tragedy* in the repertory of a number of companies, see Rosalyn Knutson, *The Repertory of Shakespeare's Company, 1594–1613* (Fayetteville: University of Arkansas Press, 1991).
23. Keith Sturgess, *Jacobean Private Theatre* (London and New York: Routledge and Kegan Paul, 1978), pp. 169, 170. A similar view of the relationship between the Hope and the court production is taken by Ian Donaldson in *The World Turned Upside Down: Comedy from Jonson to Fielding* (Oxford: Clarendon Press, 1970), pp. 48–9; 72–7; and John Creaser, 'Enigmatic Ben Jonson', in *English Comedy*, ed. by Michael Cordner, Peter Holland and John Kerrigan (Cambridge: Cambridge University Press, 1984), pp. 100–18.
24. Quoted in Jesse Franklin Bradley and Joseph Quincy Adams (eds), *The Jonson Allusion Book* (Oxford: Oxford University Press, 1922), p. 356.
25. 'Prologue to the King's Majesty', in H&S VI, p. 11 (1. 4).
26. Leah Marcus, *The Politics of Mirth: Jonson, Herrick, Milton, Marvell, and the Defense of Old Holiday Pastimes* (Chicago: University of Chicago Press, 1986), pp. 24–63. She has recently recanted this view of the play in her article 'Of Mire and Authorship', in *The Theatrical City: Culture, Theatre and Politics in London, 1576–1649*, ed. by David L. Smith, Richard Strier and David Bevington (Cambridge: Cambridge University Press, 1995), pp. 170–81.
27. Marcus, *The Politics of Mirth*, p. 61.
28. See Andrew Gurr, 'Three Reluctant Patrons and Early Shakespeare', *Shakespeare Quarterly*, 43 (1992), 159–74; and Richard Dutton, *Mastering the Revels: The Regulation and Censorship of English Renaissance Drama* (Basingstoke: Macmillan, 1991), pp. 41–73.
29. *Dramatic Records in the Declared Accounts of the Treasurer of the Chamber, 1558–1642*, ed. by David Cook (Oxford: Malone Society Collections, VI, 1962), p. 60.
30. Quoted from the declared accounts of the Pipe Office, in Chambers IV, p. 183; quoted in H&S IX, p. 245.
31. See Cook, Malone Society Collections VI, pp. 90–124, for a list of such routine payments.
32. Malone Society Collections X, pp. 25–6.
33. Quoted in Chambers II, *The Elizabethan Stage*, pp. 246–7.
34. The fate which Tucca wished on the players who were unsuccessful in London. See *Poetaster*, III.iv.168. The condescension with which metropolitan playwrights viewed provincial playing is another of the

marketing myths of the London theatres. It has been analysed by Peter Greenfield in 'Professional Players at Gloucester: Conditions of Provincial Performing', *Elizabethan Theatre*, 10 (1983), 73–93.

35. On the economics and the limits of city legislation against playing, see William Ingram, *The Business of Playing: The Beginnings of the Adult Professional Theatre in Elizabethan London* (Ithaca and London: Cornell University Press, 1992), ch. 5.

36. See Andrew Gurr, *The Shakespearean Playing Companies* (Oxford: Clarendon Press, 1996), ch. 6.

37. Chambers II, *The Elizabethan Stage*, p. 250.

38. See H.N. Hillebrand, *The Child Actors: A Chapter in Elizabethan Stage History* (New York: Russell and Russell, 164), pp. 160–63.

39. Ibid., p. 267.

40. On the willingness of some parents to apprentice their children to the Choristers but also to the playing companies, see Hillebrand, *The Child Actors*, pp. 158, 197–99.

41. See William Ingram, 'The Playhouse as Investment, 1607–14: Thomas Woodford and Whitefriars', *Medieval and Renaissance Drama in English*, 2 (1985), 9–30.

42. Chambers, II, *The Elizabethan Stage*, p. 250.

43. See H&S I, p. 195; Chambers, III, *The Elizabethan Stage*, p. 372.

44. See Malone Society Collections VI, p. 58 (and *passim*, for examples of the £10 fee being divided between the Council and the King).

45. H&S I, p. 195.

46. See Hillebrand, *The Child Actors*, pp. 189–97.

47. Quoted in Philip J. Finkelpearl, '"The Comedian's Liberty": Censorship of the Jacobean Stage Reconsidered', *English Literary Renaissance*, 16 (1986), p. 136.

48. H&S I, p. 197.

49. Dutton, *Mastering the Revels*, p. 178. See also Ingram, 'The Playhouse as Investment', pp. 176–85 for the controversial suggestion that the connection between *The Isle of Dogs* and the restraint of playing in 1597 was coincidental.

50. Compare the similar case of the revivals of *Every Man In His Humour*, discussed in Knutson, *The Repertory of Shakespeare's Company*, pp. 75–8.

51. See Jean Howard's particularly persuasive account of this movement in *The Stage and Social Struggle in Early Modern England* (London and New York: Routledge, 1994), ch. 1.

52. See Paul Yachnin, 'The Powerless Theatre', *English Literary Renaissance*, 21 (1991), 49–74

8

Hell for Lovers: Shades of Adultery in *The Devil is an Ass*

Helen Ostovich

Jonson represents the London of November 1616 in *The Devil is an Ass* as a hellhole of greedy consumerism where Satan and his devils are outwitted by more sophisticated sinners. Frances Fitzdottrel, an abused wife in that hell, must choose between her tyrannical fool of a husband and her sensitive admirer – essentially a choice between being perceived as honest (by sticking to her marriage vows), or dishonest (by reaching out for love and rational companionship). In this dilemma, Jonson stresses that she has every justification for preferring adultery: hence, the difficulty of her decision. Her desire for independent self-government in sexual matters is closely bound up with her desire for independent control of her real property, both impossible in common law where the marital authority over both sexuality and property is the husband. Despite Jonson's modern reputation for misogyny, his sympathetic treatment of Frances suggests that his relationships with women in London – in particular, I will argue, the Sidney women – alerted him to complex models of female behaviour. In *The Devil is an Ass* he acknowledges what compromises a woman's ability to make decisions when trapped in unhappy marriage and tempted to commit adultery. How does a woman resist the gender ideologies of her day, define her identity as separate from her husband's, or locate a private space where she may discover and act on her own values? To be chaste, silent, and obedient for the sake of a fool seems ludicrous, especially when it entails or forecasts considerable financial privation.

Frances Fitzdottrel's response to her predicament owes a debt to decisions made by several wives of Jonson's acquaintance who in desperation defied patriarchal rules and flirted with scandal. These women, whose lives are adumbrated in legal, social, and literary documents *circa* 1616, provide shadow-texts which we may read as corroborating marginalia edging Jonson's dramatic text and giving it a perspective based on realities of the day. The single most important shadowing figure in that regard is Mary Wroth. In choosing Wroth as my focus, I am asserting only a shadowy relation between Wroth and Frances Fitzdottrel, although the emphasis of my argument may make it appear more exact or direct. Wroth is simply the most persuasive positive model among many women whose situations parallel Frances's, and whose examples, positive and negative, provide a context for Frances's decision to remain chaste, if not always silent or obedient. That context includes positive models like Anne Clifford, or Elizabeth Sidney, Countess of Rutland, and notorious figures like Penelope Rich or Honora Denny, all women in Wroth's social sphere. The negative example most explicitly contemplated in the play is Frances Howard, who, in the play's framework of Satan, Iniquity, and a personal demon, certainly represents the road not taken; witchcraft, suit for divorce, and murder. But Mary Wroth, both as woman and artist, represents a special case for Jonson.

Let me place Wroth first in a highly speculative, even circuitous and digressive, relation with Jonson and his creation of Frances Fitzdottrel in *The Devil is an Ass*. According to *Conversations with Drummond*,[1] a record of opinions Jonson voiced in 1618/19, Jonson wrote his 'Song: That Women are but Men's Shadows' (*Forest* 7) as the 'penance' demanded by the Earl of Pembroke's 'lady' for supporting the Earl's argument that women have no will of their own, but merely react to the strategies of male desire:

> Follow a shadow, it still flies you;
> Seem to fly it, it will pursue:
> So court a mistress, she denies you;
> Let her alone, she will court you.
> (ll. 1–4)

Was the lady in question the Countess of Pembroke, Mary Talbot, whom Pembroke married, not very happily, for her money, or the lady with whom he shared a life-long love affair and friendship, his cousin Mary Wroth? Is the song a conventional reiteration of male superiority – hardly the 'penance' an opinionated lady would exact – or a tease anticipating rebuttal? Jonson's apparent misogyny in the poem, turning on a simple gender binary – 'playful antagonism' towards women combined with 'delicate deference' to his patron[2] (Pembroke sent him £20 a year for books) – demands reinterpretation in the light of his admiration for the women of the Sidney circle. Perhaps *The Devil is an Ass* represents 'penance' of another kind, an acknowledgement of a woman's right to challenge and change the inequities of her life. Frances Fitzdottrel claims that female agency by exerting tautly rational control over her desires, placing a premium on peace of mind over transient pleasures of the flesh. Many of Wroth's sonnets in *Pamphilia to Amphilanthus*, written and revised between 1612 and 1621, illustrate the same tension between yearning and resolve, as when Pamphilia admonishes herself 'Fly traiter joye whose end brings butt dispaire', recognizing that 'Thus faine thou wouldst bee kind, butt must deny'.[3] What I am suggesting is that, by dint of their social and artistic proximity, in which the roles of patron, mentor, and poet mingled, Jonson may have found himself tracing Mary Wroth's outline in his creation of Frances Fitzdottrel.

Jonson's admiration for all the Sidney women is evident in his many dedications, masques, poems, and conversations on record. Some women in the Sidney circle, such as Mary Wroth's aunt, Philip Sidney's sister, Mary, Countess of Pembroke, or her best friend and cousin by marriage, Susan, Countess of Montgomery, receive conventional praise for their beauty and virtue. Jonson considered Wroth's first cousin, Elizabeth, Countess of Rutland, 'nothing inferior to her father s[ir] P. Sidney, in poesy' (*Conversations*, 205–6), and praises her in *Epigrams* 79 as nature's way of improving on the reproduction of a merely male heir. In *Forest* 12 he salutes her for her 'dowry', the poetic power that 'alone, can raise to heaven' (41), and thus may compensate her for her own childlessness in her marriage to Roger Manners, Earl of Rutland, who was thought to be impotent. According to Drummond (*Conversations*, 206–14), Sir Thomas Overbury was in love with her, and asked Jonson to read her his poem 'A Wife now the Widow', apparently as part of an effort to seduce her into a liaison. She refused wittily by quoting his poem back at him: 'He comes too near, who comes to be denied.' The Earl of Rutland, resentful of Jonson's friendship with his wife, 'accused her that she kept table to poets', and 'intercepted' their correspondence, but did not go so far as to challenge him (*Conversations*, 361–4).

For Mary Wroth herself, Jonson's admiration is profound, whether he addresses her directly as a Sidney whose name implies her status as 'fair crown of your fair sex' (*Epigrams* 103), or as 'Nature's index' of beauty, creativity, and talents attributed only to goddesses in the past (*Epigrams* 105), or as a Venus whose verse contains 'all Cupid's armory' and whose 'readers take,/For Venus' ceston, every line you make' (*Underwoods* 28). This last poem compliments her with the highest praise one writer can extend to another: that her work has enriched his understanding and improved his art. Jonson not only lauds her in her favourite poetic form, the sonnet (a form he otherwise never used), but also claims that after copying out her sonnets he has become 'A better lover, and much better poet'. Mary Ellen Lamb describes Jonson's sonnet as a 'sexual response to a seductive text',[4] but she perhaps makes too much of Jonson's use of the word 'lover', a term he frequently chooses to describe friendship, as in the closing address of the dedicatory letter prefixed to *Epicoene*. W. David Kay has suggested that Mary Wroth might be the Charis of Jonson's *A Celebration of Charis in Ten Lyric Pieces*, and points out the similarity between the chaste Venus of the fifth lyric, 'His Discourse with Cupid', and *Epigrams* 105.[5] The transfer of verses from the fifth and fourth lyrics to *The Devil is an Ass* (II.vi), and the stalemated love affair in the finale of both play and poem, make other suggestive links with Wroth, of whom Jonson told Drummond, 'My lord Lisle's daughter, my Lady Wroth, is unworthily married on a jealous husband' (*Conversations* 359–60). But to see the bond between Wroth and Jonson as essentially erotic is, I think, to miss the esteem Jonson clearly feels for her within the larger cultural context of the Sidneys as artists, participants,[6] and patrons, admiration expressed in the dedication to *The Alchemist*, and in Jonson's excursions into the pastoral mode in *The May Lord*, now lost, and *The Sad Shepherd*, left unfinished at his death. Barbara Smith has pointed out that Jonson and Wroth shared such poetic practices as using classical models and names, preferring the plain style, and, especially, writing to affirm their sense of self during personal setbacks (troubled marriages, alienation from court, accusations of slander).[7]

Frances's dilemma in *The Devil is an Ass* seems to owe something to Wroth's, especially in Jonson's perception of the difference between the social role a woman performs and her private self whose hidden resources enable her to act against or subvert conventional male labels limiting women's identity to maid, wife, widow, or whore – that is, limiting her to her sexual relations with men.[8] If Jonson discussed her projects with her, or had access to early versions of *Urania,* which she may have begun writing as early as 1615, although the consensus is that she wrote most of it between 1618–20, then he would have had an understanding of how Wroth dealt with her anger at the constraints imposed on her gender: she was writing, or intending to write, a romance about heroic women whose 'expressions of permissible female sexuality are not always confined to the marriage bed' and who demonstrate their worth through their psychological victories over their own rage[9] – a stoical strength with which Jonson could identify, and which he renders in Frances Fitzdottrel.

In the gender wars activated by unhappy marriage in early modern life, the chief question regarding wives seems to be whether women have the right to rearrange their lives, as Jonson suggests in *The Devil is an Ass,* or must submit to male authority. In the Fitzdottrel marriage, like many others of the period, property and sexuality coalesce as the chief factor contributing to the wife's discomfort. Conduct books and sermons debate the equality of the sexes with predictable results: usually the wife is considered to be at fault if it happens that she is more competent or more intelligent than her husband in money matters; her job is to endure, and her only recourse is prayer.[10] But clergymen are not always aware of shifting attitudes in their flocks: when William Gouge preached in Blackfriars against a wife's disposing of family goods without her husband's consent, 'much exception was taken' in his congregation.[11] Despite the common law fiction of coverture, that a wife or *feme covert* had no independent legal identity apart from her husband, in practice wives maintained during marriage substantial property interests of their own, usually depending on their husbands' good will and on property settlements made before marriage.[12] But unhappy marriage put a strain on the wife and the property. Anne Clifford's struggle to gain control of her estate in Westmorland, ultimately successful after 40 years and two marriages, was a constant bone of contention in her marriage to the Earl of Dorset, who wanted her to accept a cash settlement and sign a statement giving up her rights to her male Clifford relatives. During May 1616 when Anne 'would not consent to the agreements', her husband barred her from Knole, the principal marital residence, separated her from her child, refused conjugal visits, and warned her repeatedly that she 'was undone for ever' if she did not concede – all this during the month in which her mother, her chief supporter, was dying. Although Anne had support from the queen and a few of her ladies, she was repeatedly harassed not only by Dorset and the Cliffords, but also, in January 1617, by the king, his most eminent advisers, and his lawyers. Significantly, Anne did not submit, even though the king himself 'grew in a great chaff'.[13] In this case, dispute over a wife's property, and male appropriation of the heiress's right, led to a punitive and demoralizing marital situation. Lady Elizabeth Hatton experienced similar struggles with her second husband, Sir Edward Coke, in part (like Frances Fitzdottrel) because of an inadequate marriage settlement, despite the fact that her family, the Cecils, abounded in competent legal minds. Coke took legal control of Lady Hatton's rents, conveyed some of her property to his own servants and family, defrauded her of income for herself and her children, and, against her will, used her Hatton stepdaughters as pawns in arranged marriages to further his own ambitions. Coke's breaches of trust, including physical violence and kidnapping, made a mockery of their marriage, much of which she spent living apart from her husband.[14] Interestingly enough, she rejoined him for moral support during the period of his disgrace: Coke was removed from the bench on 16 November 1616 as Lord Chief Justice after his arrogant mishandling of the Overbury murder trials, his implication in the Cockayne project, and his peculation of Crown funds in the matter of Sir Christopher Hatton's bond – all instances in which his own self-serving conduct destroyed his credibility with the king and various court factions. Jonson satirized him as Sir Paul Eitherside in *The Devil is an Ass*.[15]

Where adultery rather than property was the apparent primary issue in an unhappy marriage, the sexual double standard blames the wife, no matter what the marital provocation. Dorothy Leigh, in *The Mother's Blessing*, 1616, gives the standard view of female comportment: 'Some of the Fathers have written that it is not enough for a woman to be chaste, but even so to behave her self that no man may think or deem her to be unchaste'; that is, she is responsible for how others think of her, and the injustice of her predicament is irrelevant. But Leigh modifies this position by arguing that men force women to be idle and immodest in dress (as indeed Fitzdottrel forces Frances), and the result is that 'The vain words of the man and the idle ears of the woman beget unchaste thoughts oftentimes in the one, which may bring forth much wickedness in them both.'[16] Nevertheless, adultery was perceived as essentially a woman's crime, because the consequence of a wife's adultery (a spurious child) was a threat to social order and degree.[17] The good wife of conduct books, like Frances Fitzdottrel in Act I of *The Devil is an Ass*, is enclosed and silent: 'As her body is locked within the walls of the house, her tongue is locked in her mouth.'[18] Her antithesis is the wife who objects to abuse and finds solace in another union, as Frances Fitzdottrel contemplates. When Penelope Rich, following judicial separation from Lord Rich for adultery in 1605, married her lover, Charles Blount, in a ceremony officiated by William Laud, King James refused to recognize the match, because she was the guilty party and merely separated, not divorced. Although the legal status of the marriage was never clear, the scandal branded Lady Rich a whore, and when Blount died the following year, she was denied all rights at the funeral and in the settlement of his estate, despite his will.[19] In a later scandal 'barely veiled' as fiction in *Urania*,[20] Mary Wroth related the story of Lord Hay's marriage to Honora Denny, who, unhappy with her abusive husband, committed adultery; her own father, Sir Edward Denny, retaliated by trying to kill her. Denny later accused Wroth of libelling him 'in that spitefull and scornfull passa[g]e', and generally of spreading 'lascivious tales'; her book was withdrawn from the market.[21]

Wroth's representation of her own marriage in *Love's Victory* and the shadowing of her own love triangle (Sir Robert Wroth, Mary Wroth, and William Herbert, Earl of Pembroke) with her uncle's (Lord Rich, Penelope Rich, Sir Philip Sidney) in *Urania* suggest the correspondences between Wroth's marital difficulties, both actual and fictionalized, and Frances Fitzdottrel's dilemma in Jonson's play. Both writers represent a woman who loves one man, while married to another. This extramarital longing does not incur authorial disapproval, in fact, the story reflects badly on the husband, a crude insensitive boor who reaps the anger which the situation sows. Both construct their stories within a complex world of sophisticated topicality, deliberately recalling other scandals of the period in order to create a social and metaphysical spectrum of right and wrong, in which a sincere love, even if adulterous, seems nobler than any alternative. Although Jonson does not allude directly to Wroth's personal history in *The Devil is an Ass*, the many intersections are suggestive. The Wroth/Pembroke love affair, sufficiently well-known in 1616 that Queen Anne expelled Wroth from court, may have begun as early as 1603, perhaps the cause of the rift between Pembroke and his mother, Mary Sidney Herbert.[22] (Jonson makes it clear that Wittipol's love for Frances is of long standing, though undeclared). This prior emotional commitment may also explain the 'unkindness' between the Wroths only two weeks after their wedding; Sir Robert Sidney wrote to his wife, after meeting their new son-in-law by chance, of 'somewhat that doth discontent him; but the particulars I could not get out of him, only he protests that he cannot take any exceptions to his wife, nor her carriage towards him. It were very soon for unkindness to begin.'[23] But Robert Wroth's complaint came as no surprise, since the Sidneys had already noticed problems. Mary had appended 'words of grief' to the end of one letter from her mother to her father, and both parents discussed it later as 'a great misfortune to us all', and prayed for 'amendment of it' in time.[24] Neither the Wroths nor the Pembrokes, both married in 1604, had children for a decade or more: Mary Wroth's legitimate son James, born one month before her husband's death in 1614, died in 1616; the Pembrokes had one son who died at birth in 1616, and another who died in infancy in 1620. The survivors of this foursome were the illegitimate children Mary Wroth had with Pembroke: William, born in 1615, and Katherine, born in 1619, both supported by the Sidney circle. In a letter to his wife, Wroth's father wrote: 'You have done very well in putting Will away, for it had been too great a shame he should have stayed in the house.'[25] The foster mother with whom the child was 'put away' may have been Judith Fox, who in her 1636 will left William £10 for a memorial ring (a more substantial amount than her bequests to her own brothers) and the residue of her estate to Katherine, with Mary Wroth acting as executor.[26]

This evidence of enduring family loyalty is pertinent to the treatment of adultery in *The Devil is an Ass*. As far as can be determined from the birth of her children, Wroth decided not to consummate her love affair with Pembroke until after her husband's death, a decision Jonson seems to reflect in Frances Fitzdottrel's decision to reject Wittipol's suit. This conjecture finds support in Robert Wroth's will (14 March 1614), specifically stating that he was on good terms with his wife, whose 'sincere love, loyalty, virtuous conversation, and behaviour towards me, have deserved a far better recompense.'[27] Mary undertook to repay his debts of £23,000, even after most of his estate, with the death of their son, passed to Robert Wroth's brothers. Her behaviour echoes what Josephine Roberts sees as the 'repeated pattern of a stoical feminine triumph over enforced marriage' that characterizes *Urania*, as in the stories of Bellamira, Melasinda, Lisia (whose parents marry her to a great lord 'so dull a piece of flesh as this, or any Country need know', [p. 599]), and particularly Limena, whose husband tortures her when she confesses to loving another man, even though 'that unseparable love I beare him, was before I knewe you, or perfectly my self, and shall be while I am, yet alwayes thus in a vertuous, and religious fashion' (p. 12). Although she survives his abuse (which Roberts explains as a 'metaphorically expanded' version of Wroth's marital distress) and ultimately marries her lover, Limena illustrates 'the sensational suffering that a woman must undergo in order to have her own choice'.[28] John Leeke, one of Mary Wroth's servants, reveals the misery of her married life in his description of a relative's husband as 'the foulest churl in the world: he hath only one virtue, that he seldom cometh sober to bed; a true imitation of Sir Robert Wroth.'[29] Wroth's depiction of her husband in her play, *Love's Victory*, like Jonson's Fitzdottrel in *The Devil is an Ass*, is broadly comic: as Rustic, he is a clown who features in many worth/Wroth and cozened/cousined puns, tellingly during the mock-funeral for Musella/Mary Wroth and Philisses/ Pembroke:

> *Lacon*: No worth did live, which in her had not spring,
>   And she thus gone, to her grave worth doth bring.
> *Rustic*: I liked her well, but she ne'er cared for me,
>   Yet am I sorry we thus parted be.
>   (V.v.24–7)

> *Rustic*: When Venus wills, men cannot but obey,
>   Yet this I'll swear, I'm plainly cozened here!
>   But 'tis all one, the bargain may prove dear.
>   (V.vii.116–18)[30]

In his critique of Jonson's 'To Robert Wroth' (*Forest* 3), Gary Waller reads Jonson as delivering a back-handed compliment that progresses to a final sneer, in praising Wroth for a bucolic way of life that his wife scorns, particularly in seeming to commend him for not being Pembroke.[31] Although many readers may resist Waller's interpretation, or want to avoid seeing too direct a relation between dramatic characters and historical persons, *Love's Victory* depicts in the husband/husbandman Rustic a man without wit or art, close in spirit to Jonson's philistine Fitzdottrel:

Rustic: Truly, I cannot riddle, I was not taught
        These tricks of wit; my thoughts ne'er higher
                                                wrought
        Than how to mark a beast, or drive a cow
        To feed, or else with art to hold a plough,
        Which if I knew, you surely soon would find
        A matter more of worth than these odd things,
        Which never profit, but some laughter brings;
        These others be of body, and of mind.
Philisses: Spoke like a husband ...
                                        (IV.i.391–9)

Whether we see Mary Wroth's marriage as tragic or comic, the
excuse for adultery is plain, but so too are the personal scruples
that prevent a virtuous woman from betraying herself, even when
life has apparently betrayed her.

In *The Devil is an Ass*, Frances is similarly conscientious, and
Jonson emphasizes her ethical stand by placing her story in the
morally debased context of the Frances Howard trials, still in
process when the play was first performed in November, 1616.
Frances Howard's transgressions (and those Fitzdottrel begins to
accuse his wife of in V.viii when he is 'possessed') include witchcraft, adultery, and murder, vices which breed so rapidly in
London that even Satan finds them hard to top:

            We still strive to breed
    And rear 'em up new ones; but they do not stand
    When they come there: they turn 'em on our hands.
    And it is feared they have a stud o' their own
    Will put down ours. Both our breed and trade
    Will suddenly decay, if we prevent not.
                                        (I.i.105–10)[32]

During the Essex divorce trial of 1613, Frances Howard, then
Countess of Essex, sought an annulment of her marriage on the
grounds of the Earl's impotence, which some thought to be the result
of *maleficium*, especially when a search revealed that the Countess's
virginity was still intact after three years of cohabitation. Mary
Woods, a wisewoman, accused Howard of approaching her for a
powder to poison her husband, and other evidence suggests that
Howard had been considering poison as early as 1610.[33] Anne

Turner, 'a shady individual rather like Jonson's Lady Tailbush ... a fashion adviser and confidante' of Howard's, was believed to have conspired on her behalf with Dr Simon Forman to destroy Essex's sexual powers by witchcraft, and was later executed for her participation in the murder of Sir Thomas Overbury, the man Howard feared would prevent her marriage to Robert Carr, Earl of Somerset, once her divorce from Essex was obtained.[34] Fitzdottrel invokes the names of Gresham, Forman, Franklin, and Savory, all implicated in the Overbury case, when he tries to conjure the devil (I.ii.2–3), and even promises to lend the devil his wife, 'If he had a mind to her' (I.ii.45–50). Ironically, Pug does appear after this promise of adultery, but is beaten (II.ii) when he tries to claim it. Not all of Howard's contemporaries believed her capable of, or wholly responsible for, the vices attributed to her. Sir Simonds D'Ewes records a Captain Field's testimony that she was 'of the best nature, and the sweetest disposition of all her father's children; exceeding them also in that delicacy and comeliness of her person.'[35] Anne Clifford wrote in her diary for 24 May, 1616, that Frances Howard had been arraigned after confessing, and was 'much pitied by all beholders', but that Somerset 'stood much upon his innocency'.[36] The implied criticism of Somerset reappears in Mary Wroth's account of the story in *Urania*. She too presents a compassionate view of Frances Howard, and places the blame squarely on Somerset. According to Wroth, Howard loved Somerset before she married Essex; presumably Wroth means before the marriage could be consummated. Although Frances Howard had been married in 1606 at age 13 to Essex, then 15, they did not cohabit for three years, while Essex travelled abroad and she participated in court life, dancing in masques as Wroth and Anne Clifford had done.[37] Subsequently, between 1609–12, she remained a virgin. The crime, in Wroth's retelling, is that Somerset 'so wrapt in the heaven of it, as he cannot contain himself', boasted to Overbury of this 'wench he lov'd, and who so dearly loved him, as for his sake she has liv'd a Maiden-wife, and would have ever, had she not enjoyd him'; Howard, furious at how 'cruelly, vildly, and scornfully' he had 'defamd' her, vowed revenge (pp. 564–5). Wroth does not include the murder of Overbury – in her version, Howard avenges herself directly on the tattling lover by having him whipped – but she does sympathize with Howard as a victim of passion and treachery.[38]

As a foil to Frances Fitzdottrel, Frances Howard represents a formidable prospect for the would-be adulteress. David Lindley puts the case clearly both for the Essex divorce and the Overbury murder trials:

> By suing for divorce at all Frances Howard flouted the doctrine of wifely obedience; and by charging her husband with impotence she raised the fearful spectre of male inadequacy. At the same time her action in bringing matters to open court challenged the conventional requirements of female silence and chastity.
>
> ...
>
> For ... dishonoured women there were but two alternatives, to suffer in silence, or to visit revenge upon themselves by taking their own life. Lucrece by her suicide becomes the truly heroic female, passive and quiescent; Frances Howard, on the other hand, by attempting her own revenge becomes the type of the malicious woman.[39]

Even if Jonson felt some sneaking sympathy for her, since he himself had quarrelled with Overbury over the propositioning of the Countess of Rutland, he still uses Frances Howard as a tacit bugbear to frighten Frances Fitzdottrel with public exposure and trial should she leave her husband. Perhaps we might have learned more if Jonson's pastoral *The May Lord* were extant: it is not clear whether this piece was a verse satire, a prose narrative, or a play, but clearly it was topical: 'His own name is Alkin, Ethra the Countess of Bedford, Mogibell Overbury, the old Countess of Suffolk [Frances Howard's mother] an enchantress, other names given to Somerset's lady, Pembroke, the Countess of Rutland, Lady Wroth'.[40] On a more positive note, he didn't expunge the masques written for Frances Howard from the 1616 Folio, and may even have admired her stoical and perhaps misplaced loyalty to Somerset in accepting sole responsibility for the murder. He may also have had the opportunity to assess her guilt privately: when the murder charge was first laid in 1615, Somerset was sent to the Tower, but Frances, pregnant, was confined to the home of Jonson's patron and near neighbour, Lord D'Aubigny, in Blackfriars.

So what freedom should a wife be permitted? The freedom to choose virtue is quite different from the imposition of virtue on a wife as her husband's chattel. Fitzdottrel keeps his wife locked up and sets his servant to watch her. In policing his marriage, he demonstrates the ills of a bad husband, as Rachel Speght describes them in *A Mouzell for Melastomus*: he despises the wife's good advice, keeps her idle so that she cannot use her talents to the 'comfort of her owne soule', and forces her to 'fulfill the evill command of her husband',[41] as when he pushes Frances to wear cosmetics like Ladies Tailbush and Eitherside, or to take lessons in seductive behaviour from the Spanish Lady. Fitzdottrel maintains Frances in such elaborate dress that even the devil is confused by the contradiction between her chaste demeanour and provocative array: 'Hell! Why is she so brave?' Pug asks, 'No woman dressed with so much care and study,/ Doth dress herself in vain.' (II.v.11, 22–3). Speght also argues that, since marriage is intended as a 'mutuall love', 'husbands should not account their wives as their vassals, but as those that are heires together of the grace of life' (p. 22). When Fitzdottrel's desire for a new cloak outweighs any consideration for his wife, his cupidity pushes her to reappraise her married life, in which mutuality and equal benefit have no place. Her first action on stage is to blush (I.vi.1). Over her objections, her husband forces her to participate in his charade despite the gossip it will provoke; he, in a broadly topical gibe, claims that all 'great houses' have done something in any seven-year period to warrant being 'laughed at' (I.vi.18–21). Although his 'one main mortal ... fear' is to 'prove a cuckold' (I.ii.12–13), he sells fifteen minutes of his wife's time to Wittipol, and thinks that merely by forbidding 'all lip-work ... melting joints and fingers' (I.ii.191, 199–100), he has prevented adultery. Only the material world weighs with him: words, ideas, feelings, none of these intangibles register. Wroth's Rustic shares this insensitivity in *Love's Victory*:

> *Philisses*: Rustic, faith, tell me, hast thou ever loved?
> *Rustic*: What call you love? I've been to trouble moved,
>   As when my best cloak hath by chance been torn,
>   I have lived wishing till it mended were,
>   And but so lovers do.
>
>   (II.i.85–9)

Wrapped up in his magnificent second-hand cloak, 'convinced he has made a brilliant deal',[42] Fitzdottrel simply cannot register the erotic exchange of the cloak scene, in which Wittipol's adulterous offer to 'but reach a hand forth to her freedom' (I.vi.117) seems heroic, not tainted.

As if to offset the ostentatious richness of the cloak, Wittipol's rhetoric depends on an argument from starkness, stillness, reticence, and absence, a negative verbal strategy that mirrors Frances's mute restraint. He employs his time 'thriftily' (I.vi.76) and persuades by implication, describing the tactics he will not employ. He refuses to speak of her beauty: 'I'll save myself that eloquence of your glass/Which can speak these things better to you than I' (I.vi.80–81). He seeks 'no witnesses to prove' (I.vi.91) her husband's inadequacies and her own frustration, abandoned to 'cold/Sheets' by night (I.vi.92–3), and by day 'Locked up all from all society' (I.vi.101). Wittipol's depiction of the emptiness of Frances's life, his consciousness of her 'own too sensible sufferings' (I.vi.105) and his offer of love 'in equality' (I.vi.126), woo with stunningly erotic effect, particularly when Wittipol *speaks for her* (SD, 153). His act goes beyond ventriloquism, because he does not treat her as a dummy (Fitzdottrel does that): Wittipol stands in physically as well as verbally for Frances, simulating her posture and her pitch as he echoes her thoughts. It is cross-dressing transferred to voice and stance, and a prelude to his later cross-dressing as the Spanish Lady. When Fitzdottrel forbade 'all lip-work', he could not have imagined the seductive foreplay Frances experiences when Wittipol metaphorically puts his tongue in her mouth. Without her uttering any complaint, he knows her 'unequal, and so sordid match', her 'bondage' to a 'moonling' who has 'let his wife out to be courted,/And at a price, proclaims his asinine nature.' (I.vi.155–65 *passim*), and offers himself as a gallant rescuer from a life of humiliation. His final words project a fantasy of future fulfilment far more arousing than any mere embrace, because he has ignited her imagination, long dulled by the boredom imposed by Fitzdottrel:

> Do not think yet, lady,
> But I can kiss, and touch, and laugh, and whisper,
> And do those crowning courtships too, for which
> Day and the public have allowed no name.
> (I.vi.199–202)

In advocating Frances's right to be loved by a sensitive and perceptive soul-mate, Wittipol is 'on the make' undoubtedly, but differently from Jonson's usual competitively aggressive males. In this scene, Wittipol is not posturing to impress other men; although Manly acts as his second in the duel of wits, Fitzdottrel is not equipped to respond in kind. Instead, Wittipol speaks directly to Frances like one of Mary Wroth's sympathetic men in *Urania*, who 'cross gender boundaries to deny the construction of compassion as a primarily female trait'.[43]

Through Wittipol's compassion, Frances Fitzdottrel identifies two goals necessary to her survival: agency and equality. In Constance Jordan's words, she needs to establish that 'performance is distinct from position and posture: a competent, courageous woman is not a virago and her autonomy need not invariably entail rebelliousness'.[44] Jonson uses Frances to design a plot that also appears repeatedly in Mary Wroth's works:[45] a woman determined to shape her destiny first alerts her audience to the harmful effects on women of continual subordination. One effect is to create a woman vulnerable to adultery; another is to justify the abrogation of her marriage vows and her choice of another by demonstrating the abuses she suffers. In the Fitzdottrel household, the husband denies his wife any role appropriate to her education and rank: she is not allowed to manage their domestic affairs nor even to choose her own wardrobe, has no say in the family finances, no social life, no companion or waiting-woman, no establishment nor expectation of children. She is not allowed to show any initiative whatsoever. Her husband's unreasonable and objectifying jealousy undermines her self-respect: she becomes 'a fruit that's worth the stealing,/ And therefore worth the watching' (II.i.159–60). Visitors might secretly 'convey letters', or 'youths, disguised/Like country wives, with cream, and marrow-puddings' might seduce her into bawdy acts (II.i.164–5). Fitzdottrel contains her in a back room for fear she will flirt from the window with a gallant in the street, refuses her 'paper, pen, and ink', searches her food for messages (II.ii.90–102), and eavesdrops 'planted i'your hole' on the stairs or behind the hangings (II.iii.6–7). Overwhelmed by the opportunity for sexual revenge on 'such a nupson' (II.ii.77), Pug propositions his mistress in a lecherous parody of Wittipol's discreet wooing, promising to take her 'To plays, to masques, to meetings and to feasts', where she can show off her 'rigging and fine tackle' and spread her 'nets', 'fishing' for new lovers (110); Pug, like Lollio in *The Changeling*, only wants a share of her favours. But Frances spies an opportunity of another kind, and means to take advantage of it, although her natural delicacy makes her immediate goal hard to fathom. Wittipol's charms have been occupying her mind:

> I cannot get this venture of the cloak
> Out of my fancy, nor the gentleman's way
> He took, which though, 'twere strange, yet 'twas handsome
> And had a grace withal beyond the newness.
>
> (II.ii.24–7)

She cannot bear to leave him with 'no return' for his venture, and only hopes he is bright enough to interpret the apparent refusal she sends by Pug as an invitation to a rendezvous at her upstairs window behind Lincoln's Inn, thus realizing one of her husband's jealous fears – and her own refusal to be silenced. Otherwise, her wit will have 'Done the worst defeat' upon herself (II.vi.21).

Even while asserting her own agency, Frances is unable to assert her equality as unequivocally, because gender differences may make Wittipol misjudge her. Once the lovers meet, she fears that her appearance at the window will strike Wittipol as an iconographic admission of 'easiness' (51) for which her unfortunate marriage may not supply sufficient 'excuse', let alone 'reason' (56,57). He sees Frances as 'Nature violenced' (59), but first as 'Love' and 'Beauty' (58), and his desire is to possess her, not necessarily to help her empower herself. She seeks legal support for her right to protection from an abusive husband who should not have unlimited prerogatives before the law. Nevertheless, particularly in the window scene, she craves Wittipol's caresses. She wordlessly responds to his love-making over 56 lines, while '*He grows more familiar in his courtship, plays with her paps, kisseth her hands, &c*' (SD 70), a stage direction that reads as disturbingly vulgar, but should not be played that way, because nothing in Wittipol's language or her silence suggests vulgarity.[46] And Frances is quite capable of voicing protest, as she did when Pug, 'Your little worm that loves you', threw himself at her to claim a kiss (II.ii.125–32). But with Wittipol, Frances accepts his argument that the unworthy Fitzdottrel is 'the cause/Why anything is to be done upon him:/ And nothing called an injury, misplaced.' (II.vi.63) – the same argument Jonson uses in 'Elegy 19' (ll. 22–3) – and drinks in his passionate appreciation of breasts, hands, hair, face, skin, chin, lips, and eyes, a paean that rises to song, borrowed heavily from the fourth and fifth lyrics of *A Celebration of Charis*. What brings her back to earth and reminds her of the real issues – legal autonomy and her own agency in asserting it – is, ironically, the sudden appearance of her husband. For her, the lure of adultery is considerably diminished by the wife-beating that follows, an incident in which the lover is helpless to protect the woman he loves, except by withdrawing. Even more humiliating is that Fitzdottrel does not beat her for entertaining a lover; he beats her to protect himself from Wittipol, who intimidates him: 'Slight, if you strike me, I'll strike your mistress. *He strikes his wife*' (II.vii.16SD). Caught in a compromising situation which bears out the worst construction of women's behaviour, seduced by Wittipol's gentleness and admiration, having not yet decided what to do or at what speed to do it, Frances is persuaded by the shame of this final experience to seek a remedy which will give her independence. Fitzdottrel's threat of divorce – 'I could now find i' my heart to make/Another lady duchess and depose you' (II.vii.40–41) – is the last straw at a time when adultery was cause for a husband to bring suit, but cruelty was no cause for a wife.

In Frances's quest for agency and equality, the most persistent stumbling-block is that women are victims of contradictory binary reasoning. If she wants legitimacy in love, she has to accept Fitzdottrel, not Wittipol; if she wants to commit adultery, she has to identify with Ladies Tailbush and Eitherside, not her own finer feelings. In her particular hell of black and white choices, there are no other discretionary shades for solace. She comes to realize, as Gary Waller argues of Mary Wroth's heroines, that she may empower herself only 'with the emotional and physical retreat ... into the roles that have been assigned to her as a woman', on the understanding that her action 'may be tactical, not merely reactive'.[47] The crux is Fitzdottrel's decision to send Frances to an 'academy for women' (II.viii.20) to learn to be fashionable, although fashion and public life imply harlotry in the cultural assumptions of the day. The double-bind of cultural expectations for fashionable women appears in the story told by Wittipol, in his disguise as the Spanish Lady:

I'll tell you, madam, I saw i' the court of Spain once,
A lady fall i' the King's sight, along.
And there she lay, flat spread as an umbrella,
Her hoop here cracked; no man durst reach a hand
To help her, till the guarda-duennas came,

Who is the person only'allowed to touch
A lady there: and he but by the finger.
                                    (IV.iv.79–95)

In this anecdote, the fallen woman is displayed voyeuristically as a
helpless erotic object, with no agency of her own and no protection
from a rigid code. The English ladies protest such control by
arguing for an opposite extreme of 'liberty':

Eitherside: We may have our dozen of visitors, at once,
      Make love to us.
Tailbush: And before our husbands!
Eitherside: Husband?
      As I am honest, Tailbush, I do think
      If nobody should love me but my poor husband,
      I should e'en hang myself.
                                    (IV.iv.93–8)

The fashionable focus is on vanity and promiscuity, not on love and
mutuality. Adultery in this social circle begins as 'light' behaviour
that imitates 'dishonesty' and progresses to coach travel, dance,
wanting to 'Hear talk and bawdy', and finally to 'do anything' provided a woman has 'young company' who are 'brave, or lords'
(IV.iv.158–68). Now educating himself as a duke, Fitzdottrel agrees,
'It is civility to deny us nothing' – much to the devil's admiration:
'You talk of a university! Why, Hell is/A grammar school to this!'
(IV.iv.169–71). Fashion converts the world of black and white
choices into a world of blacker and blacker choices, as Fitzdottrel
now instructs his wife that 'bawdry' is civil discourse, and that
she must be 'coming', that is, sexually aggressive, or lose 'all her
opportunities/With hoping to be forced' (IV.iv.181–2).
     Wittipol has shared with Frances the labyrinthine difficulty of
making choices by speaking in her voice in I.vi. and by suffering in
her helplessness in II.vii. His impersonation of the Spanish Lady
moves him away from the inversions of Jonson's London, where
men and women become equals in baseness, and instead lets him
experience the alternative gender equality theorized by the Sidney
family. In Sir Philip Sidney's *The New Arcadia*, androgyny appears
to be 'the foundation for a defence of woman and more especially
of woman's rule';[48] the story of Pyrocles, who cross-dresses as the
virile maiden Zelmane in order to be near the woman he loves,

illustrates how a man gains strength from the feminine principle and becomes a more compassionate, sensitive male. Although Musidorus, Pyrocles's best friend, fears that love, 'the basest and fruitlessest of all passions', has made 'reason give place to sense, and man to woman',[49] transforming Pyrocles into an Amazon, Pyrocles rejects 'the primacy of the man over woman and male over female interests'[50] – a concept Manly endorses in the last lines of *The Devil is an Ass* – by insisting that women 'are framed of nature with the same parts of the mind for the exercise of virtue as we are'; he believes that the love of a virtuous man is for the virtue he recognizes in the woman and thus love is the 'highest power of the mind' (pp. 72–3), not the lowest. The device on Zelmane's shield (Hercules with the distaff in his hand, as commanded by Omphale, with the motto, 'Never more valiant') emblematizes this union of masculine and feminine as the basis of a couple's true understanding. In borrowing this story, Jonson makes some significant changes in his treatment of adultery. Wittipol disguises himself for love, but he loves another man's wife, not his daughter, and the morality of the situation subtly alters. When Philoclea responds to her love for Zelmane, she despairs because she thinks Zelmane is a woman: 'Sin must be the mother, and shame the daughter of my affection … It is the impossibility that doth torment me; for unlawful desires are punished after the effects of enjoying, but unpossible desires are punished in the desire itself' (p. 149). Her difficulty in imagining a lesbian liaison is not identical to Frances Fitzdottrel's distress at rejecting an all-too-easily imagined adulterous liaison. The callous father Basilius, like Fitzdottrel, falls in love with the drag-male, but whereas Fitzdottrel is punished with a property-trick, Basilius is punished with a bed-trick, in which his own wife substitutes for Zelmane. The adulterous desire, even though nullified in the act, resides in the lewd patriarchal husband of Sidney's story, not in the sincere lovers of Jonson's play, and therefore does not test virtue or judgement in the same way. Like Frances in her rejection of Wittipol, Philoclea decides against a dishonourable life with Pyrocles, once she finds out who he is, and for very similar reasons: 'For dissimulation – my Pyrocles, my simplicity is such that I have hardly been able to keep a straight way; what shall I do in a crooked?' (p. 430). The sexual passion of the two lovers, in Sidney as in Jonson, remains unconsummated, even though it endures. So too in Mary Wroth's cross-dressing story in *Urania* (pp. 426–36): Leonius adopts the dress of a shepherdess to

be near his love Veralinda, and the two, recognizing their similarity, form a close friendship, including erotic play, but only on
Veralinda's understanding that they both are women. Only much
later, after lengthy separation, does Leonius reveal his masculine
identity and propose marriage.

The significant parallel in these cross-dressed lovers – Pyrocles/
Zelmane, Leonius/Leonia, and Wittipol/Spanish Lady – is that all
three attain a 'female wit' that converts them into friends. Despite
Fitzdottrel's claim, 'I ha' my female wit/ As well as my male!'
(IV.iv.154–5), when he joins the ladies for a good gossip about
fashionable life, the rest of the play illustrates that he is incapable of
balancing male and female strengths beneficially. Earlier, he had
succumbed to the masculine excesses of the abusive husband,
whose jealousy isolates, controls, and blames the wife, shifting
from verbal assault, in the shape of insults, putdowns, and threats,
to physical attack. Now, he succumbs to the worst of feminine
weakness in himself: in a reversal of conventional marital roles, he
is reduced to hysteria (in the 'possession' scene), legal containment,
and silence under the wardship of his wife. Wittipol, however, is
able to make the transition to 'most true friend', as Frances
redefines it: 'And such a one I need, but not this way.' (IV.vi.4–5).
She confesses her attraction to his 'brain and spirit', but wants to
'employ them virtuously' to save her fortune:

> 'Tis counsel that I want, and honest aids:
> And in this name I need you for a friend!
> Never in any other, for his ill
> Must not make me, sir, worse.
> (IV.vi.25–8)

Once Wittipol promises that he can love Frances's 'goodness' even
more than her beauty, he crosses the threshold into de-gendered
friendship that recognizes her right to an independent existence
and goals that have nothing to do with him. In withdrawing from
sexual entanglement to deal with her desires alone, Frances tacitly
agrees with Mary Wroth's refusal to accept herself as a prisoner of
gender, reliving myths of woman helpless in love:

> Why should wee nott loves purblind charmes resist?
> Must wee bee servile, doing what hee list?

Noe, seeke some hoste to harbour thee: I fly
Thy babish trickes, and freedome doe profess.
(P16, 9–12)

Determined to see falling in love as infantile, self-centred, and
destructive, Frances rationalizes her rejection of Wittipol, at least as
a present possibility. She prefers to be constant to her own image of
herself, capable and virtuous in her own right, outside authoritarian control, rather than make herself vulnerable to the abuses of
conventional gender assignments. Fitzdottrel, in his adulterous
pursuit of the Spanish Lady, signs over his estate to please 'her'
because, he claims, Wittipol has seduced his wife: 'I fear/The toy
will'not do me right' (IV.vii.57–8). When Wittipol sheds his disguise, Fitzdottrel understands the revelation as evidence:

Fitzdottrel: Am I the thing I feared?
Wittipol: A cuckold? No, sir,
    But you were late in possibility,
    I'll tell you so much.
                                (IV.vii.61–3)

Fitzdottrel does not believe him.

In one way or another, life in London is predicated upon adultery. The rise of capitalism and the development of monopolies,
exhaustively parodied in Merecraft's schemes, represent Londoners
as philanderers seducing the country into a destructive process that
will lay England waste. Even Wittipol describes Frances Fitzdottrel
at first as an exploitable landscape with a 'brave promontory',
'valley', 'crisped groves', and 'banks of love' (II.vi.74–87), although
he does not match the crudeness of Merecraft's, 'We poor gentlemen that want acres,/Must for our needs turn fools up, and plough
ladies/Sometimes to try what glebe they are' (III.iv.45–8).[51] This
predatory linking of sexuality and property is the polar opposite of
the trust Frances seeks. Her prodigal husband abuses her worth
because he cannot understand honour as a spiritual value; he wants
instant material gratification. Merecraft and the play's other busi-
nessmen have only customers, not friends; even kinship, represented by Merecraft and Everill, is extortionate. As Manly remarks,
'ill men's friendship/Is as unfaithful as themselves' (IV.ii.34–5). In
commenting on her debased marriage, Frances Fitzdottrel condemns both parties for the contract that allowed her husband to

spend her 'wealthy portion' because 'through my friends' neglect, no jointure [was] made me' (IV.vi.22–3). In this revision of adultery as a husband's spending his wife's rights on another, what the husband fears at home as physical betrayal, the wife experiences as economic betrayal. Although English common law deemed a wife's property belonged to her husband, the court of chancery established the married woman's equitable rights: the device of the trust allowed a wife the use of her own separate estate through a third party, who was compelled by law to fulfil his obligation to her. Egerton, Lord Chancellor and thus presiding judge in the court of chancery in 1616, gave his opinion on such trusts:

> that if a feme covert doe purloyne her husbands money or goods and putteth such money into other men's hands whoethere with doe buy land to her use – he [Egerton] will not releeve the heyre or Exec[utor] of that husband to have the Lands or the money restored neither such a husband himself. But said he satt not there to releeve fooles and buzzards that cannot keepe theire wives fingrings or that cannot be good enough for theire wives.[52]

Such a trust is not necessarily a sign of a woman's emancipation or independence in a modern or feminist sense; Amy Erickson points out that it may simply 'be a means of removing marital property from liability for the husband's debts',[53] and this certainly seems to be Frances's object. Trust, legally and spiritually, is what Frances wants from Wittipol, an ideal of equitable friendship that affirms the possibility of a non-sexual relationship between men and women. The cultural bars to such a friendship are significant: males associated with other males for intellectual and social intercourse (as Wittipol does with Manly), and associated with females for sexual intercourse.[54] A contemporary verse written during the Somerset case, for example, laments the fact that the Earl 'preferred the love of a woman to the true affection of his male friend, Overbury.'[55] What Frances achieves in her friendship with Wittipol, however, validates the worth of both in a virtuous voluntary bond between equals, based on a reciprocal exchange of faith. As Robert Evans points out, Jonson distinguishes between true and false friendship in 'An Epistle to Master Art[ur] Squib' (*Underwoods* 45) by warning against 'a kindred from the purse' (l. 10):

Those are poor ties, depend on those false ends,
'Tis virtue alone, or nothing that knits friends.
(ll. 11–12)

In the financial imagery of the poem, friendship is, like money, a
powerful currency that purchases social credit.[56] In *The Devil is an
Ass*, friendship tells the 'truths' that secure Frances's 'equal right'
(V.viii.155, 165).

How does this rate as a happy ending? Wittipol, as critics seeking
a romantic conclusion remark, demonstrates proof of 'his commitment, ardour and tender care' as a lover by performing the only
decent act available to him.[57] But this view focuses on Wittipol's
loss, rather than Frances's gain. Her achievement is a measure of
contentment in a situation that otherwise defies peace of mind.
Frances embarks on a period of virtual autonomy in which she can
prove herself capable of constancy, as Mary Wroth did in defer-
ring the consummation of her love for Pembroke until after her
husband's death. She cannot choose a lover because she already has
a husband, although Fitzdottrel's sickbed finale suggests that he
may not be around for long. The stage-icon of Fitzdottrel, in bed
for the last scene, presents him as ill and dispossessed in two
senses: dispossessed of property and of demons. Both possessions
were false, because he ignored his proper role as husband and his
opportunity for real possession by Pug. Like Morose at the end of
Epicoene, Fitzdottrel has lost all his status as a functioning male. He
looks sick, feels sick, and is deemed sick and worthless by others.
The final vision of the bedridden husband, surrounded by not
exactly well-wishing survivors of his schemes, strongly favours the
idea of Fitzdottrel as virtually dead and incapable of resurrection.
Pseudo-widowhood is Frances's happy ending. Her self-respect
demands that she repudiate adultery as personified by Mistresses
Tailbush and Eitherside, or as implied by Frances Howard's crimes;
clearly no lover at all is better than an association with that vora-
cious trio. The play is comprehensible in light of Mary Wroth's
choices: first, as a wife, and then as a widow, with power over her
estates and the determination to decide her own future as a lover, a
mother, and a writer. Gary Waller describes Mary Wroth, particularly in the decade after 1614, as a woman who 'carved out of a
disadvantageous situation an unusually independent life' and
whose writings leave a record of 'a determined, even stubborn,
woman, intent on maintaining her independence wrestling with

legal and manorial negotiations, not afraid to use her court contacts and very much standing on her dignity.'[58] Frances too refuses to be passive and merely decorative: she resists new entrapment, no matter how enticing, in order to remain true to herself. What the 'too worthy' (V.viii.160) Frances gains at the end of the play is her self and a private space in which she can maintain an integrated identity. When Pamphilia returns home near the end of Book III in *Urania*, she grieves over her losses, 'yet she lost not her selfe; for her government continued just and brave, like that Lady she was, wherein she shewed her heart was not to be stirr'd, though her private fortunes shooke round about her' (p. 484). Closure is not a feature of *Urania*; Pamphilia's story is not over yet, and neither is Frances Fitzdottrel's. Her retreat into estate management allows her a legitimate means of asserting herself and recuperating her losses, before – in the tradition of the Sidney romance – setting forth again.

Notes

1.   Ben Jonson, *The Complete Poems*, ed. by George Parfitt (London: Penguin, 1975), Appendix 2, pp. 459–80, ll. 368–71. References are to lines in *Conversations*. Henceforth all citations included within parentheses in the text. All citations of Jonson's poetry are also from this edition.
2.   Robert C. Evans, *Ben Jonson and the Poetics of Patronage* (Lewisburg: Bucknell University Press, 1989), p. 127.
3.   'Sonett [F6]' in Josephine A. Roberts (ed.), *The Poems of Lady Mary Wroth* (Baton Rouge/London: Louisiana State University Press, 1983). All references to Wroth's poem are cited parenthetically by number, as in this edition. Roberts suggests (p. 42) that Wroth may have been circulating the poetry in this collection among her friends, including Jonson, from as early as 1612.
4.   Mary Ellen Lamb, *Gender and Authorship in the Sidney Circle* (Madison: University of Wisconsin Press, 1990), pp. 154–5.
5.   W. David Kelly, *Ben Jonson: A Literary Life* (Basingstoke: Macmillan, 1995), pp. 134–5.
6.   Wroth danced in *The Masque of Blackness* (1605) and *The Masque of Beauty* (1608), in the latter being particularly praised for her gracefulness; the compliment as well as the charm of the masque itself prompted her father, Sir Robert Sidney, to purchase several copies of it for the pleasure of reading the verse and giving it to his friends. See Roberts, *Poems of Lady Mary Wroth*, pp. 13–14.
7.   Barbara Smith, *The Women of Ben Jonson's Poetry: Female Representations in the Non-Dramatic Verse* (Aldershot, Hants.: Scolar Press, 1995), pp. 70–71.

8. For a fuller discussion of women's 'doubleness' as enabling agency, see Heather L. Weidemann, 'Theatricality and Female Identity in Mary Wroth's *Urania*', in *Reading Mary Wroth: Representing Alternatives in Early Modern England*, ed. by Naomi J. Miller and Gary Waller (Knoxville: University of Tennessee Press, 1991), pp. 191–209.

9. Lamb, *Gender and Authorship*, pp. 142–3.

10. Margaret R. Sommerville, *Sex and Subjection: Attitudes to Women in Early Modern Society* (London: Arnold, 1995), p. 41. See also Constance Jordan, 'Renaissance Women and the Question of Class', in *Sexuality and Gender in Early Modern Europe: Institutions, Texts, Images*, ed. by James Grantham Turner (Cambridge: Cambridge University Press, 1993), esp. pp. 93–4; and Anthony Fletcher, *Gender, Sex, and Subordination in England, 1500–1800* (New Haven and London: Yale University Press, 1995), esp. pp. 161–70.

11. Amy Louise Erickson, *Women and Property in Early Modern England* (London and New York: Routledge, 1993), p. 9, citing Susan Amussen.

12. Erickson, *Women and Property*, pp. 19, 101, and 236.

13. Anne Clifford's diary entries for 1616–17 are reprinted in Elspeth Graham, Hilary Hinds, Elaine Hobby and Helen Wilcox (eds), *Her Own Life: Autobiographical Writings by Seventeenth-Century Englishwomen* (London and New York: Routledge, 1989), pp. 35–53. See especially pp. 41–5.

14. Laura Nosworthy, *The Lady of Bleeding Heart Yard: Lady Elizabeth Hatton, 1578–1646* (London: John Murray, 1935), pp. 8–72.

15. In addition to Nosworthy, see Robert C. Evans, *Jonson and the Contexts of His Time* (Lewisburg: Bucknell University Press, 1994), pp. 64–71 and 77–86; and David Lindley, *The Trials of Frances Howard: Fact and Fiction at the Court of King James* (London and New York: Routledge, 1994), pp. 145–93.

16. Dorothy Leigh, *The Mother's Blessing; or, The Godly Counsel of a Gentlewoman Not Long Since Deceased, Left Behind Her For Her Children* (London, 1616), in *Daughters, Wives, and Widows: Writing by Men About Women and Marriage in England, 1500–1640* (Urbana and Chicago: University of Illinois Press, 1992), pp. 297, 296.

17. Sommerville, pp. 147–8.

18. Ann Rosalind Jones, 'Nets and Bridles: Early Modern Conduct Books and Sixteenth-Century Women's Lyric', in *The Ideology of Conduct; Essays in Literature and the History of Sexuality*, ed. by Nancy Armstrong and Leonard Tennenhouse (New York and London: Methuen, 1987), pp. 39–72 (p. 52).

19. Lawrence Stone, *Road to Divorce: England 1530–1987* (Oxford: Oxford University Press, 1990), p. 307; and Lindley, *The Trials of Frances Howard*, pp. 87–8. This case is an extreme example of the ills caused by enforced marriage: Penelope Rich had been for years, in all but legal fact, Blount's wife, and had borne him several children, before Lord Rich took them to court.

20. Lady Mary Wroth, *The First Part of the Countess of Montgomery's Urania*, ed. by Josephine A. Roberts (Binghamton: Medieval and

Renaissance Texts and Studies, 1995), pp. 515–16. Henceforth *Urania* and page numbers cited parenthetically within the text.

21. Roberts, *Poems of Lady Mary Wroth*, pp. 32, 239.
22. Gary Waller, *The Sidney Family Romance: Mary Wroth, William Herbert, and the Early Modern Construction of Gender* (Detroit: Wayne State University Press, 1993), p. 80.
23. Roberts, *Poems of Lady Mary Wroth*, pp. 11–12. I have modernized the spelling here and in other correspondences.
24. Waller, *The Sidney Family Romance*, p. 114.
25. Roberts, *Poems of Lady Mary Wroth*, p. 25.
26. Roberts, in Wroth, *Urania*, pp. lxxiv–lxxv.
27. Roberts, *Poems of Lady Mary Wroth*, pp. 22–3.
28. Josephine Roberts, '"The Knott Never To Bee Untide": The Controversy Regarding Marriage in Mary Wroth's *Urania*', in Miller and Waller, *Reading Mary Wroth*, pp. 109–32 (pp. 112–13).
29. Roberts, in Wroth, *Urania*, pp. xc–xci.
30. *Love's Victory*, in *Renaissance Drama by Women: Texts and Documents*, ed. by S.P. Cerasano and Marion Wynne-Davies (London and New York: Routledge, 1996), pp. 91–126. The autobiographical element in the play is frequently commented on by Wroth's modern critics.
31. Waller, *The Sidney Family Romance*, pp. 117–18.
32. Ben Jonson, *The Devil is an Ass*, ed. by Peter Happé (Manchester: Manchester University Press, 1994). All references are to this edition, cited parenthetically.
33. Lindley, *The Trials of Frances Howard*, pp. 81, 43–4.
34. Leah S. Marcus, *The Politics of Mirth: Jonson, Herrick, Milton, Marvell, and the Defence of Old Holiday Pastimes* (Chicago and London: University of Chicago Press, 1978), p. 89.
35. David Lindley, 'Embarrassing Ben: The Masques for Frances Howard', in *Renaissance Historicism: Selections from 'English Literary Renaissance'*, ed. by Arthur F. Kinney and Dan S. Collins (Amherst: University of Massachusetts Press, 1987), pp. 248–64 (p. 252, 6n).
36. Graham, *et al*, p. 43. Anne Clifford records a year later (19 May 1617) that Frances sent her a 'token' from prison, possibly in memory of Anne's mother, who had died on the day of Frances's arraignment the year before.
37. Frances Howard (along with Anne Clifford, and Mary Wroth's cousin Susan Herbert, Countess of Montgomery) took part in Jonson's *Masque of Queens* in 1609. Howard later caused some embarrassment by refusing to dance with masquers in *Love Restored*, 1612. Jonson wrote wedding masques for both her marriages: *Hymenaei* in 1606 for the Essex Wedding, and *A Challenge at Tilt* and *The Irish Masque at Court* in the 1613–14 Christmas season for the Somerset wedding.
38. Roberts, *Poems of Lady Mary Wroth*, pp. 35–6.
39. Lindley, *The Trials of Frances Howard*, pp. 104, 175.
40. *Conversations*, ll. 399–403. Some suspected that the Countess of Suffolk had supplied the poison herself; others suspected that Overbury's was a natural death made to look like murder for political reasons.

41. Rachel Speght, *A Mouzell for Melastomus*, 1617, in *The Polemics and Poems of Rachel Speght*, ed. by Barbara Kiefer Lewalski (New York and Oxford: Oxford University Press, 1996), pp. 19, 20 and 24. Lewalski points out that the book was entered into the Stationers' Register 14 November 1616, and may have been printed at that time, although the title-page says 1617 (p. xxxii).
42. Richard Allen Cave, *Ben Jonson* (Basingstoke: Macmillan, 1991), p. 125.
43. Lamb, *Gender and Authorship*, p. 175.
44. Constance Jordan, *Renaissance Feminism: Literary Texts and Political Models* (Ithaca and London: Cornell University Press, 1990), p. 295.
45. For the most succinct analysis of Wroth's arguments, see Carolyn Ruth Swift, 'Feminine Self-definition in Lady Mary Wroth's *Love's Victorie* (c. 1621)', *English Literary Renaissance*, 19 (1989), 171–88.
46. The Royal Shakespeare Company's 1996 production of *The Devil is an Ass* (dir. Matthew Warchus) at the Swan managed a very sensual window scene without much touching. Douglas Henshall (Wittipol) relied on passionate speech and gestures: he almost touched Joanna Roth (Mistress Fitzdottrel) with every mention of a body part, his hands approaching within centimetres and then skittishly avoiding contact, as though he was trying not to go too far, not to frighten her. He conveyed extreme desire with great delicacy and almost balletic elegance. She was mesmerized, almost swooning in response, as was the audience.
47. Waller, *The Sidney Family Romance*, p. 206.
48. Jordan, *Renaissance Feminism*, p. 220.
49. Sir Philip Sidney, *The Countess of Pembroke's Arcadia (The New Arcadia)*, ed. by Victor Skretkowicz (Oxford: Clarendon Press, 1987), p. 71. Citations henceforth included parenthetically within the text. My argument does not fit *The Old Arcadia's* Pyrocles, a far more sexually aggressive lover whose *nom de travesti*, 'Cleophilia', suggests his transgressive version of femininity. The revised *Arcadia* expresses Sidney's changed attitudes towards women's influence and integrity.
50. Jordan, *Renaissance Feminism*, p. 224.
51. Marcus, *The Politics of Mirth*, pp. 85, 87.
52. Maria I Cioni, *Women and Law in Elizabethan England with Particular Reference to the Court of Chancery* (New York and London: Garland, 1985), pp. 158, 162–3. Chancery supported such trusts to protect women and their dependent children from grasping or spendthrift husbands, and in fact gave a wife the legal standing to sue her husband and/or others without her husband's permission if she could prove that he was in collusion to defraud her of her estate, as Fitzdottrel attempts in his dealings with Merecraft. Cioni cites several cases: 'Dame St. John *v.* Englefield, Mich. 1616: A bill preferred without the privity of her husband allowed'; 'Rivet *v.* Lancaster, 1596/7. The wife sueth her husband'; or 'Joan Hawes *v.* Hawes and Pyers', in which Joan successfully sued her husband because he had deceived her, although she lost the suit against the trustee Pyers (p. 169).
53. Erickson, *Women and Property*, p. 107. Nevertheless, she also suggests (pp. 127–8) that emotional constraints on women not to contest and

not to speak out against husbands, or only under terms of apology and concession, effectively prevented protest against marital abuse. Even women brave enough to fight and win, like Frances Fitzdottrel, were hobbled by latent expectations of restraint and overt injunctions to be subservient.

54. Sommerville, *Sex and Subjection*, p. 131.
55. Lindley, *The Trials of Frances Howard*, p. 190.
56. Evans, *Ben Jonson and the Poetics of Patronage*, pp. 198–9.
57. Cave, *Ben Jonson*, p. 133.
58. Waller, *The Sidney Family Romance*, pp. 121–2.

9

Print, Popular Culture, Consumption and Commodification in *The Staple of News*

Julie Sanders

Jonson's late plays are too often presented as acts of nostalgia, dramatic and political, promulgated by an ageing dramatist out of favour with the Caroline court.[1] This underestimates the richness and topicality of playtexts such as *The New Inn* (1629), *The Magnetic Lady* (1632), and *A Tale of a Tub* (1633), as well as the continuing exercises in dramatic experimentation which these plays represent in the Jonsonian canon.[2] My focus in this essay will be on just one of those late plays: *The Staple of News* (1626) which in its proactive concern with the emergent print culture of the early seventeenth century opens up for debate ideas about politics, gender, and commodification that have resonance for our own era as well as that for which the play was written.

The Staple of News concerns itself with the innovative idea for a stage-play of the burgeoning print culture of the early seventeenth century. Partly set in a news-office, or 'Staple of News', the play deftly manages to combine the ancient and traditional tale of the prodigal son with a topical exposition of the nature of the press and popular culture. It constitutes a sustained consideration of the social and political impact in the Caroline era of the emergence of the print industry.

The play opens with Pennyboy Junior's coming-of-age and his inheritance, on his birthday, of the family wealth; an event due, we later learn, to his father's recent death. The reports of that 'death' soon turn out to have been greatly exaggerated, as we witness Pennyboy Junior's father, now in disguise as Pennyboy Canter,

183

subjecting his profligate son to a moral testing. Alongside this moralistic 'prodigal play', the rather more complex play about the news-office proceeds apace (interestingly, the news-staple is said to have been established in the very same house as that in which Pennyboy Junior himself has rooms (II.ii.31–5)[3]). In addition, we are introduced to the related tale of the Princess Pecunia, the desirable female icon of wealth and value, who is held under virtual house arrest in the abode of Pennyboy Senior, the prodigal's miserly uncle. The play thus draws on a morality tradition that pitted prodigality against avarice, but employs that structure as an enabling rather than a constrictive framework. All of these scenes are interspersed with the comments and interjections of the onstage audience of gossips with whom Jonson has furnished his play. They have their own humorously reductive account of the plot to offer:

> *Expectation*: Here's nothing but a young prodigal come of age, who makes much of the barber, buys him a place in a new office i'the air, I know not where; and his man o'law to follow him, with the beggar to boot, and they two help him to a wife.
>
> (I. Intermean, ll. 2–7)

The Staple of News was thought an important play in terms of its treatment of print culture, not least because it brought into the public domain the question of exactly what news constituted for society at large. The very use of the term 'news' in this play to refer to numerous forms of literary production complicates the general critical understanding of what has previously been understood as Jonson's elitist literary politics. Jonas Barish may have implied that Jonson established a literary hierarchy in which plays and theatrical ephemera were fairly low on the ladder of importance, regarding the publication of the 1616 Folio as the act of a literary exclusionist,[4] yet in the context of *The Staple of News*, 'news' as a phrase brings into play news-sheets, pamphlets, ballads, prose, poetry, plays, and puppetry, and it potentially legitimizes them all.[5] What is fascinating about *The Staple of News* is that it only delegitimizes a resistance to print; it does not necessarily endorse the theory that Jonson established a printed text in contradistinction to the protean theatrical script in 1616 and that he was therefore allegorically rejecting popular festivity and theatricality.[6]

Expensive and expansive folio publications are not the central concern of *The Staple of News* however: that honour falls to printed news items, pamphlets and *corantos*. News to a large extent occupies an intermediate position between manuscripts and books: its essential ephemerality, however, renders it discrete from both forms. Its ephemeral nature meant that like public theatre play performances it was more affordable than the permanent document that was a book. As a result, it might be interesting to consider *The Staple of News* as a mediatory comment upon the changing relationship between writer and text, audience and availability, made through the mediums of theatre and print.

The tangible effects of an advancing print culture on the availability of news can and has been dated to the decade of the 1620s – the decade in which this play was composed and first performed.[7] That decade witnessed the circulation of *corantos*, (single sheets of news in folio size) which began to appear in London with some regularity, deriving from and reporting upon events occurring on the Continent, in particular the Thirty Years' War.[8] It also saw the transition towards domestically printed newsbooks. Increasingly the single-sheet *corantos* yielded their market dominance to the weightier quarto newsbooks that were often between 16 and 24 pages in size.

The triumphant triple repetition of 'News, news, news!'[9] that ushers the Heralds onto the court-stage before King James VI and I in Jonson's 1620 masque, *News from the New World Discovered in the Moon*, conjointly announced an interest in, and a concern with, the emergent medium of print that would continue throughout the decade. Pamphlets and broadsheets had long been in existence and were accessible to the literate sector of the populace, but the 1620s, on the very cusp of which this masque stood, was a decade that witnessed the arrival of regular newsbook journalism. Additionally present onstage with the Heralds are the diverse literary figures of a Printer, a Factor, and a Chronicler: all producers of this 'news' in some respect, but all possessing startlingly different, indeed completely antithetical, understandings of their art or trade. The Heralds are astounded that the Printer enquires as to the cost-price of their news; such nascent capitalism seems anathema to them. The Printer on the other hand appears to harbour no such qualms:

Indeed I am all for sale, gentlemen, you say true. I am a printer, and a printer of news, and I do hearken after 'em wherever they

be, at any rates; I'll give anything for a good copy now, be't true
or false, so't be news.

(ll.14–17)

The element of snobbery and hierarchism in the Heralds' dismissal
of the Printer as a 'dull tradesman' does not escape attention. The
Factor (a newspaper columnist) is quick to express the egalitarian
qualities of print: 'I have friends of all ranks and of all religions'
(l. 36). For these 'friends', the Factor maintains an 'answering catalogue', and he has ambitious plans to expand his enterprise:

And I have hope to erect a staple for news ere long, whither all
shall be brought and thence again vented under the name of
staple-news, and not trusted to your printed conundrums of the
serpent in Sussex, or the witches bidding the devil to dinner at
Derby – news that, when a man sends them down to the shires
where they are said to be done, were never there to be found.

(ll. 41–7)

Jonson would of course erect his own staple for news within a few
years of this masque, but this time for public rather than court consumption. Writing was clearly metamorphosing, both economically
and politically, into a new commodity, a fact acknowledged in the
capitalistic tones of the Printer in *News from the New World* and in
the carefully chosen terminology employed to describe the Staple
emissaries: 'Men employed outward, that are sent abroad/ To fetch
in the commodity' (I.ii.50–51).

The printing trade in its earliest days certainly possessed vast
and untrammelled potential. A 'responsible' form of journalism
might after all establish a close, if not liberating, communication
with 'ordinary people'.[10] Elizabeth Eisenstein has demonstrated
how print culture rendered ideas far more widely accessible, discussing the potential democratization represented by the pre-
servative powers of the print: 'it secured precious documents not
by putting them under lock and key, but by removing them from
chests and vaults and duplicating them for all to see ... .'[11]
Eisenstein's description unwittingly evokes the stage destiny in *The
Staple of News* of Pecunia, who is lifted out of virtual captivity in the
household of Pennyboy Senior (the names of her ladies-in-waiting –
Statute, Band, and Mortgage – stressing the financial and emotional
constraints involved in that incarceration: we later hear of sexual

and physical abuse on the part of their 'master') and transported into the space and sphere of possibility that constitutes the Staple news-office (although as we later learn this expansion of opportunity may be of greater benefit to her 'readers' than to Pecunia herself).

Comparable happenings within the print industry in the early seventeenth century have antithetically been viewed as liberating and potentially democratizing in their provision of news for a wider audience,[12] or, in their Protestant bias, as an example of the susceptibility of news to such contentious issues as 'censorship' and 'propaganda'. These terms require, and are thankfully now receiving, newer and more thoughtful definitions in their application to the early modern period. Censorship was frequently the result of arbitrary whims or decisions, or of the political 'moment', rather than an established policy or regime. Propaganda in our modern understanding suggests a manipulative state operation: no comparable notion of 'state' existed in the early seventeenth century. In *The Staple of News*, Jonson interrogates his own understanding of the print as a commodity open to the usual interpretations and fetishizations of commodification. He does this by exploring the role of propaganda and the control of ideas within the staple-office itself, but also mediates these ruminations through the fetishized and commodified body of Pecunia. Pecunia, whose name means money (in full it is Aurelia Clara Pecunia, or Golden Bright Money), is an object of considerable desire within the play. The various investors in the Staple-office compete for the control of her body and her finances (the former of course being emblematically representative of the latter) and in turn find themselves in competition with Pennyboy Senior – an instance perhaps of the new world of capitalism in collision with the values of the feudal past. Pennyboy Junior, the emerging victor in all of this, proves as profligate with his affections, and the object of that affection, as he is with the tailors' bills we see him so readily accepting in Act I (as Canter observes with cynicism: 'I say 'tis nobly done to cherish shopkeepers/ And pay their bills without examining thus.' (I.iii.44–5)). Ultimately Pennyboy Junior's extravagant dreams founder on the hyperbolic notion he develops of creating a Canters' College (a linguistic extravagance which, like Pecunia, he intends to control) and Canter reveals his true identity in order to chastise his son publicly and abduct Pecunia away from him. The tale does end happily (although not before the Staple-office has exploded) with Pecunia restored to a significantly chastened Pennyboy Junior, but what rests unresolved by the end is the future of the transitional society which Jonson has so expertly surveyed in the course of the play.

In the process of all this pluralistic and interlinked activity, Jonson employs the trope of the news-office as a means of interrogating a culture based on the patriarchal power to purchase people and ideas. *The Staple of News* does not then satirize the press *per se* but rather explores the politics of certain responses to it and its commodification.[13] In this way Jonsonian politics turn out not to be opposed to censorship but to depend upon new forms and understandings of the term. Jonson seeks to expand the range of discourses through the medium of 'news' and to regulate them critically.

The inclusivity of a term like 'news' in this play highlights the unsatisfactory nature of polarized oppositions such as 'popular' and 'elite' when discussing cultural operations such as the print. Both Bob Scribner and Tessa Watt have expertly refuted the applicability of a two-tier model when discussing the history of culture, and in particular print culture, in this period.[14] Scribner questions whether we are in fact, when we are talking about 'popular culture', even discussing a 'culture of the masses', standing in opposition as it were to that of a political or educational elite; he talks rather of 'shared values'. Jonson's play evidences the fluidity of the boundaries between sections of society within a medium such as the print and the 'vertical antagonisms' that this produces.[15] It is not the case that Jonson uses *The Staple of News* simply to deride 'popular culture' – as has often been suggested in critical accounts of the play;[16] what he demonstrates, through the complex interactions and interrelations of his manifold characters, is how the print industry bridges socially differentiated readers and groups. By its very nature then, acting as a mediator between manuscript and books, printed 'news' – of interest to variant sectors of society as the multifarious visitors to the Staple-office indicate – made precarious the boundary between aristocracy and lower gentry.[17] Jonson is exploring that increasing fluidity and permeability of societal boundaries and frontiers in *The Staple of News* – not least as it manifested itself within the burgeoning space and locale that was urban seventeenth-century London; this was also his subject in the play that preceded *The Staple of News* a decade earlier: *The Devil is an Ass*, in which commodification, not least of women, also features (interestingly, this is the one play that the theatre-going gossips of *The Staple of News* Intermeans identify by name (I.Intermean, ll. 39–42)). Here though, instead of monopolies and projections in their entirety, which were the focus of that ethical 1616 drama, the specific monopoly of the print and the publication of 'news' is his concern. Jonson is exploring both the possibilities and the potential drawbacks of the porous parameters of print culture, and popular culture is therefore inherent to his project rather than the target of it.

'Popular' literary forms may include broadsheets, chapbooks, plays (religious and secular), and artefacts of mass consumption. All of these figure in the drama and stage properties of *The Staple of News*: it is no mere coincidence, for example, that our three male leads share the title of Pennyboy: the printed broadside was the cheapest form of print available and could be had for just a penny.[18] This rendered this particular form of print accessible to the lower orders and, in terms of the naming of Jonson's triad of male protagonists (part of a family which surely views itself as significant within the community of the play), once again emphasizes the blurring of boundaries between seemingly separate sections of society that is effected by the medium of print. Ballads and so-called 'cheap print' were subject to exploitation in the period, as is a figure of wealth such as Pecunia within the play. In 1624 a syndicate was formed calling itself the 'ballad partners' which indicates the development and increasing specialization and centralization of this trade, concomitant with events within the print industry at large.[19]

Popular culture did not stand distinct from elite culture: they inhabited shared spaces. As Scribner and Watt have evidenced, we are invariably dealing with a complex matrix of appropriation, assimilation, and interaction when we consider the roles of 'cheap print' and high culture productions in this period. The so-called 'residual' remains of popular culture, such as ballads, fairytale, folksong, myths and legends, and proverbs also feature in this play, for the most part accruing around the figure of, or constructions of the figure of, Pecunia. Since these constructions are the products of self-promoting men, be it the miserly Pennyboy Senior, the figure of conspicuous consumption that is his nephew, or the professionally ambitious jeerer Cymbal, who is also governor of the Staple, they are undoubtedly unreliable as representations of Pecunia. What is intriguing in this play is that when this allegorized and over-determined figure speaks, it is with clarity, strength, and vision. Her indictment of the physically and emotionally abusive Pennyboy Senior is devastating and irrefutable by comparison with the hyperbolic and spurious language of her male counterparts.

Scribner has spoken of the untrustworthy nature for the historian of source material deriving from sites of 'popular culture', in that, by the time they are available for interpretation, they have often been removed from their original location or social site, such as the tavern in the individual instance of alehouse gossip.[20] Once again Jonson's play expertly evidences those acts of appropriation on the part of the upper echelons of society, and its attendant blurring of cultural demarcations. The onstage gossips in the play-intermeans are astute theatre-goers: they therefore carry street or tavern gossip into the more 'elite' space of the Blackfriars theatre. In a related gesture, Lickfinger the epicurean cook of the play proper will purchase this theatre gossip for consumption at one of his banquets (inevitably therefore to be consumed and reconstituted by the aristocracy). The 'news' industry is merely a specialization and centralization of the societal tendency towards gossip; from the 1590s onwards presses in Stationers' Hall had been established near to London's principal centres of trade and gossiping discourse.[21]

It could be argued that *The Staple of News* was in 1626, like the female gossips' rehearsal of street-news they have heard, being performed in a transitional space: that of the Blackfriars theatre. As with the location of the Staple-office within the same household as Pennyboy Junior's apartment, Jonson is clearly dealing with the aligned spaces of the Blackfriars of the playhouse and the Blackfriars of the play – the locale for a number of important Stationers' groups in the 1620s. This trope of spatial proximity was one that he had previously employed to great topical, political, and theatrical effect in *The Alchemist* in 1610 and *The Devil is an Ass* in 1616.[22] The private theatre audiences were a site of social fluidity and commingling, more so than 'elitist' readings of these theatre-houses have in the past suggested.[23] Jonson once again mirrors and reflects his audiences within the complex stage relationships of his play. He is himself a mediator between differentiated social groups with his ostensibly discrete works intended for public or private theatre consumption and for the court in the elite form of the masque. It has been suggested that by the time of writing his so-called 'late plays' Jonson had effectively rejected his public-theatre background in favour of a more court-deferential form, but the complexity of his treatment of that popular 'public' inheritance in these late plays, let alone their process of assimilating (and redefining) the masque form, must give us pause. Jonsonian politics are neither so easy to trace nor to categorize in these rich and complex playtexts. What we are witnessing in any enactment of *The Staple of News* are the contradictory politics of print and the contradictory politics of Ben Jonson, dramatist.

With *The Staple of News*, it is not a simple case of seeing Jonson as an advocate of, or for, popular culture – too many complex acts of appropriation have occurred for that process to be either explicit or even emergent. Print culture, as we have seen, is essentially fluid and so too is the process of interplay and reinterpretation in Jonson's dramatic creations: '"Print culture" is both being formed and modified as a phenomenon, and above all interacting with existing forms of popular culture while we are observing it.'[24]

Democratic arguments in favour of early modern print culture are generally countered by the suggestion that censorship enacted its own restraints upon the press – some critics arguing that royal control was exerted over this form, rendering it less than populist, if not quasi-absolutist, in content. Such readings are however generally more indicative of our own era in which there exists a sense of the news as being manipulated by a minority in control, be it due to financial power (witness the Rupert Murdoch/Robert Maxwell phenomenon in the 1980s) or political power (witness government limitations on war reportage). D.F. McKenzie states that the popular press in the early modern period was a reflection of an egalitarian movement, as well as immensely educative in forming a new language for talking about politics,[25] at a time when, as Anthony Parr has put it, 'people were ready to learn the language of that debate'.[26] Blair Worden has reassessed the contribution of censorship in this period to the freedom or otherwise of speech in print.[27] He declares that 'the problem of censorship is vulnerable to distortion'[28] and questions whether the freedom of the press was even a debated issue in the period, whilst also conceding that Jonson is an interesting case for any consideration of the effects of such policies.[29]

Undoubtedly the Crown frequently intervened in the print industry tending to grant patents, for certain classes of publication, to the monarch's favourites. English printing patents were broad grants and often proved extremely lucrative. The print medium existed uneasily between the worlds of royal licence and oscillating market forces; this forms part of the antimasque debate in *News from the New World* and also constitutes a central topos of *The Staple of News*.

Like many other seventeenth-century authors, Jonson recognized the new opportunities proffered by the printed book, not least its capacity to reach far wider audiences than manuscripts: its capacity to perform the function of being a carrier of social relationships. Combined material and artistic success was Jonson's objective, as his sharply registered disappointment(s) at the poor reception(s) of his plays indicates. Yet in acknowledging, and possibly even catering for, the new 'popular' potential of his work, Jonson continued to make ostensibly elitist and exclusive gestures through the medium of books, displaying the 'neurotic' personality he has been accused of, if not necessarily the pre-established elitism Stanley Fish has credited him with.[30] McKenzie regards *The Staple of News* as 'the hardening point of Jonson's isolation,'[31] partly because, he argues, the dramatist may be pushing for the political awakening of the *'menu peuple'* but he makes no allowance for the struggle and the difficulty this would entail. In his very gesture of accommodation towards the general public, McKenzie feels Jonson abstracts himself from the situation in hand:

> Jonson evidences the same virtues and limitations of all whose passionate defence of minority culture is beyond criticism so long as it remains in a condition of high-minded self-abstraction from mass civilization.[32]

Contradictory drives of this nature characterize the writing profession and the volumes it produced in the seventeenth century: 'There was a tension, often quite explicit in these volumes between the intellectual elitism claimed for authorship, and the broader appeal required if authorship were to prosper in the marketplace.'[33] Wendy Wall has suggested that the period also witnessed a debate about privacy which was embodied within the anxieties surrounding emergent print culture. The reader as voyeur became a focus of concern and exploitation. *The Staple of News* is a play which questions the concept of sight from a number of perspectives. The Prologue berates the gossips for attending the play merely to see (and not hear or understand) the play:

> You come to see who wears the new suit today, whose clothes are best penned (whatever the part be), which actor has the best

leg and foot, what king plays without cuffs and his queen
without gloves, who rides post in stockings and dances in boots?

(Induction, 40–44)

As well as the obvious references to the fashions of the moment
(interestingly referred to in textual terminology: 'whose clothes are
best penned'), this speech makes covert allusion to the shocked
responses of members of the court audience for Jonson's 1605
masque, *The Masque of Blackness*, in which a six-month pregnant
Queen Anne of Denmark appeared blacked up and without
gloves.[34] Reasons for Jonson's alluding to this masque some twenty
years later can only be speculated upon, but it does add credence to
the general reinterpretative role of the masque genre within this
play and in turn to potentially subversive readings of this play's
performative princess, Pecunia.

In Jonson's infamous quarrel with Inigo Jones over the masque
form, the dramatist had derided the notion that the visual spectacle
of the masque exceeded the words or the text in importance.[35] He
therefore stresses through the Prologue's representations to the
audience of gossips (and note that the audience 'audits' rather than
'spectates' a play) that it is the words and the texts of *The Staple of
News* which are important. As if to further emphasize the point, we
witness the prodigal Pennyboy Junior engrossed in Act I in adorn-
ing himself superficially with the latest fashions and failing to read
the associated texts (that is to say, the bills for their commission). In
the address to the Readers which precedes Act III, Jonson stresses
their superior opportunity to interpret the play aright (correcting
as it were the misjudgements of original audiences):

In this following Act, the Office is opened and shown to the
prodigal and his princess Pecunia, wherein the allegory and
purpose of the author hath hitherto been wholly mistaken, and
so sinister an interpretation been made, as if the souls of most of
the spectators had lived in the eyes and ears of these ridiculous
gossips that tattle between the Acts.

(ll.1–6)

On the surface then the text rather than the performance of *The
Staple of News* is being valorized. But as the Induction and the
opening scene indicate, we are surely being instructed to mistrust
surfaces – and so, despite Jonson's instructions to us to avoid

allegorical or topical interpretations of the play, and in particular the Staple office, we should surely proceed to do just that: to read into the events of the play.

Behind the extravagant and complex 'surface' iconography of the court masques a similarly political vein of reference is now beginning to be teased out by critics.[36] In the context of this critical development, the time is surely ripe to review readings and interpretations of Pecunia's role and function in *The Staple of News*. It is nothing new to state that she is representative of money in a tradition that stemmed from classical and medieval sources.[37] Her relationship to the allegorical (silent) female figures of the court masques has also been amply demonstrated (her royal progress to the Staple office and the staged display of her to its workers are obvious examples of this treatment). But Pecunia, as has already been mentioned, is in truth far from silent, and is rather assertive and self-conscious in her statements and actions within the playtext. We never witness any submission on her part to Pennyboy Senior's attempts at control: she rather resists and struggles against his imprisonment, calmly questioning the self-punitive aspect of his sexual and financial obsession:

Why do you so, my guardian? I not bid you.
Cannot my grace be gotten, and held too,
Without your self-tormentings and your watches,
Your macerating of your body thus
With cares and scantings of your diet and rest?
                                        (II.i.21–5)

A fuller consideration of Pecunia's operation within this text may be liberated by the correlative potential for subversion and resistance now being traced within the Jacobean court masques written by Jonson. Many of those texts were commissioned by Anne of Denmark (alluded to, as we have seen, in the Induction to this play) and contain at the very least limited potential for criticism of her husband's policies and regime.[38] Jonson's invocations of masque in his late plays may then be a less submissive gesture than has previously been presumed, and may conversely contain the potential for radical critique.

In addition to allegorically depicting money or wealth, Pecunia functions as a representative of the print. Cymbal and Fitton hope to win her financial support for the business by wooing her; in that respect she contains the synecdochical potential to represent the press. She is, in relation to this, an object both of desire and acute anxiety, and as a result her various male suitors attempt mastery of her throughout the play. This control is invariably attempted through language as her 'readers' produce and reproduce appropriating poetic blazons on her body (and her wealth).

Wendy Wall has persuasively explored the language of manuscript and printed sonnet sequences in the late Elizabethan and early Jacobean period, suggesting that patterns of economic and sexual exchange can be traced within these textual exchanges. Unprinted Elizabethan sonnet sequences often circulated in manuscript form: another token of significant semiotic exchange. A central trope of these sequences as well as a focus of their exchange was the female body, figured as it was in the poetic blazon. That body was deconstructed and re-membered by the power of the male wit as a commodified and fetishized object:[39]

> As the poem moved into the blazon section proper – the praise of eyes like sapphires, an ivory white forehead, apple-like cheeks, lips like cherries ... – the woman became arrayed as an object of consumption for other men, flaunted before an audience as something not only there to be looked upon, but eaten ...[40]

Jonathan Sawday's account here of the blazon has obvious resonance for *The Staple of News*. The jeerers constitute the grotesque extreme of the male competition of wit which Sawday is detailing. It is surely no coincidence that a number of Pecunia's suitors (also jeerers) appropriate the emblazoning language of those courtly sonneteers and romance emblems in order to woo her; Madrigal, Cymbal, and Pennyboy Junior indulge in these acts of linguistic and cultural appropriation. Pennyboy Junior recites an almost identical catalogue of properties to those listed by Sawday:

> Please her but to show
> Her melting wrists or bare her ivory hands,
> She catches still! Her smiles, they are love's fetters!
> Her breasts his apples! Her teats strawberries!
> Where Cupid, were he present now, would cry,
> Farewell my mother's milk, here's sweeter nectar!
> (IV.ii.42–56)

Sawday stresses the etymological origins of the term '*blason*' in chivalric literature: it was a term for a shield. The female form is thus recounted by the poet in quasi-heraldic terms; significantly, Pecunia is also wooed by a herald or '*blasonneur*', Piedmantle. Sawday's employment of metaphors of digestion in his account of the operations of the blazon make actual the themes of consumption which are predominant in the treatment of Pecunia and the society of *The Staple of News* as a whole. Lickfinger the cook-poet (his extravagant culinary concoctions are deliberately described in terms originating from masque (IV.i.19–37)) caters directly to that consumerist and competitive society with his opulent and performative dishes.[41] Once again, the masque is being invoked as emblematic of conspicuous consumption and a vehicle for the emblematic display of the female form, either as allegory or as flesh.

Pecunia is an emblem herself and in that sense she is representative of a certain type of text that was circulating in this period: emblem books which were extremely popular with a wide audience. Emblem books like masques were a complex combination of the visual and the textual. Intriguingly Jonson himself used that archetypal emblematic tale of reader/spectator voyeurism – the myth of Diana and Actaeon – elsewhere in his writing.[42] But Pecunia is no mere emblem – Jonson's act of characterization, of making her flesh as it were, carries out a process of 'unmetaphoring',[43] of making the iconic real. This complicates any fixed reading of her character or function within the play. Her body, her corporeality, is very much our focus as well as that of her suitors.

Seventeenth-century print culture has been described as an era of increasing specialization. Tessa Watt has focused on the Protestant or godly output at this period, but also prevalent were medical and scientific textbooks, as the culture of anatomization and the so-called 'new science' gained force. As Wendy Wall and Jonathan Sawday have indicated, these expressed a particular interest in interiority and the human, and often specifically female, form. This led to an identification of text and body:

> Books were composed of parts that could be read and interpreted in the same way that bodies were made up of parts that exhibited signs of their health or decay to the skilled reader – the physician – who 'interpreted' the signs of the body.[44]

Textbooks depicting dissection did exhibit a particular interest in exploring the female form and its differences from the dominant male sex. This contributed to a process which could be seen as a controlling impulse: the private spaces of women were thus made public, commodified. Subtle cultural codes can be seen to be in operation here. Since masculinized notions of authorship undoubtedly dominated in the period (and have contributed in their turn to masculinized readings of Jonson, readings which are Folio, rather than performance, dominated), printers used the female body as a metaphor for the newly commodified book[45] – the object, artefact, or recipient of male creativity – like the womb-vessel described in so many of the medical textbooks: 'The relationship [of woman to her womb] was analogous to the print allegory …The woman was the *locus* for the 'matrix' from which is drawn the infant, or the printer's font.'[46] The Staple-emissaries undoubtedly sexualize their acts of publication; the public chronicler is described as having 'the maidenhead/Of all the books.' (I.v.33–4).[47]

The text as an erotic as well as an economic commodity renders it a direct parallel to Pecunia herself. Commodification need not necessarily mean control but the gendering of commodification and cultural practice and production in this play implies that patriarchal gestures at control were manifest in the print industry. The opening scene of Pennyboy Junior's coming of age is not unconnected. The play's induction has already introduced us to the idea that to be well-dressed or fashionably attired was to be well-penned, and to 'come of age' was to 'write man'. Masculinity and print were inherently associated. Wendy Wall has demonstrated how to be a 'man in print' meant to be in publication: 'To be represented as 'a man in print' in the Renaissance, as the phrase implies, belied a nervousness about one's ability to be perfectly and completely a man at all.'[48] Pennyboy Junior and Cymbal's rivalry for both Pecunia and the control of language is surely further confirmation of this nervousness.

Wall continues, 'To be "a woman in print" was to call into question the logic that shifts social and class issues easily into the frame of sexuality and gender' (p. 347). Pecunia is a transgressive figure for that reason: her wealth provides her with status and importance within the press, a position that her femininity might otherwise deny her. The boundaries of gender as well as of rank are notably disturbed or disrupted by the events of this play. Pecunia contains the potential for the social mobility and disruption that Catherine

Belsey, Ania Loomba, and others have seen as being so critical to male dramatic representations of femininity and female subjectivity in this period.[49] In *The Staple of News* Pecunia does not represent a single text – she exists in numerous versions. Men reinterpret and differentiate Pecunia in order to assert some personal claim over her. This can be viewed as a parallel to what Richard Burt has designated 'censorship as "fetishism"'.[50] Each character seeks to liberate Pecunia from one defining reading only to impose on her another version; she is never allowed full entrance into the social field as an uncensored whole; instead each character produces a partial and censored reading which is both dependent upon, and a departure from, that of her previous interpreter. By the end of the play however, Pecunia has stepped out of the allegory she has been assigned a role in: she performs 'unmetaphoring' and resists fixity.

The notion of print as a fixing agent in the early seventeenth century, preserving texts and regulating spellings and layout has been explored by Eisenstein and others. Joseph Loewenstein has stressed that the age of print witnessed a regulation of English writing: uniform orthography and appearance became pressing concerns.[51] But print is not necessarily a stable medium – Jonson's revisions and amendments to previous quarto copytexts of his own plays and his suppression of details no longer relevant or now simply embarrassing in his 1616 Folio, are indicators of the instabilities of texts, printed or otherwise. Print can then be a destabilizing medium – a medium that can mobilize, change, or protest; it can prove to be a liberating force within society at large.

If the expanding print industry drew attention to the problematized and potentially conflictual area of 'rights' in the realms of politics and literature, it also began substantially to alter author–reader relationships from their pre-existent states, creating, not least, a forum for debate, both political and theatrical. As Parr observes, popular culture was in some sense appropriated for this purpose by the newsmakers:

> Broadside ballads had long been a profitable way of exploiting public curiosity about current sensations, but the growth of literacy and awareness of the world at large, especially as England became more involved in Continental politics, created the conditions for a new kind of journalism, one that might demand a more sustained effort from the reader and mediate responsibility between news and its recipients.[52]

Jonson was both struggling to cope with these redefinitions and striving to harness them for his own benefit; possibly this lies behind his efforts to contain and control the more wayward performative energies of his texts in his careful oversight of their journey into print. Jonson was engaged with the potential of print in both its advantageous and disadvantageous sense: *The Staple of News* is an effort to explore the problems of the medium in literary, political, and sociological terms.

In Act V Sc.i Thomas announces: 'Our Staple is all to pieces, quite dissolved.' (V.i.39). The news-office in an extreme act of self-combustion (self-censorship?), has blown-up:

Shivered, as in an earthquake! Heard you not
The crack and ruins? We are all blown up!
Soon as they heard th'Infanta was got from them,
Whom they had so devourèd i'their hopes
To be their patroness and sojourn with 'em,
Our emissaries, Register, Examiner
Flew into vapour; our grave governor
Into a subtler air, and is returned
(As we do hear) grand-captain of the jeerers.
I and my fellow melted into butter
And spoiled our ink, and so the Office vanished.
(V.i.40–50)

In truth though, Thomas has not melted into butter; this is simply a metaphor for his loss of position and, as such, part of a general pattern of butter puns in the text which play on the name of the famous printer Nathaniel Butter, part of a syndicate of British printers formed in the 1620s and who was reportedly not amused by Jonson's jokes. This pattern of references also implicitly questions the assumed fixity of print, assumed even by the Staple's workforce:

Fitton: O, sir, it is the printing we oppose.
Cymbal: We not forbid that any news be made
But that't be printed; for when news is printed,
It leaves, sir, to be news. While 'tis but written –
(I.v.46–9)[53]

Such opinions are regularly cited as if they were simply further evidence of Jonson's personal and authoritarian view, suggesting that he was directly opposed to the new print culture,[54] but this seems a wholly false strategy. In her article on the masques of the early 1620s, Sara Pearl remarks that *News from the New World* is a text that parodies the capitalistic print culture[55] but this same argument cannot be extended easily to describe *The Staple of News*. This is not a play that satirizes printed news; it attacks rather certain interpretations and appropriations of the press. For all the potential democratization and liberation of print, the Staple office is by and large scornful of its target population:

> *Register*: 'Tis the house of fame, sir,
>   Where both the curious and the negligent,
>   The scrupulous and careless, wild and staid,
>   The idle and laborious; all do meet
>   To taste the *cornucopiae* of her rumours,
>   Which she, the mother of sport, pleaseth to scatter
>   Among the vulgar. Baits, sir, for the people!
>   And they will bite like fishes.
>   (III.ii.115–22)

In an interesting pun, the Register declares, 'The people press upon us.' (I.ii.111); as if to prove his point a variety of customers duly arrive. Cymbal resists putting the material desired by many of these clients into printed form; this is a ridiculous stance for the governor of a news-office to take. There is no possible way in which the Staple can succeed thus as a financial venture. A news-office that resists the new print culture is doomed to failure.[56] The employees' written contracts barely prove more durable; ink after all can run and dissolve. The description of the office explosion is a variation on the overblown, hyperbolic accounts (such as that of Spinola and his eggs (I.iv)) that have indeed been its staple diet and production; it is an exaggerated account of financial dissolution, a company going as we still say 'into liquidation' after failed attempts to woo investors.[57]

A disinterest in the harsh fiscal consequences of his behaviour is a mark of the conspicuous consumption of the prodigal son figure, but to proffer this as a sole reading of Pennyboy Junior is inadequate. He demonstrates occasional depth of understanding, not least of the central topos of the press. Whilst he does seem to pour money into the Staple with little regard, purchasing positions at will for his friends, he is also manifestly sympathetic towards the consuming public (perhaps because he empathizes with them as consumers), unlike the jeering Fitton who wishes to deny them their printed stories:

> Why, methinks, sir, if the honest common people
> Will be abused, why should not they ha'their pleasure
> In the believing lies are made for them,
> As you i'th'Office, making them yourselves?
> (I.v.42–45)[58]

Milton's *Areopagitica* will not sound so different a few decades later:

> Nor is it to the common people less than a reproach; for if we be so jealous over them, as that we dare not trust them with an English pamphlet, what do we but censure them for a giddy, vicious, and ungrounded people; in such a sick and weak estate of faith and discretion, as to be able to take nothing down but through the pipe of a licencer … .[59]

Areopagitica is undergoing critical revision itself at present. Many critics have argued that it is a response to an increasingly capitalistic system, a demand for individual liberties and rights, but critics such as Burt and Norbrook argue that Milton (like Jonson) was not anti-censorship *per se* but rather demanding new forms of it. Norbrook in particular sees *Areopagitica* as a defensive text, a comment on the ideological struggles occurring in contemporary Europe, and says that we should view it against the background of Renaissance republicanism rather than later liberalism.[60] For a re-reading of Milton's pamphlet, he argues that we need to connect the development of Parliament, political theory, literary history, and a study of the mass media. This is exactly what I would argue is necessary for a re-evaluation of *The Staple of News*; it needs to be seen as a response to the political crises of its own time and as an intervention in the debate over press and censorship, rather than as either a purely supportive or oppositional text.

Pennyboy Junior's debate with Fitton and Cymbal over the press prefigures modernist and post-modernist dilemmas about the fixity of form. For Fitton and Cymbal, the written as opposed to the printed retains a sense of being corruptible (that is possible to corrupt in the same way as their jeering corrupts language and conversation), yet in the text itself printing is regularly associated with waxen or melting metaphors and this would seem to deny their sense of rigidity. Words may not fit; symbols (cymbals?) may be multivalent. Print as a controlling force then only ever constitutes a superficial understanding of the form. In this play all constraints and controls prove to be artificial. Pennyboy Senior cannot maintain his oppressive regime over Pecunia any more than Pennyboy Junior proves able to buy and keep her attentions; with the kissing game the latter is as prodigal in love relationships as in all else. *The Staple of News* in this respect is also investigating the commodity of gender and its attendant fetishizations in a sophisticated manner.

In terms of its historicity *The Staple of News* is a remarkable dramatic document. In addition to capturing the emergent medium of the print and providing considerations of the new monarchy, it attends to complex questions of democracy, constitutional change, and social, civic, and intellectual property rights. Like the newssheets that provide its subject-matter, this play, with a heightened sense of its own politicized (and consumed) discourse, offers 'news' of its time and manner of production.

Notes

I would like to thank Kate McLuskie and Richard Burt for their invaluable comments on earlier drafts of this essay. My thanks also to Sue Wiseman for illuminating insights into the role of 'news' in this period.

1. See Anne Barton, *Ben Jonson, Dramatist* (Cambridge: Cambridge University Press, 1984) for an influential account of the 'nostalgia' theory. This in turn shaped Michael Hattaway's reading of *The New Inn* in his edition for the Revels series (Manchester: Manchester University Press, 1984). The account of *The Staple of News* as a prodigal play in Jill Levenson, 'Comedy', in *The Cambridge Companion to English Renaissance Drama*, ed. by A.R. Braunmuller and Michael Hattaway (Cambridge: Cambridge University Press, 1990), pp. 263–300 (esp. pp. 288–9), does little to redress the balance. See also Douglas M. Lanier, 'The Prison-House of the Canon: Allegorical Form and Posterity in Ben Jonson's *The Staple of Newes*', *Medieval and Renaissance Drama in England*, 2 (1983), 253–67.
2. Articles that have begun the process of recuperating these texts for politicized readings of this nature include Martin Butler, 'Stuart Politics in *A Tale of a Tub*', *Modern Language Review*, 85 (1990), 12–28;

and his 'Late Jonson', in *The Politics of Tragicomedy*, ed. by Gordon McMullan and Jonathan Hope (London: Routledge, 1992), pp. 166–88; Julie Sanders, '"The Collective Contract is a Fragile Structure": Local Government and Personal Rule in Jonson's *A Tale of a Tub*', *English Literary Renaissance* (forthcoming); '"The Day's Sports Devised in the Inn": Jonson's *The New Inn* and Theatrical Politics', *Modern Language Review*, 91(1996), 545–60; and Helen Ostovich, 'The Appropriation of Pleasure in *The Magnetic Lady*', *Studies in English Literature, 1500–1900*, 34(1994), 425–42.

3. Ben Jonson, *The Staple of News*, ed. by Anthony Parr (Manchester: Manchester University Press (Revels), 1988). All quotations from this edition henceforth cited within parentheses in the text.

4. Jonas Barish, *The Anti-theatrical Prejudice* (Berkeley and London: University of California Press, 1981). This book has been employed in quasi-doctrinal fashion to label Jonson as anti-theatrical and elitist in his politics. Stephen Orgel endorsed the theory in 'What is a Text?', in *Research Opportunities in Renaissance Drama*, 24 (1981), 3–6. This theory has been wrongfooted recently by John Creaser in 'Enigmatic Ben Jonson', in *English Comedy*, ed. by Michael Cordner, Peter Holland and John Kerrigan (Cambridge: Cambridge University Press, 1994), pp. 100–18.

5. Richard Burt, *Licensed by Authority: Ben Jonson and the Discourses of Censorship* (Ithaca and London: Cornell University Press, 1993) and 'Licensed by Authority: Ben Jonson and the Politics of Early Stuart Theatre', *English Literary History*, 54 (1987), 529–60.

6. See Wendy Wall, *The Imprint of Gender: Authorship and Publication in the English Renaissance* (Ithaca and London: Cornell University Press, 1993), p. 18. For further discussion of the stability or otherwise of Jonson's folio text, see *Ben Jonson's 1616 Folio*, ed. by Jennifer Brady and W.H. Herendeen (Newark, NJ: University of Delaware Press, 1991).

7. See David Norbrook, '*Areopagitica*, Censorship, and the Early Modern Public Sphere', in *The Administration of Aesthetics: Censorship, Political Criticism, and the Public Sphere*, ed. by Richard Burt (Minneapolis and London: University of Minnesota Press, 1994), pp. 3–33. See in particular p. 7.

8. See the introductory essay to Anthony Parr's edition of *The Staple of News*, op. cit. Quotations from this essay, henceforth Parr.

9. *News from the New World Discovered in the Moon*, l. 1. All quotations from the masque are from *The Complete Masques*, ed. by Stephen Orgel (New Haven and London: Yale University Press, 1969; repr. 1975), henceforth *News from the New World*.

10. The use of such a term is inherently problematic. The issue is expertly weighed in Natalie Zemon Davis's essay, 'The Print and the People', in her *Society and Culture in Early Modern France* (London: Duckworth, 1975).

11. Elizabeth Eisenstein, *The Printing Press as an Agent of Change: Communications and Cultural Transformations in Early Modern Europe* (Cambridge: Cambridge University Press, 1979), p. 80.

12. See Norbrook, '*Areopagitica*', p. 7:
     There was a significant expansion in the political public sphere,
     especially from the 1620s onwards, an emergent civil society whose
     means of communication – reports of parliamentary debates, news-
     letters, satires, and so on – circulated horizontally, cutting across
     the vertical power structures emanating from the court.
13. Tom Hayes, *The Birth of Popular Culture: Ben Jonson, Maid Marian, and
     Robin Hood* (Pittsburgh PA: Duquesne University Press, 1992, p. 49):
     Print did not replace the theater as the central legitimizing medium
     in early modern England. It expanded the influence of writing ...
     The increase in popular literacy worked against monolithic, central-
     ized authority, against the idea that there was one legitimate voice
     in the text.
14. See Bob Scribner, 'Is a history of popular culture possible?' *History of
     European Ideas*, 10 (1989), 175–92 (p. 175) and Tessa Watt, *Cheap Print
     and Popular Piety, 1550–1640* (Cambridge: Cambridge University
     Press, 1994).
15. See Tim Harris, 'The Problem of Popular Political Culture in
     Seventeenth-Century London', *History of European Ideas*, 10 (1989),
     43–58 (p. 43).
16. Parr to a certain extent repeats this formula in his edition.
17. Wall, *The Imprint of Gender*, p. 12.
18. From Henry Peacham, *The Worth of a Penny* (1641), cited in Watt,
     Cheap Print and Popular Piety, p. 11:
     For a peny you may have all the Newes in England, of Murder,
     Flouds, Witches, Fires, Tempests, and what not, in one of Martin
     Parker's Ballads.
19. See Watt, *Cheap Print and Popular Piety*, p. 39. A court order in the
     same year requested the formal registration of ballads which had
     heretofore gone unlicensed. This again indicates an increasing pro-
     fessionalization and centralized control of the print industry in all its
     manifestations.
20. Scribner, 'Is a history of popular culture possible?' p. 176.
21. See Parr, *The Staple of News*, p. 24. See also Bernard Capp, 'Separate
     Domains? Women and Authority in Early Modern England', in *The
     Experience of Authority in Early Modern England*, ed. by Paul Griffiths,
     Adam Fox and Steve Hindle (Basingstoke: Macmillan, 1996), pp. 117–45.
22. See, for example, Keith Sturgess, *Jacobean Private Theatre* (London and
     New York: Routledge, 1987); Andrew Gurr, *The Shakespearean Stage,
     1574–1642*, 2nd edn (Cambridge: Cambridge University Press, 1980);
     and Martin Butler, *Theatre and Crisis, 1632–42*. (Cambridge:
     Cambridge University Press, 1984). See also Kate McLuskie's article in
     this volume.
23. Although Butler, *Theatre and Crisis*, has gone a long way to redefining
     this.
24. Scribner, 'Is a history of popular culture possible?', p. 180.
25. See D. F. McKenzie, '*The Staple of News* and the Late Plays', in *A
     Celebration of Ben Jonson*, ed. by William Blissett, Julian Patrick and
     R.W. Van Fossen (Toronto: University of Toronto Press, 1973),

pp. 83–128, although he registers considerable doubt as to Jonson's participation in any such movement.

26. Parr, *The Staple of News*, p. 25.

27. See Blair Worden, 'Literature and Political Censorship in Early Modern Europe', in *Too Mighty to be Free: Censorship and the Press in Britain and the Netherlands*, ed. by A.C. Duke and C.A. Tamse (Zutphen, De Wallburg, 1987), pp. 45–62. For examples of texts which present the monolithic understandings of censorship which Worden attacks, see Annabel Patterson, *Censorship and Interpretation: The Conditions of Writing and Reading in Early Modern England* (Madison: University of Wisconsin Press, 1984) and Janet Clare, *Art Made Tongue-Tied by Authority: Elizabethan and Jacobean Dramatic Censorship* (Manchester: Manchester University Press (Revels), 1990). For an argument related to Worden's, see S.L. Lambert, 'The Printers and the Government, 1604–1640', in *Aspects of Printing from 1600*, ed. by Robin Myers and Michael Harris (Oxford: Oxford Polytechnic Press, 1987), pp. 1–29.

28. Worden, p. 45.

29. Richard Burt has made a valuable contribution to the currently raging censorship debate, creating a new model that involves not removal and replacement by the censoring body but rather dispersal and displacement. He argues that censorship was a far more collaboratory and complicit series of actions than monolithic notions of 'Censorship' allow. Just as no Ur-text can be uncovered in terms of authorial intention, neither does there exist some Ur-pre-censorship text; he argues that the text will always prove castrated, feminized, and therefore disappointing to those who seek such an artefact. Those who seek some original, radical politics are also likely to be disappointed: see Burt, *Licensed by Authority* and '(Un)Censoring in Detail: Thomas Middleton, Fetishism, and the Regulation of Dramatic Discourse', forthcoming. My thanks to Richard for permission to use this article in advance.

30. See Stanley Fish, 'Authors–Readers', where he argues, admittedly in the context of Jonson's poetry, that the author played the game of excluding members of an already defined elitist readership, thus denying any potential 'populism' in the Jonsonian text, although he concedes that the plays are a separate issue.

31. McKenzie, '*The Staple of News* and the Late Plays', p. 111.

32. Ibid., p. 113.

33. Leah Marcus, *Puzzling Shakespeare: Local Reading and its Discontents* (Berkeley: University of California Press, 1988), p. 21. Frontispieces in particular simultaneously represented inclusive and exclusive gestures.

34. See Clare McManus's essay within this volume.

35. Stephen Orgel, '"To Make Boards to Speak": Inigo Jones's Stage and the Jonsonian Masque', *Renaissance Drama*, n.s. 1 (1968), 121–52.

36. See, for example, Martin Butler and David Lindley, 'Restoring Astraea: Jonson's Masque for the Fall of Somerset', *English Literary History*, 61 (1994), 807–27; and Martin Butler, 'Ben Jonson and the

Limits of Courtly Panegyric', in *Culture and Politics in Early Stuart England*, ed. by Kevin Sharpe and Peter Lake (Basingstoke: Macmillan, 1994), pp. 91–115.

37. See Parr's detailed explanation of this in *The Staple of News*.

38. See for example, Barbara Kiefer Lewalski, 'Enacting Oppositions: Queen Anne and the Subversions of Masquing', in her *Writing Women in Jacobean England* (Cambridge, MA and London: Harvard University Press, 1993), pp. 15–43; and Marion Wynne-Davies, 'The Queen's Masque: Renaissance Women and the Seventeenth-Century Court Masque', in *Gloriana's Face: Women, Public and Private, in the English Renaissance*, ed. by S.P. Cerasano and Marion Wynne-Davies (Hemel Hempstead: Harvester Wheatsheaf, 1992), pp. 79–104. For a refutation of this subversive potential, see Suzanne Gossett, '"Man-Maid Begone!": Women in Masques', *English Literary Renaissance*, 18 (1988), 96–113.

39. See, for example, Nancy J. Vickers, '"The Blazon of Sweet Beauty's Best": Shakespeare's *Lucrece*', in *Shakespeare and the Question of Theory*, ed. by Patricia Parker and Geoffrey Hartman (New York and London: Methuen, 1985), pp. 95–115 and 'Diana Described: Scattered Woman and Scattered Rhyme', in *Writing and Sexual Difference*, ed. by Elizabeth Abel (Brighton: Harvester, 1982), pp. 265–79.

40. Jonathan Sawday, *The Body Emblazoned: Dissection and the Human Body in Renaissance Culture* (London and New York: Routledge, 1995), p. 199.

41. See Patricia Fumerton, *Cultural Aesthetics: Renaissance Literature and the Practice of Social Ornament* (Chicago: University of Chicago Press, 1991). She examines the way in which masques displaced the consumption of sweets and confectionery following a banquet – 'consuming the void' as it was known – and how the idea of that ritual – a withdrawal into privacy – was replaced by an act of exposure, the masque. The banqueting halls for the purpose accordingly grew in size.

42. Most notably in *Cynthia's Revels* – see V.ix 12–27 in C.H. Herford, and Percy and Evelyn Simpson (eds), *Ben Jonson*, 11 vols (Oxford: Clarendon, 1925–52), IV.

43. The phrase was coined by Rosalie Colie in describing the work of Andrew Marvell. Cited in Parr, *The Staple of News*, p. 39.

44. Sawday, *The Body Emblazoned*, p. 136. See also Wall, *The Imprint of Gender*, p. 226.

45. Wall, *The Imprint of Gender*, p. 281.

46. Sawday, *The Body Emblazoned*, p. 215.

47. On the figuring of male authorship as 'birth', see Katherine Eisaman Maus, 'A Womb of His Own?: Male Renaissance Poets in the Female Body', in *Sexuality and Gender in Early Modern Europe: Institutions, Texts, Images*, ed. by James Grantham Turner (Cambridge: Cambridge University Press, 1993), pp. 266–88. See also her *Inwardness and Theater in the English Renaissance* (Chicago: University of Chicago Press, 1995). In the Induction to *The Staple of News*, the Prologue describes himself as the 'man-midwife' to the poet's dramatic project (ll.57–9), and

Pennyboy Junior refers to the staple-emissaries as midwives (I.v. 77–9).

48. Wall, *The Imprint of Gender*, p. 347.
49. See Catherine Belsey, *The Subject of Tragedy: Identity and Difference in Renaissance Drama* (London and New York: Methuen, 1985); and Ania Loomba, *Gender, Race, Renaissance Drama* (Manchester: Manchester University Press, 1989).
50. See Burt, '(Un)Censoring in Detail'.
51. Joseph Loewenstein, 'For a History of Literary Property: John Wolfe's Reformation', *English Literary Renaissance*, 18 (1988), 389–412.
52. Parr, *The Staple of News*, p. 24.
53. See *News from the New World*, ll.53–6. The lines in *The Staple of News* are clearly derivative, as they are elsewhere in the text. *Neptune's Triumph* is also a regular source – an indication of Jonson's dealings with the problematic ephemerality of these masques and their particular brand of 'news' in this ephemerality-focused public theatre play.
54. See McKenzie, '*The Staple of News* and the Late Plays'.
55. Sara Pearl, '"Sounding to Present Occasions": Jonson's Masques of 1620–25', in *The Court Masque*, ed. by David Lindley (Manchester: Manchester University Press, 1984), pp. 60–77.
56. Fumerton, *Cultural Aesthetics*, in a section entitled 'Tearing down the Masque: Towards an Aesthetics of Consumerism', suggests that the masque form underwent a process of self-combustion or deconstruction as the age of capitalism took hold.
57. Commentaries on the play since Herford and Simpson have made this point but have produced it as confirmation of Jonson's opposition to news-offices such as the Staple and the dissolution therefore as an act of wish-fulfilment. I take issue with this reading.
58. See *News from the New World*, ll.48–51.
59. John Milton, *Areopagitica; For the Liberty of Unlicenc'd Printing, To the Parlament of England* (1644), ed. by William Haller in *The Works of John Milton*, IV, gen. ed. Frank Allen Patterson (New York: Columbia University Press, 1931), ll. 16–22, p. 328. Spellings modernized.
60. See also George Orwell and Reginald Reynolds (eds), *British Pamphleteers* (London: Wingate, 1948), I.

10

'The Eccho of Uncertaintie': Jonson, Classical Drama and the English Civil War

Susan Wiseman

I

The Ghost of *Sylla* rises.
Dost thou not feel me Rome? not yet!
...
Can Sylla's ghost arise within thy walls,
Less threatening than an earthquake,
(Catiline, I.i.1–4)

As the presentiments of civil discord which open *Catiline* indicate, Jonson's tragedies, sources of controversy in his own lifetime, have obvious resonances in the Civil War period. This essay discusses the implications of the reworking of those plays, especially *Catiline*, *Epicoene*, and *Sejanus*, rather than discussing the plays themselves in detail.[1] Jonson's texts were variously reworked during the period 1640–60, but these rearticulations imply that 'Jonson' or 'his' texts occupied a disputed, rather than agreed, cultural place. Moreover, the narratives Jonson used were reused in a range of texts which did not necessarily invoke his name, such as *The Powerful Favourite* (1628) which used the narrative of Sejanus to discuss the Duke of Buckingham.[2] Civil War uses of 'Jonson' suggest a continuum of cultural reworking from the invocation of his name to emulation of his textual strategies.

The dominant way in which criticism has traced the influence of Jonson during the Civil War by finding 'allusions' to him and his work, is, for the Civil War period, a potentially self-defeating way to understand the transmission and circulation of Jonsonian texts and the narratives that they dramatize. When is an allusion not an allusion? G.E. Bentley, when collecting 'allusions' to Jonson and Shakespeare, apparently 'rejected large numbers of previously reported "allusions" which were not really allusions at all'.[3] As this implies, the category of 'allusion' brings with it a focus on authorship, the proper name and literary usage whereas Civil War uses of Jonson are political, intertextual, tendentious, and do not necessarily involve allusion to his proper name. *The Jonson Allusion Book* delineates the literary-political process of Jonson's canonization, but in doing so it offers a totemic 'Jonson' stabilized as transhistorically politically conservative, classicizing, and part of the Restoration shaping of literary culture.

This essay argues that during the Civil War and Protectorate and at the Restoration, engagement with Jonson's texts was more complex and problematic than the listing of highly literary invocations suggests. The official literary genealogy excludes more fraught, lengthy, and complex engagements with 'Jonson' provoked by *Catiline*, and to a lesser extent *Sejanus*, in the writings of the Civil War and Protectorate. These texts were reworked because of their attention to conspiracy and to the possibility of imaging a more perfect commonwealth; such texts were not automatically the property of any of the groups fighting in the wars.

Indeed, that Jonson's texts were read as complexly inviting an audience to take pleasure in subversion as well as negating that pleasure by affirming the rule of law is suggested by the career of another of Jonson's plays: *Epicoene*. With its gendered thematization of the rule of law and its subversion, *Epicoene* (first performed in 1609 and later at court in February 1636) was the first of Jonson's plays to be performed at the Restoration. Mentioned by Pepys in June, performances followed in November and December 1660 and, on 19 November, General Monck (until recently, of course, Cromwell's general) arranged a performance at the Whitehall Cockpit.[4] The play's popularity is a clue to the complexity of the political and aesthetic status of Jonson's plays in the Civil War and Protectorate. Edward Kynaston played Epicoene in the 1660 version, and in terms of its address to the new dispensation, its blending of styles, and its implicit framing of rebellion as gender inversion the play presents an appropriately ambivalent start to the Jonson of the Restoration.

That *Epicoene* was revived at the moment of Restoration also suggests some of the changes in theatrical production that took place between 1640 and 1660. Not only did the play's gender thematics obliquely address the Civil War (often figured in terms of the wife's domestic rebellion), but Kynaston's presentation of Epicoene seems like an ironic comment on the changed ideologies of female performance. *Epicoene*'s theatre career indicates that it was not only 'Jonson' that was refashioned in the 1640s and 1650s, as 'man' and canon, but also questions of taste, politics, and the aesthetics and ethics of performance. As Pierre Bordieu puts it, 'taste, [becomes] one of the most vital stakes in the struggles fought in the field of the dominant class and the field of cultural production' – a struggle inevitably more violent in the unstable time of Civil War.[5] It is this struggle over both taste and the politics of Jonson's plays that the study of 'allusion' has effaced from the post-Restoration understanding of the dramatist and his canon.

During the 1640s, because of the transformed relationship between print and theatre following the strictures against theatre in 1642, print itself, and printed plays, performed an important role in the aesthetics and politics of Jonsonian transmission.[6] In this market playtexts were also printed texts, sold and read alongside pamphlets, news, and other books. Thus, the story of Catiline, rather than Jonson's play specifically, was in circulation as a narrative against which to measure the Civil War conflict: Catiline was flexible enough to be used by all sides. Simultaneously though, aesthetic claims and conflicts were imbricated with political positions. Jonson's proper name and his texts were claimed for particular values: George Daniel comments: 'This, this was Jonson; who in his owne name/Carries his praise'. But any discussion or emulation of Jonson which exceeded mere assertion of the proper name was problematic, as is evident in the political and aesthetic commentary and reuse of Jonson in the 1640s and, differently, in the post-regicidal 1650s. In the claiming and reworking of this contradictory cultural capital the period saw texts which engage more nuancedly than has sometimes been acknowledged with the 'troubling power' of Jonson's writing.[7] In sum, to trace Jonson's texts in the Civil War – from an invocation of his name to complex reworkings of the same narratives – involves tracking a series of pairs thrown into exaggerated tension by changed circumstances: decorum versus subversion; aesthetics and politics; print and theatre.

II: THE 1640s: TRAGEDY, SATIRE, PRINT

Jonson's ambiguous place in terms of taste and politics in the new
circumstances of the print trade is made evident in the way he
was invoked, on the one hand, and emulated, on the other, in the
political pamphlets and playlets of the 1640s.
In *The Great Assises Holden in Parnassus by Apollo and his Assessors*
(1645) the figure of Jonson is used to focus on his ethics of print.
The newswriters of the Civil War – *Mercurius Britanicus, Mercurius
Aulicus, The Scottish Dove* and others – are arraigned before Apollo
for profaning print. As Scaliger, the 'Censor of manners in
Parnassus' tells Apollo:

Needs must wee those advantages confesse,
Which we reape from the literary Presse,
...
This engine of the Muse doth disperse
Arts best achievement, both in Prose and Verse.[8]
The question is:
How *Typographie* doth concerne your state,
...
This instrument of Art is now possest
By some, who have in Art no interest.

(A2r)

Those who have no interest in art are the newswriters. The debate
over the relative aesthetic and to an extent political values of 'art'
and newswriting is held when the newswriters are rounded up to
be tried by a jury of more or less literary writers – 'Thomas May,
William Davenant, Joshua Sylvester, George Sandes, Michael
Drayton, Francis Beaumont, John Fletcher, Thomas Haywood,
William Shakespeare, Philip Massinger' (A2r). Although the
newswriters are condemned (only to be reprieved by Apollo's
intervention) the evidence suggests that poetry, translation and
other arts cannot be clearly distinguished from news and its
untruthful pleasures. Jonson, significantly, features neither
amongst the poets nor the jurors, but as 'Keeper of the Trophonian
denne'. So often himself a prisoner, he plays Apollo's gaoler where
the newswriters are 'laid in Irons cold'. Jonson, with John Taylor
the Water Poet, features as Apollo's henchman. He is 'sowre Ben'
who 'by his belly, and his double chinne/ Hee look'd like the old

Hoste of a New Inne' (p. 9) – uncouth, yet absolute in the service of Apollo. So, keeper of the prison-house of literary value on the one hand, indecorous grotesque on the other, Jonson's posthumous role in relation to 1640s print journalism is here characterized by coercion and contradiction. The familiar arbitrating, aesthetically policing, *decorous* Jonson – the Jonson Richard Dutton in this volume traces into the Restoration – is combined in this instance with the huge consumer, excessively physical and even grotesque.

The contradictory presence of 'Jonson', as cultural censor and as exceeding the decorum his own work implies, permeates the uses to which Jonson and his texts are put in the short pamphlet plays of the 1640s. The 'classical' Jonson was transformed by the Civil War popular pamphlet market. The ambivalence about processes of government evident in both tragedies meant that contemporaries felt that they were applicable to the circumstances of the 1640s, though not clearly the political or aesthetic property of a specific group. *The Players Petition to the long Parliament, after being long Silenc'd, that they might Play again* (1642), emphasizes this felt applicability, though not exactly *how* the plays would comment on the situation:

> We will not dare at your strange Votes to jeer,
> Or personate King *Pym* with his state fleir:
> Aspiring *Catiline* shall be forgot,
> Bloody *Sejanus*, or who ere else could plot
> Confusion 'gainst the state.[9]

As Kate McLuskie argues elsewhere in this volume, the politicized implications of plays is determined by their immediate context of production. At its first performance, *Sejanus* (1603), Jonson's first tragedy, had been suspected of referring to the Essex rebellion, and perhaps to Raleigh,[10] but though that past may give the texts resonance they are here seen as commenting on the present. The *Petition* indicates that in the 1640s the two tragedies were a politically volatile and ambivalent part of the occluded theatrical repertoire; the very story of Catiline gestured towards both royalist and republican understandings of government.

The engaging qualities of Catiline as conspirator and usurper were explored in detail by a source used by Jonson and others, Sallust's history. Sallust makes Catiline a vivid empathetic centre of his narrative, describing him in terms of the misuse of virtues –

'Bold of Spirit, Subtle, Waywarde, a deepe dissembler, greedy of another mans Thrift, Prodigall of his owne; Talkative enough, voide of wisedom, of an high mind, accompanied with desires unsatiable, incredible, too too ambitious.'[11] Although from the very opening of the play Jonson's Catiline is cynically using those who think themselves his friends (I.i.), Sallust's scheming Catiline was in some ways more readily adaptable to the readings of Cromwell as a Machiavel than Jonson's less engaging figure. Sallust's Catiline 'neither cared he how, or by what meanes he had it, so he were sole-Lord in possession (p. 59), and Sallust's attempts to account for the apparently secret seductions of the usurper and his accumulation of power in terms of desire and gratification produce a charismatic corrupter of public virtue and value:

> And therefore by observation of every mans humour, some he would acquaint with beautiful Harlots, upon other some he would bestow Dogges of pleasure, and upon others galant horses, sparing for no cost, ... first to engage their allegiances and afterwardes to make use of their disloyalties. (p. 68)[12]

The privatization of social processes, such as gift exchange, and the imbrication of luxurious desires with social and ultimately political rebellion is central to Sallust's Catiline. Jonson's play, however, while using many of the scenes from Sallust, does not emphasize the seductive potential of the conspirator to the same degree, fighting shy of making the conspirator unequivocally the audience's point of identification.[13]

If Jonson's Catiline is to some extent an inert presence, neither wholly seductive nor completely repellant, Civil War recensions of the story made the meanings of 'Catiline' both topical and explicit in a range of ways, and Catiline's association with an unstoppable force – 'Though hills were set on hills, and the seas met seas to guard thee' (I.i.) – meant that in the 1650s both royalists and those who felt that the Protector had betrayed the Commonwealth could link Catiline and Cromwell.

Print genres, such as Civil War pamphlet playlets on the question of usurpers, reuse Sallust and Jonson's analyses of usurpation by hybridizing Senecan tragedy and satire. For example, *Craftie Cromwell* and *The Levellers Levell'd* – a pamphlet playlet probably played by the journalist and later republican theorist, Marchmont Nedham – rework Senecan drama as satire and in doing so make links amongst Jonson, Catiline, *Catiline*, Senecan drama, and the 1640s. Both playlets had a print circulation but it is not known whether they were performed. Certainly, their satiric recension of Jonsonian classical drama has several implications. First, insofar as these plays are returning to Jonson's *Catiline* they transform the emotional dynamic of reception, not simply from theatre performance to reading – a large transformation in itself – but from tragedy into topical satire, melding news, politics and dramatic pleasures. Amongst other things they rework the tragic dynamic which Rebecca Bushnell finds between the 'masculine king' and the 'effeminate usurper'.[14] In the very re-creation of Jonson's text as satire, they foreground the exciting aspect of Catiline, offering the audience a satiric thrill similar to those found elsewhere in Jonson's dramatic writing – particularly, of course, in *Epicoene*'s self-conscious thematization of the perverse pleasures of gender transformation. While not necessarily offering close reworkings of Jonsonian texts, such playlets from the Civil War use Jonson to suggest a strong ambivalence about whether the classical tragedies participate in the 'decorous' or subversive aspects of Jonson's writings.

In *The Levellers Levell'd* Senecan tragedy becomes satire, using 'England's Genius' to predict the chaos of war where 'rebellious hands are everywhere imployed to root out Loyalty'.[15] When the conspirators swear to assassinate Charles, Conspiracie 'pulls forth a picture':

> *Conspiracie*: ... here's *Catiline's* Effigie; if you intend to prosecute your wishes through bloud and vengeance, and to reach your glories maugre the furie of the world, sweare by this sacred Relique.
> *They lay hands upon the picture*
> *Omnes*: Most religiously.
> *Conspiracie*: By the fam'd memorie of this brave spirit, that once made Rome to tremble at his nod, who took the horrid sacrament in blood to level her proud battlements, sweare not to lay down armes till King *Charles* be sent to the invisible land, till all Lawes are repealed and abrogated, *meum* and *tuum* on pain of death not mentioned.
>
> (I.ii. p. 204)

This scene parodies Catiline's invitation to the conspirators to swear by human sacrifice: 'I have killed a slave,/And of his blood caused to be mixed with wine' (I.i.), with an 'effigie' replacing the sacrifice. The production of an 'effigie' (puppet?) Catiline on stage – or in a scene to be imaginatively staged by the reader – gestures towards both comic play and the rituals of witchcraft, suggesting diabolic practices but also a quasi-farcical reworking in the present – as a puppet show – of a plot which in its classical and Jonsonian origins was serious.[16]

The Levellers Levell'd and *Craftie Cromwell* make strategic use of Jonsonian tragic genre. Jonsonian classical decorum is invoked ironically, transformed into satire so that the reader or audience (for such dialogues may perhaps have been read aloud) understands the use of Jonson within the framework of satire. Thus *Craftie Cromwell*, the second part of which ends up with the crowning of Cromwell, takes up the form of Jonson's tragedy, transforming it into a citizens' plot. It utilizes the Senecan ghost in a way that lays claim to the classical discourses, high tragedy and satire – simultaneously – and which suggests the bathos of the mere citizens being described in such high discourses.[17] The Prologue of the play/newsbook, circulating to be read as news and as drama, explicitly relates genre and political circumstances:

An ordinance from our pretended State,
Sowes up the Players mouths, they must not prate
Like Parratts what they're taught upon the Stage.
Yet we may Print the Errors of the Age:
All their projections cannot hinder so,
But if we write, the Presses needs must goe.
That, that alone, heales our dejected Sense,
We can divulge our pen'd Intelligence:[18]

Craftie Cromwell is not in any sustained sense a reworking of *Catiline*, but is related to the earlier tragedy through semi-parodic satiric gestures.[19] The opening scene of the two-part playlet calls attention to the contemporary situations; like *The Great Assises* it emphasizes the important politics of print:

1 *Cit* What Newes is stirring?
2 *Cit* None, but what Fame speaks i'the nose by the Lyurnall, and the rest o' the Gazets.
1 *Cit* And what speake they?

2 *Cit* Why, that you and I, and all must be undone by our
Machiavellians, they will not yet accept their Soveraignes
proffer, nor hearken to any name of Peace, 'lesse that he take
his Crowne from off his head and place it at their feet; and this
they tearme the Subjects Libertie, and privilidge of Parliament.
1 *Cit* The name of Libertie hath ever been the watch-word us'd
before Rebellion, the idle eccho of uncertaintie.

(p. 3)

The playlet's status as participating in the news and engaging with
contemporary populist political discourse is explicit. Moreover, it
frames the play's use of the Senecan genre in Act II, where
Cromwell is renewed by the ghostly energies of 'the ghost of Pym':

Cromwell: Is not my Body now a walking Armour, my Ribbes are
Barres of Brasse, my hands of Iron?
...
Nor need I doubt to bring my ends to passe, since now I have
new cast the *timerous State*, made up my Faction all the
Kingdom o're, Imprison'd *Charles my King*, exil'd his Friends;
what let's me then that I ascend a throne –

(II, pp. 6–7)

The hyper-masculine personal qualities of the conspirator-usurper
are here given to Cromwell by supernatural intervention. Echoes of
Catiline are present, but the point of these allusions is to enrich the
journalistic contemporary reference of the piece.

Did the Civil War satiric transformation of Jonson's texts and
genres and narratives used by Jonson make the political implications of 'Jonsonian' and related texts more or less certain?
Obviously, providing an immediate, contemporary target for the
use of classical forms reworked as satire could be seen as refocus-
ing and therefore stabilizing any ambivalent political implications
to be found in Jonsonian classical drama, placing them immediately
and thoroughly within contemporary political discourse. This
recension as satire itself, of course, registers, even as it reformu-
lates, the politically volatile nature of Jonsonian classical tragedies.
Certainly, the classical drama replayed as satire has a sharpened
polemical topicality marked by an excitement about the possibility
of rebellion and the figure of conspirator or usurper as exciting. The
political language Jonson's plays offered could be applied to a

number of ends; if history and political theory was to make sense by 'application', to whom was Catiline comparable? As these satires indicate, Cromwell was, at points, figured as Catiline. But that did not necessarily stabilize the values of the plays as royalist; the royalists at Oxford were described as 'whelps of Catiline'.[20] As the Civil War dialogues suggest, a complex range of political positions and readers existed during the 1640s rather than a simple binary division between, say, parliamentarians and royalists.

Arguably then, by the time that the Civil War began, Jonson's texts occupied an unusual and uncomfortable position as texts for the commercial theatre and, equally problematically, as texts related to readings of classical tragedies. Jonson's texts – in an important sense 'his' – were part of culture in a way that was, to say the least, unusual for dramatic texts. But plays alone of these have the additional tension of existing in two media – print and played – and of articulating the language of politics not only through narrative but through the building blocks and emotional dynamics of the different Renaissance genres – tragedy, tragicomedy, and (in different ways) comedy. So Civil War writers engaged Jonson's texts in a number of different ways. They formed an ambivalent cultural capital rather than an inheritance with a stable meaning. First, writers and readers in the 1640s were conscious of Jonson's texts as taking up the similar ambivalent political status as some classical histories, such as Tacitus over whom Deagory Wheare comments, 'the most eminent of the Critics differ'. Secondly, as the next section investigates, they formed an ambiguous inheritance because of the emerging political implications of the realm of the aesthetic as a cultural capital in high and popular culture.

III: 1649: INVOCATION VERSUS EMULATION

As several critics have noted, royalist poets asserted rights over the Stuart cultural heritage. Charles I's side was taken by poets known to Jonson and sons of Ben and contributors to *Jonsonus Virbius* (1638), such as Suckling, Herrick, Howell, Cleveland, William Cartwright, Henry Vaughan, John Beaumont (made into a royalist icon by the 1647 folio with its politicization of the Jonsonian understanding of authorship).[21] This association between Jonson and royalism was taken up in two critical accounts of the last days of

Charles I. *Perfect Occurrences* no. 104 for 22–30 December 1648 – just before the execution – claimed that 'the King is pretty merry, and spends much of his time in reading of Sermon Books and Ben Johnsons Playes.' In 1651, well into the republic, an account called 'The None-such Charles his Character' retold the story, claiming that Charles was 'more fixt on Ben's verses ... during the time of his imprisonment, then on these holy writs, wherein salvation is to be sought.' If Jonson was claimed by royalists, the subversive pleasures offered by his plays were also used to discredit Charles and his supporters.

At this time a range of plays invoked Jonson as part of royalist claims to history. *The Famous Tragedy of Charles I* positioned itself as part of a truly royalist body of writing and a royalist cultural aesthetic by claiming both theatrical status and authors:

> Though *Johnson, Shakespeare, Goffe,* and *Davenant,*
> Brave *Sucklin, Beaumont, Fletcher, Shirley* want
> The life of action, and their learned lines
> Are loathed by the Monsters of the times;
> Yet your refined Soules, can penetrate
> Their depth of merit, and excuse their Fate.[22]

This makes explicit the royalist claim to a mixture of taste and virtue, and within that framework, to Jonson as first amongst markers of royalism.[23]

However, at the moment of the regicide and as the 1640s turned to the 1650s, as 'royalism' became an empty category and republicanism began to be developed as an official discourse, apparatus of government, and to an extent iconography, Jonson's texts took on a newly ambivalent set of meanings. 'Jonson' was indeed claimed by royalists but the contradictory understandings of his writings is evident in the pages of newsbooks discussed above. The crisis and inversion of 1649, the moment of the regicide may – though the evidence is sketchy – have precipitated changes in critical readings of 'Jonson'. The plays, and Jonson's ambivalent political legacy, were made accessible and problematic in new ways by the emergence of the new state. At this point, *Catiline* was reused as tragedy rather than satire; Robert Baron took the legacy very seriously when he actually modelled *Mirza* on *Catiline*. Moreover, the struggles of the republic also brought new potential to cultural use of *Catiline* in terms of the complex position of Cicero in that text.

As Markku Peltonen has argued, the post-regicidal emphasis on republican thought did have a background in some strains of earlier seventeenth-century humanistic and classicizing political thought. The reworking of Jonson's drama, both alone and as part of a corpus of classical narratives, suggests that such material was understood by contemporaries as available to be reorganized as part of a more explicitly republican project.[24] This happens in *The Tragedy of the Famous Orator Marcus Tullius Cicero*, where the legacy of Jonson's *Catiline* is reshaped to chart Cicero's later failure to secure democracy and the consequent rise of Antony. At the end of Act I, the Chorus comments:

A King is but a Royall slave,
And Rule a Vassalage more brave;
A Scepter's but a glorious name,
A Crown the burden of the same
Proud front which it adorns
...
Unhappy *Rome*, did Julius die
For affected Tyranny?
And must *Antonius* inherit
The aimes of his ambitious Spirit?[25]

Such questions have ready applications to the state of the republic in 1650, especially the tendency of the overthrow of tyrants to produce new tyrants rather than a new order of government, something the play emphasizes, reiterating it, for example, in this exchange between Salvius and Cicero, when Salvius has supported Antony:

Salvius: Alas good *Cicero*, 'twas not hate to you
Nor love to *Antoninus* that I did it,
But pure devotion to my Countrey's cause.
Cicero: But my immoderate hate of Antony
(I now confesse it) blinded my discretion,
And carried me too inconsiderately
Unto this dangerous planting of *Octavius*.
(Act III)

Cicero concludes, 'Sure some superior power has order'd this,/ And made us instruments of our own subversion' (Act III). Thus the play engages in a complex way with the possible future of the Commonwealth and Cicero emerges as a crucial, if not politic, figure in the play's sympathetic articulation of republican values. Acting as a kind of sequel to *Catiline* (in a different way from the satires of the 1640s) this play makes decisions about how *Catiline* can be reused, working a Jonsonian drama into an implicitly republican reading of the fortune of Rome.

The Tragedy of Cicero used Jonsonian drama to articulate the dangers likely to undermine republican government. Insofar as it can be seen as a sequel to Jonson's treatment of Cicero, this play claims a 'Jonson' rendered, through emulation rather than invocation and assertion, officially republican. Printed during the republic, the tragedy indicates that Jonson's *œuvre* was not, as the history of Jonsonian allusion and the post-Restoration readings of Jonson seem to suggest, self-evidently part of royalist cultural capital. In addition, at the moment of publication *The Tragedy of Cicero* places the attention to political conflict in Jonson alongside, rather than in opposition to, the notion of Jonsonian decorum to produce them as part of the culture of the republic.

As in the pamphlet dramas of the 1640s, Jonsonian drama is only part of the play's referentiality and works in tandem with other sources and ideas, particularly in this case of Roman history. Rome as remembered during the English Civil War was in some ways like the Rome momentarily proposed by Freud as a model for the psyche – a many-layered presence into which the present could quarry in search of identificatory and political models; the landmarks of republican Rome had been replaced by 'ruins, but not by ruins of themselves but of later restorations made after fires or destruction'.[26] The Rome of *Marcus Tullius Cicero* is in part an archaeological salvage, working with material from ancient sources and with Jonsonian reworkings.

Such salvaging and use of classical history as a framework within which to imagine the future took place in the royalist camp, too. Greek models, like Roman history and to an extent Jonson's own plays, played a cultural role that fused history, dramatic tragedy, and typology. Taking up classical drama, translators like Edward Sherburne and Christopher Wase translated Greek drama as an explicit address to contemporary politics and as the Civil Wars drew to a traumatic close Wase looked to a range of genres, including Greek tragedy, to articulate a vision of a possible future 'restoration'. The implicit link between the rereading of history and royalist politics can be seen in the literary and political career of Sherburne who published *Medea* in 1648 and was later involved in the royalist uprising at Rufford, Nottinghamshire. As Annabel Patterson suggests, Civil War political allusion might be oblique, but Wase's *Electra* eschewed ambiguity.[27] Its full title, which was *Electra of Sophocles Presented to Her Highnesse the Lady Elizabeth; with an Epilogue Shewing the Parallel in Two Poems, 'The Return' and 'The Restauration'*, indicates that the play was absolutely to be understood in terms of the present. The binding in of the two final poems was integral to this process.

Wase applied the quasi-Jonsonian method of citation, as found in *Sejanus*. However, where the question of political relevance was dynamically suspended by Jonson's *Sejanus* (in terms of the applicability of the text to both Essex and Raleigh in the 1605 version and in the speech of Cordus on the discovery of relevance in history), Wase's *Electra* consistently attempts to turn the translation to the present. The fact that *Sejanus* – annotated by Jonson – was found by contemporaries to be politically allusive may possibly inform Wase's deliberate use of annotation to make contemporary reference. At any rate, Wase is at pains to make annotation politically, rather than aesthetically productive.

Wase published Sophocles's *Electra* annotated to prophesy a restoration of the Stuart line. Accordingly, this *Electra* was 'presented to Her Highnesse the Lady Elizabeth'.[28] Although the annotations tell us that the play fits the English situation really well: 'Our Agamemnon's dead, Electra grieves./The only hope is that Orestes lives', there is one problem: this leaves Henrietta Maria as Clytemnestra – proof indeed as the sixth annotation notes 'that similitudes run not upon all foure' (I. p. 5). This inconvenient detail delays Wase's insistence that the story of Electra, a dramatic lesson from history, speaks to the present for but a moment.[29] He writes, 'Plays are the Mirrours wherein Mens actions are reflected to their own view' and the playtext is presented as offering self-reflexive potential for the times.

The poems concluding the text rework Jonson explicitly. They seem to be intended to provide a sequel to the play and to return the reader to the present. Wase appends 'The Epilogue' showing in parallel the two poems 'The Return' and 'The Restauration'. 'The Return' uses the metaphor of marriage between king and country, asserting that the parliamentarian forces can force the body but not the will of the people:

… though their grim Horsemen tread
Upon the Quaking Countrey's head;
…
Force can but in a rape engage,
'Tis choice must make it Marriage.
                              (pp. 2–3)

The true marriage of king and people Wase presents as an act
'impregnable' except by a 'Conveyance' which:

… must enchant our conscious hands,
To slumber in like guilty bands,
While like the froward Miltonist,
We our old Nuptiall knot mistrust.
                              (p. 3)

Milton's divorce writings here imply his – for Wase – negatively
inflected republican politics, as familial divorce is taken as standing
for the country's adultery with parliament. Such language is familiar from the pamphlet controversies of the later 1640s, but what is
of interest is that Milton is implicitly set against Jonson in Wase's
two poems. The Jonsonian turn suggested in the annotation of
the play appears much more strongly in the second poem, 'The
Restauration'. This, the final poem in the volume, prophesies the
events of an imagined restoration in a poem addressed to Princess
Elizabeth. Amongst the future scenes that the poem imagines is
Elizabeth's 'Brother on his Throne', surrounded by 'a bright Array
of Peers' (pp. 8, 10). For Elizabeth, and the true reader, this means
'spotless joy' and the poem envisions feudal relations reinstituted:

Thus mark in Halls of great resort,
At Penshurst, or some Prince's court
If my Lords angry Gentleman
(The Upper House of his great train)
Or some big steward shall crush down
His fellows with perpetual frown;
The House, because he domineers,
And takes upon him o're his Peers,
Think the Yoke too hard to be born;
Not for the Burden, but the Scorn.
When if the wiser Lady soon

Spy and remove the grief, anon
You may a chearfull duty see
Flit through the busie Family.
No Monster is so much abhorr'd,
As an Inferiour surly Lord.

The Villagers their knees shall bow,
Not aw'd by a stern troopers brow.

(p. 11)

This rewriting of 'To Penshurst' acknowledges the potential for dissent and aggression within the social body. The 'house' in question seems to allude to parliament as well as Penshurst. Yet, as in Jonson's poem, the social body is ideally to be reharmonized by acknowledgement of such dissent. The solution proposed is in the lord's removal of 'the grief' – though through the agency of the lady, and ideal figure (again presumably hinting at Elizabeth). Thus the poem seems to be using Jonson to project a vision of a 'restorated' England in which what is restored is in part feudal hierarchy. Wase locates the problems in the social order with the ambition of the intermediary classes – stewards and 'inferior' lords and proposes a vision of the future in which such symptoms of social division are erased and the idealized social relations of Penshurst are restored. Wase's play and poem are strenuously 'royalist', yet leave out Charles, and, within the reworking of 'To Penshurst' as a vision of a 'restored' future, the poem opens up a discussion of political divisions and the problems of social hierarchy.

In this instance, a royalist text evidences a complex engagement with Jonson, contrasting with the uses of Jonson as though the proper name stood self-evidently for a set of aesthetic and political positions. This detailed intertextuality again contrasts with the invocation of a name suggesting that Jonson's texts required a complex engagement to turn them to the various political ends of Civil War writers. Where the proper name asserts a certain set of positions, reworkings such as the republican Cicero or Wase's concluding poem to *Electra* take up Jonson's methods as part of a political and aesthetic regime, commenting – from several positions – on the events of the 1640s and 1650s, and as such are made productive in a richer and perhaps more ambivalent way than our understandings of Restoration Jonson have suggested.

IV: 1660: EMULATION, INVOCATION, AND THE CANON

Restoration canonization of a decorous, aesthetic, above-all *coherent* Jonson made Jonson central to the aesthetic regime in which 'taste classifies and it classifies the classifier'.[30] Critical comparison focused on the relative reputations of Jonson and Shakespeare has reproduced a concentration on the invoked rather than the emulated Jonson discussed here. The emphasis on the invoked Jonson which finds its apotheosis in the still covertly influential allusion-hunting of the early twentieth century has, to an extent, effaced the emulatory and politicized uses of Jonson which take account of the politically and aesthetically contradictory implications of Jonson like those discussed above.[31]

Restoration Jonson, then, began with a return to production and with *Epicoene*. The significance of 'Jonson' as royalist cultural capital and as a signifier of royalism is indicated by the fact that one of his plays is the first to be put on: *Epicoene* was sponsored by General Monck (the Duke of Albemarle). Although he was the military architect of the Restoration, Monck had very recently been Cromwell's general; in 1660 he was still a strangely ambiguous figure.

The Prologue to the performance of *Epicoene* commissioned by Monck, however, insisted on the connection between royalty and theatres:

Greatest of Monarchs, welcome to this place
Which Majesty so oft was wont to grace
Before our Exile, to divert the Court,
And ballance weighty Cares with harmless sport.
This truth we can to our advantage say,
They that would have no King, would have no Play:
The Laurel and the Crown together went,
Had the same Foes, and the same Banishment.

The link between theatre and royalty was facilitated by the banishment of each, and in the 'interregnum' fanatics ruled: 'This spacious Land their Theater became' (p. 210). The prologue, like Wase's vision of a restoration, asserts a similarity between pre-war and post-war cultural politics effacing the critical potential of the theatre and the changes in social relations wrought by the wars evident in the career of the very patron of the play, let alone the way in which *Epicoene* had new resonances for restoration sexual politics including the question of the use of actresses on the public stage.

In *Epicoene*, the political question of subversion is thematized as a gendered sexual mistake. Pepys comments on Edward Kynaston's Epicoene that he appeared 'as a poor woman in ordinary clothes, to please Morose; then in fine clothes, as a gallant, and in them was clearly the prettiest woman in the whole house, and lastly, as a man; and then likewise did appear the handsomest man in the house.'[32] The deceptions of desire, masculinity, and sexual subversion might be read as providing a sublimation of the critical political energies of the 1650s, but, certainly, in this staging of *Epicoene* we see a sublimation of the more problematic Jonson in a royalist account.

This performance of *Epicoene* worked culturally and politically for Albemarle and for Jonson, as one of a range of events that found both a place in Restoration culture and political ideology. At the Restoration, as Jennifer Brady argues, not only does Dryden take up Jonson in detail, but Jonson becomes a figure of political conservatism whose 'ideological heirs [could] in the aftermath of Civil War, ... project their own cultural and political nostalgia for a cherished authority.'[33] This Jonson is established most readily around authorial claims of inheritance from Jonson (like the claims of Dryden, Flecknoe, and Shadwell discussed by Brady) rather than by textual production which continued to produce conflict. Jonson's plays were in the repertoire but what to do with them was a new kind of problem; when *Catiline* was performed in the 1668–9 season it again provoked controversy when Lady Hervey thought that 'Doll Common' acted Sempronia in imitation of her.[34] Once again, culturo-political chiasmus had put 'Jonson' the courtier-poet back on the agenda and Jonson's critical tragedies were again problematic.

The influence of Jesse Franklin Bradley and Joseph Quincy Adams's *Jonson Allusion Book* (1922) as discussed in the introduction to this essay, produced a 'Jonson' in explicit rivalry to Shakespeare, but, in attempting to trace 'estimates of his genius' the compilers decided against tracking down 'mere indications of Jonson's influence upon others, in the form of imitation or quotation.'[35] As Frank Whigham has argued, emulation involves a 'structure of struggle and assimilation' whereby the later text develops a complex relationship of aesthetic and political challenge to, as well as extrapolation of, the earlier text,[36] and, as this essay has suggested, the Jonson of allusion rather than emulation is partial in several senses, though most signally problematic in producing an apparently coherent Jonson.

The tracing of 'allusions' sustains an already circular or tautologous royalist, conservative, invoked 'Jonson' but excludes precisely the more complex and diffuse generic and political encounters with Jonson's texts that have been the subject of this essay – though these are sometimes implicit in the sections quoted. It tends, therefore, to produce a royalist Jonson in the invocation of the proper name where the engagement of seventeenth-century texts with Jonson offers a different view, and one not yet organized around Jonson's reception by canonical authors.

Thus, while the use of Jonson by canonical authors has produced 'Jonson' as a figure of debate about aesthetic decorum, and has resulted in an aestheticization of the live political and subversive issues in the texts, the period analysed here, the generation after Jonson's death, suggests a more diverse reception and an understanding of Jonson's texts as providing complex problems for subsequent writers.

The uses of Jonson's texts suggested in this essay complicate the Jonson produced by both the invocatory claims of Restoration writers and literary periodicity which isolates Renaissance and Restoration drama from each other and from texts produced in the 1640s and 1650s.[37] The interregnum uses of his texts suggest that in the 1640s and 1650s, while 'Jonson' certainly was claimed as cultural capital by royalist writers, his reputation and writings also produced more complex engagements from the satirical reworkings of the pamphlet plays to the production of a serious extrapolation of the political critique facilitated in classical drama as found in *Marcus Tullius Cicero*.

During the English Civil War and Protectorate, then, Jonson's tragedies, particularly, were a vital but ambivalent legacy at a moment when a sphere, or competing spheres, of the aesthetic were being manufactured to conflicting and antithetical political ends. 'Jonson' and the two tragedies were a crucial aesthetic and political property for the generation immediately following his death and during the time of the Civil War, Protectorate, and Restoration during which both republican and royalist refashionings of the state and subject put 'Jonson', *Catiline*, *Sejanus*, and *Epicoene* to work as separate but dangerously intertwined cultural, political and pleasurable markers, commodities, and moments. This suggests a received 'Jonson' who, as Burt has argued, was 'neurotic' in the contradictory desire to 'censor himself ... and his equally powerful desire to express the censored material ... (sometimes in the same context)'[38] and whose apparent convictions – around politics, performance, and patronage – were perceived by his contemporaries and successors as problematic to the point of being riven by contradiction.

Notes

1. For an analysis of *Sejanus* and *Catiline* in the context of their moment of production, see Julie Sanders, 'Roman Frames of Mind', in her *Ben Jonson's Theatrical Republics* (Basingstoke: Macmillan, 1998).
2. P.M., *The Powerful Favourite*, 'Printed at Paris', (1628).
3. Ernest Sirluck, 'Shakespeare and Jonson among the Pamphleteers of the First Civil War: Some Unreported Seventeenth-Century Allusions', *Modern Philology* 52 (1955–6), 88–99 (p. 88).
4. C.H. Herford, Percy and Evelyn Simpson (eds), *Ben Jonson*, 11 vols (Oxford: Clarendon Press, 1925–52), IX, pp. 208–9. Henceforth H&S. According to H&S, 'The prologue preserved in a broadside, is ascribed to Denham in the Bodleian copy (Wood 398.16)' (p. 209), whereas Leslie Hotson, in *The Commonwealth and Restoration Stage* (Cambridge: Cambridge University Press, 1928), thinks that it is by Davenant: 'Although Killigrew's company was elected to act the play ... Davenant wrote the prologue to the King.' (pp. 208–9). As Jennifer Brady notes, Dryden thought *Epicoene* a 'perfect Play': see her 'Collaborating with the Forebear: Dryden's Reception of Ben Jonson', *Modern Language Quarterly* 54 (1993), 345–69 (p. 347).
5. Pierre Bordieu, *The Field of Cultural Production*, ed. by Randal Johnson (Cambridge: Polity Press, 1993), pp. 102–8; see also his *Distinction: A Social Critique of the Judgement of Taste* (London: Routledge, 1986; repr. 1996), pp. 2–7.
6. Prologue, *Craftie Cromwell* (London, 1648).
7. Richard Helgerson, *Self-Crowned Laureates* (Berkeley: University of California Press, 1983), p. 184; see also pp. 130–67.
8. *The Great Assises Holden in Parnassus by Apollo and His Assessours* (E. 269 (11)), p. 2. Subsequent references cited parenthetically within the text.
9. This version from the later reprint by Thomas Jordan, *A Royal Arbor of Loyal Poesie* (London, 1660), pp. 78–9.
10. Ben Jonson, *Sejanus, His Fall*, ed. by Philip J. Ayres (Manchester: Manchester University Press, 1990), pp. 16–22.

11. Sallust, *The Conspiracy of Catiline*, trans. by Thomas Heywood, ed. by Charles Whibley (1608; repr. London, 1924), p. 59. On Sallust's reading of Catiline, see D.C. Earl, *The Political Thought of Sallust* (Cambridge: Cambridge University Press, 1961), pp. 82–103.

12. See also Ben Jonson, *Catiline*, ed. by W.F. Bolton and Jane F. Gardner (Lincoln: University of Nebraska Press, 1972), I.i. 164–71. Barbara DeLuna claims *Catiline*, in *Jonson's Romish Plot* (Oxford: Clarendon Press, 1967), as the play most frequently alluded to in the seventeenth century (p. 361), and sees its afterlife in terms of 'anti-papist' discourse as well as topical work on conspiracy (pp. 328–59).

13. Thomas Otway's *Venice Preserved* (1682), for example, which uses *Catiline* as a source text, makes the opposite choice about how to deal with the conspirators, inviting the audience into empathetic relationships with many figures. See DeLuna, pp. 349–54, on the relationship between *Venice Preserved* and *Catiline*. More generally, John Sekora discusses Sallust's patterning of the degeneration of the state into luxury in *Luxury: the Concept in Western Thought, Eden to Smollet* (Baltimore and London: Johns Hopkins University Press, 1977), pp. 36–7.

14. Rebecca W. Bushnell, *Tragedies of Tyrants: Political Thought and Theater in the English Renaissance* (Ithaca and London: Cornell University Press, 1990), p. 118.

15. The editor of *The Levellers Levell'd* thinks that the sub-plot satirizing William Lilly is taken from *The Alchemist*: Marchmont Nedham, *The Levellers Levell'd*, ed. by Philip C. Dust, *Analytical and Enumerative Bibliography*, vol. 4, numbers 3 and 4 (1980), pp. 182–240 (p. 183).

16. Indications are that *Catiline*, performed after the Restoration, continued to be viewed as both a classical tragedy and as overblown, indicating that such a view might well have been held during the Interregnum though, in the absence of performance, would be likely to have been less explored. Thanks to Dr von Malzthen for discussing this: see *Notes and Queries* 231 (1986), 467–9.

17. *Craftie Cromwell; or Oliver Ordering Our New State* (Mercurius Melancholicus, Feb 1648, E. 246 (17)); crowning of Cromwell in part two, p. 16.

18. For a discussion of the transformation of genres by the Civil War, see Nigel Smith, *Literature and Revolution in England, 1640–1660* (New Haven and London: Yale University Press, 1994), pp. 1–44.

19. Sallust, *The Conspiracy of Catiline*, pp. 68, 76.

20. *The Character of an Oxford Incendiary*, April 1645 (E. 279(6)), p. 8.

21. Smith, *Literature and Revolution*, p. 12. See also McLuskie and Dutton in this volume. The endless commendatory poems to the Beaumont and Fletcher folio of 1647 include comparisons between those poets and Jonson, or simple invocations of Jonson's spirit by Denham, Howell, George Buck, William Cartwright, John Berkenhead, Edward Powell, Joseph Howe, Henry Harrington, Richard Brome, Henry Vaughan, and the royalist general Sir George Lisle who was later to be memorialized in *The Famous Tragedy of Charles I*.

22. *The Famous Tragedy of Charles I*, prologue.

23. See also *Cromwell's Conspiracie* (?1660) which reworks this play.
24. See for example, Markku Peltonen, *Classical Humanism and Republicanism in English Political Thought, 1570–1640* (Cambridge: Cambridge University Press, 1995).
25. *The Tragedy of That Famous Roman Orator Marcus Tullius Cicero* (1650/1), Act I.
26. Sigmund Freud, *Civilization* (New York: Norton, 1961; repr. 1989), pp. 17–18.
27. 'You can speak as openly as you wish against ... tyrants, as long as you can be understood differently, because you are not trying to give offence, only its dangerous repercussions. If danger can be avoided by some ambiguity of expression, everyone will admire its cunning', Quintilian, *Institutes*, 9.2.67, quoted in Annabel Patterson in 'Roman-Cast Similitude', in *Rome in the Renaissance: The City and the Myth*, ed. by P.A. Ramsey, (Binghamton, NY: Medieval and Renaissance Texts and Studies, 1982), pp. 382–94 (p. 383).
28. Christopher Wase, *The Electra of Sophocles* (The Hague, 1649). Elizabeth seems to be chosen to offer an identification with Elizabeth I. Wase's idea of relevance borders here on free association: the letter 'E' is enough to link Electra and Elizabeth.
29. See also Fanshawe's use of the idea of restoration in *Il Pastor Fido* (1647).
30. Bourdieu, *Distinction*, p. 6.
31. For example, Brady notes that Dryden's detailed and purposive emulation of Jonson has gone undiscussed, 'Collaborating with the Forebear' (p. 346).
32. H&S IX, pp. 208–9.
33. Brady, 'Collaborating with the Forebear', p. 346.
34. As Richard Dutton implies in *Ben Jonson: To the First Folio* (Cambridge: Cambridge University Press, 1983), emulation which recognized the politically as well as aesthetically problematic aspects of Jonson's tragedies continued even during the period of Jonson's canonization after the Restoration. *Catiline* continued to be played because of 'genuine admiration for its handling of living questions of history, politics, and ethics.' (p. 132). See also Katherine Eisaman Maus, *Ben Jonson and the Roman Frame of Mind* (New Jersey: Princeton University Press, 1984), p. 111.
35. Jesse Franklin and Joseph Quincy Adams (eds), *The Jonson Allusion Book* (New Haven: Yale University Press, 1922), v.vi. Virtually the same methodology appears in Gerald Eades Bentley's *Shakespeare and Jonson: Their Reputations in the Seventeenth Century Compared* (Chicago: University of Chicago Press, 1945).
36. Frank Whigham, *Ambiton and Privilege: The Social Tropes of Elizabethan Courtly Literature* (Berkeley: University of California Press, 1984), p. 78.
37. Brady discusses the relationship between the Renaissance and the Restoration, 'Collaborating with the Forebear', p. 348.
38. Richard Burt, *Licensed by Authority: Ben Jonson and the Discourses of Censorship* (Ithaca and London: Cornell University Press, 1993), p. xi.

Index